MAXIMIZING BUSINESS PERFORMANCE

through

SOFTWARE PACKAGES

Best Practices for
Justification, Selection,
and Implementation

MAXIMIZING BUSINESS PERFORMANCE

through

SOFTWARE PACKAGES

Best Practices for Justification, Selection, and Implementation

Robert W. Starinsky

AUERBACH PUBLICATIONS

A CRC Press Company

Boca Raton   London   New York   Washington, D.C.

Library of Congress Cataloging-in-Publication Data

Starinsky, Robert W.
    Maximizing business performance through software packages : best practices for justification, selection and implementation / Robert W. Starinsky.
            p.   cm.
    Includes index.
    ISBN 1-57444-329-1 (alk. paper)
    1. Industrial management--data processing. 2. Industrial management--Computer programs. I. Title.

HD30.2 .S7825 2002
658'.0553--dc21   2002028044

Visit the Auerbach Publications Web site at www.auerbach-publications.com

© 2003 by CRC Press LLC
Auerbach is an imprint of CRC Press LLC

No claim to original U.S. Government works
International Standard Book Number 1-57444-329-1
Library of Congress Card Number 2002028044
Printed in the United States of America 1 2 3 4 5 6 7 8 9 0
Printed on acid-free paper

DEDICATIONS

I dedicate this book to my family, especially to my wonderful and loving mother, Virginia. Her tremendous work ethic is second to none and serves as my inspiration. To my loving wife, partner in life, and closest friend, Christine, whose patience has been severely tested during this and also during my previous book writing project. Finally, to our newest family member, my 2-year-old daughter, Stefanie. Much of this book was written while she either napped or played at my side. She played a pivotal role in this book as her need for my attention made meeting my manuscript deadline challenging to say the least.

ACKNOWLEDGEMENTS

First, to everyone at CRC Press/St. Lucie Press: Thank you for your help in sponsoring this book and bringing it to life under your label. There is probably no other publisher better suited for this type of book. As I have found out first hand, few projects require as much time, patience, or energy as does the writing of a book (except for possibly implementing an enterprise-wide software package). To make all of that effort worthwhile, it certainly helps to have a publisher on board that will market the end product to the right audience.

I would also like to thank my former and current associates and colleagues in business. These individuals have been instrumental to both my thought process and my wisdom in numerous ways. It has been my pleasure to have worked with a number of outstanding individuals over the years who served as either the essential mentors or partners in my software and technology journeys, including Kay Abrams (formerly Irvine) and Donna Schwantes, Masseurs. Enrique Alvarez, Chuck Ban, José Blanco, Bill Caspers, Keith Danhoff, Mark Engleman, Terry Horner, Hal Kopke, Earl Patterson (now deceased), Don Pelka, Jim Pope, Gordon Merna, Jim Perez, Mike Schultz, Bill Stagner, and William (Croft) Walker. It was this group of esteemed associates and colleagues who challenged me to understand, deliver, and share knowledge.

Finally, special thanks are extended to Edward Zibrida, an outstanding individual whose candor and experience have earned my highest respect. Although Ed and I have been friends for many years, I am pleased to now have Ed working alongside me at Tradewinds Group. For this project, Ed has served as the litmus test for clarity and value in my writing. His disdain for both computers and for computer-related books has kept this book on target for you, the reader.

— Robert W. Starinsky

FOREWORD

It Ain't Pretty Out There

In our business, we have observed over 1500 enterprise software selection and implementation projects. We've just about seen it all and it is baffling that the same basic mistakes are made over and over again. The main culprits are little effective planning, selecting software based on an emotional review of subjective and incomplete information, putting the project in the hands of the *wrong* people, and poor senior management leadership. Any of these deficiencies can doom the enterprise software project.

It's Going to Get Better

Enterprise software projects may be the most problematic and failure-ridden activity a business can undertake. Therefore, this activity has nowhere to go but up. And it will. In 20 years our business schools will teach about "normal" practices to manage enterprise systems so they aggressively support progressive and collaborative business processes. The "Wild West" days of enterprise software experienced in the 1990s through about 2010 will be long gone. The students will laugh at this chaotic history — some won't believe it.

The Challenge

Today's chaos is acceptable — but it is not an option for those who want to be profitable in the next 5 to 10 years — or be in business in 10 to 15 years. One way or another, all organizations and businesses must take action to understand progressive business processes and to methodically adopt enterprise software that will support them.

How This Book Can Help You

In this book, Robert Starinsky offers a solid approach that can enable a firm's transformation to the discipline and control needed to effectively select and implement complex enterprise software and to manage and improve these systems over time. The efficiencies awaiting those who accept Starinsky's advice contained in this book are phenomenal and in time will be critical to your firm's survival.

Mark Engleman
President
SoftSelect Systems, LLC
www.softselect.com

PREFACE

What This Book Is About

An organization's management team faces numerous challenges today. Technology is increasingly helping business organizations to meet these challenges and compete in a changing world. The business application software package is one such dimension in today's business technology mix that is intended to improve an organization's competitiveness. In fact, the impact of business application software is so pervasive that software plays a dominant and largely understated role in most business decision making and business operational processes today.

This book focuses on the importance of this relationship between business and business application software, particularly the role of software packages in today's business world. Software packages have played a major role in reshaping our traditional business and organizational models over the past decade. They have also played a role in reshaping the traditional software development model. In fact, a central tenet of this book is that buying commercial, off-the-shelf software packages for most business applications has largely left obsolete the concept of custom or from the ground up business application software development.

Among the types of software that have rewritten the rules include the so-called back office systems, such as those providing enterprise resource planning and supply chain management capabilities and the front office systems, including those for customer relationship management and electronic commerce. The list also includes business intelligence software that provide ways to collect and analyze disparate business data from multiple systems using data warehouses and analytical analysis and reporting software.

Why Read This Book

Finding and implementing a suitable software package is not an easy task. The purchase of a software package is usually far from a commodity buy. It is a complex and gut-wrenching process. Something else that is not always well understood — the cost of the software is often only a minor portion of the overall cost when implementing the typical software package. In addition to being expensive, a major software package implementation consumes a considerable amount of an organization's time and energy. The process can be draining, maddening, and even frightening.

The selection and implementation process and the software itself can also introduce a high degree of business risk if the implementation is not carefully managed. A software package implementation is akin to a high-stakes poker game. This is especially so when the impact stretches into all aspects of an organization and perhaps outward to both its customers and suppliers. The software package implementation can represent the perfect hand for an organization if played correctly. At the same time, this hand also represents the perfect way to fail if played incorrectly.

Despite the costs and the risks, our eagerness for business application software has become a multibillion dollar industry that is today comprised of some of the world's largest, most profitable, most innovative, and most powerful businesses we know. An important question this book will answer is: "What is driving this madness, this relentless rush to software packages?"

What You Will Learn

This book focuses on the business challenges related to justifying, selecting, and implementing software packages by presenting and articulating what is referred to as the software package life cycle. To that end, it contains practical advice and insights on how to justify software packages to enable business process change or improvement, how to select a good fitting software package, and most important, how to implement the software package successfully. This book is based upon the author's industry and product knowledge, and hands-on project experience.

Who Should Read This Book

The intended audience for this book includes both business and technical audiences. This includes executive and senior level managers, business unit managers, project managers, business and systems analysts, industrial engineers, and consultants. This book will benefit individuals in organizations that are actively considering or engaged in a business improvement initiative as these often lead to a software package selection and implementation effort. It will also assist those who are already tasked with a software package selection and implementation assignment in their organizations.

It should be noted that the book's general focus makes it applicable to any type of business organization or other entity having an interest in self improvement, especially if it involves selecting and implementing a software package. But do keep in mind that middle market businesses in distribution or manufacturing that are interested in an enterprise-wide solution, such as an enterprise resource planning software package, will find this book particularly valuable.

CONTENTS

1

THE SOFTWARE PACKAGE
REVOLUTION

It is difficult to pick up any business or technical publication today without some reference to software. Although it has been said that computers have changed our lifestyles and workdays, a computer without software represents only raw potential; it is the software that revolutionizes the way we live, work, or play. In particular, software packages have brought computers into the mainstream. For instance, prior to the widespread availability of software packages, businesses had to hire their own staff or consultants to design and develop software to automate important or labor-consuming facets of their operations.

Developing one's own software was typically a costly and lengthy proposition to successfully automate an existing business process. Every organization, even those with similar processes, had to develop one-of-a-kind solutions. As a result, computer usage was limited to the largest of organizations. There had to be a better way. There was and it has become the foundation for tremendous organizational transformation and a multibillion dollar industry: the software industry. Today there are few stones that have been left unturned by the still young and entrepreneurial software industry.

WHAT KIND OF IMPACT HAS SOFTWARE HAD?

Consider how in the course of less than a decade that word processing software virtually eliminated the use of typewriters. Also consider that electronic spreadsheet software virtually eliminated adding machines, calculators and columnar pads from the desktops of accountants.

Consider a short example from my personal life: after a 10-year hiatus from the classroom, over the past year, I decided to accept an offer to teach several graduate-level classes at a local university. I was surprised to find that during my first few weeks back in the saddle, gone were the once familiar chalkboard, overhead projector, and the final grade input sheet for the school's computer system. Also, I was requested to post the course syllabus on the school's web page.

Today's classroom is equipped with a computer for me to present my lecture via Microsoft PowerPoint; I entered grades electronically, over the Internet into the school's PeopleSoft computer software. Chalkboards have been replaced by whiteboards that sense and record my strokes as I write on the board. Why? So students can also view the entire class online. Of course the classroom is also equipped with cameras and microphones to complement the whiteboard writings and my PowerPoint slides. I felt, for the first time, swept away by technology in a once familiar setting.

This combination of software and technology had transformed the classroom and the learning experience into something I never experienced previously as either a student or as an instructor. Needless to say, I was in effect a student myself, relearning and adapting to the technology-enabled classroom. The transformation of the classroom at the hands of technology is but one example of the radical transformations occurring in many industries and for any number of processes. One such element in such technology-enabled transformations is the software package.

Organizations of all types and sizes have been adopting commercially developed, off-the-shelf software packages at breakneck speed over the past decade. Software packages are the essence of the technology-based changes that have been experienced in organizations of all types and sizes. This chapter explores what is fueling this dramatic and continuing trend throughout the business world.

SO WHAT IS A SOFTWARE PACKAGE ANYWAY?

For the purpose of this book, commercially developed, off-the-shelf software (COTS) packages are preassembled business application systems that have been designed, built, and tested by someone other than your organization. Your organization buys or leases the preassembled business application system either directly from the firm, which designed and built the software, or from an authorized reseller of the software. There are numerous types of preassembled business application systems. I will now review several board categories or types of software commonly available.

Applications by Category

Software packages generally fall into specific application categories, such as enterprise resource planning (ERP), customer relationship management (CRM), supply chain management (SCM) or electronic commerce, which are also known as e-commerce or e-business applications. The categories I have noted here are those receiving the lion's share of interest nowadays. In a future chapter I will cover some of the other application categories as well.

Applications by Vertical

Sometimes software vendors have specifically chosen to target their product to a specific industry. These vendors may have specific enhancements or extensions of their software to satisfy the unique needs of that industry's unique business model or that address regulations covering a specific industry, or *vertical* as they are frequently referred to in the software business. A few typical examples of vertical industry requirements include encumbrance accounting for nonprofit and government entities or lot number and expiration date tracking of inventories for chemical and life science product distributors and manufacturers.

General Purpose by Design

Software packages are usually designed in a general way by the software vendor so that the software package can be readily adapted (although not always as easily as it may seem) for use by numerous organizations of all types and sizes. This includes manufacturers, distributions, and government entities. For instance, annual revenues are frequently used as a yardstick of company size by software vendors and their business partners and resellers.

Being general purpose in nature, software packages are usually designed to satisfy the requirements of the typical business organization. If your organization is not so typical, then the software package may not be an exact fit for your business model. In a later chapter I will discuss how to determine your business requirements and then how to evaluate a software package to determine to what degree it will fulfill your requirements.

FEATURES AND FUNCTIONS: WHERE THEY COME FROM

In the early days, the creators of a software package were not simply software engineers; they were usually business professionals — accountants, production planners, industrial engineers, and others with an idea — for a better way to do work through software.

As the market has matured and the demands on software have become increasingly complex, the task of designing and building a software system, such as an ERP package, has also become an increasingly difficult task. Today, business acumen and technical know–how must be combined to achieve world-class software design.

Software packages include features and functions that represent subsets or supersets of so-called industry best business practices or other commonly accepted business practices. For instance, they include features to address standards or regulations such as those adapted from the Uniform Commercial Code, Generally Accepted Accounting Principles, or an International Standards Organization.

In addition, software vendors often conduct focus groups with potential software buyers or existing users to elicit desired features and functions. They may create product advisory panels, comprised of business and technical experts as well as software users, to help in the design or enhancement of their software.

For many established software packages, they may have a sufficient enough number of users or a so-called "installed base" in the software industry that a user group exists for the software. The user group can in turn serve as the forum for making recommendations to the software vendor regarding product enhancements. In other cases, the vendor may itself sponsor a user group for their software. In later chapters, I'll cover more completely the enhancement and upgrade cycle and costs for a typical software package.

OPEN, LOAD AND GO? NO!

I should point out that preassembled software is not software that is necessarily ready to use. Generally speaking, some degree of configuration, or setup, is almost universally required of any software package before it will be usable in your organization. Depending on the software or your business model, this can be a significant amount of effort.

TRANSFORMING THE BUSINESS THROUGH SOFTWARE

I mentioned earlier that software packages were developed out of a need. That need was to allow a greater number of business users the ability to leverage the power of the computer to automate their business processes. That is an operational improvement. In the first wave of business automation it was a noteworthy accomplishment. However, computers also have the ability to process information faster than a human can. These analytical abilities of the computer cannot be overlooked ,and increasingly, organizations are exploiting these abilities as well. I would like to review a few of the important ways in which software is helping business organizations transform their businesses.

IT IS ABOUT CONSTANT REINVENTION

Business process reengineering is not a revolutionary idea. Though by the accounts of some authors you may have been lead to believe otherwise, businesses have always been engaged in this constant renewal process, which I refer to as the need for constant reinvention. Driven by a desire to maximize shareholder value and competitive pressures, most businesses are constantly reinventing themselves. Call it what you want — business transformation, change, reinvention, or business process reengineering — the end result is the same — businesses change constantly.

There are a number of ways through which business change can occur. Though this is not an exhaustive list, some examples of significant business change, drawn from a wide realm of possibilities, include: a merger, acquisition, or even a bankruptcy filing; a rationalization or downsizing of the business, expansion into a new market segment; the introduction of a new product; going global; or opening up a new marketing channel, the most pervasive of which lately for most businesses has been Internet-based marketing. Finally there is business process reengineering, which is all about streamlining business processes, eliminating redundancies and other nonvalue-adding steps.

IT IS ABOUT TIME TO MARKET

If the revolution in business is not about reinvention, then what is it all about? It is about time. In short, business change is occurring at a much more rapid pace today – more so than at any time in the past. In order to compress time, businesses are increasingly focusing on their core competencies. Many businesses are finding the quickest way to change is to not rely on their own capabilities and processes to design, build, or distribute things, including business processes and systems, but on alliances with suppliers, who can fulfill their business needs on an out-of-the-box basis.

The concept of time suggests another question: Why is timeliness so important? Actually, the notion of timeliness suggests that a business can operate along two dimensions. One dimension is that a business can be proactive, dictating its own agenda and course of action. The other state of affairs is to be reactive, responding, on an after-the-fact basis, to business and marketplace events.

IT IS ABOUT COLLABORATION

Organizations are increasingly forming tighter relationships with their suppliers. Suppliers are hoping these tighter relationships with key customers will keep their production lines busy for a longer period. In turn, customers expect cost concessions and consistency in both product quality and delivery schedules. For example, software packages supporting collaboration are being credited with shortening new product development cycles, reducing component complexity and improving end-product manufacturability. All of these factors contribute to reducing costs, improving margins, and reducing the market risk associated with a late product rollout.

IT IS ABOUT RUNNING LEAN

Today, virtually every organization is trying to reduce both the amount of inventory held in dollars and the duration, or elapsed time, that inventory stocks are actually held before delivery to the customer occurs. Increasingly, organizations are forming alliances and partnerships with customers and suppliers alike. These fast-emerging business alliances are increasingly built on an important, fundamental principle: information-sharing.

Supply chain management is all about the implementation of best business practices that are intended to reduce inventory levels across the supply chain while, at the same time, minimizing transportation costs and minimizing transit times. Some of the best business practices that are changing inventory dynamics include just-in-time inventory deliveries to the plant floor, cross-docking (the near simultaneous receipt and shipment of goods), and third party fulfillment. Therefore, being able to look up and down the entire supply chain, including the whereabouts of stock-in-transit, is an increasingly important business requirement that is being fulfilled by software packages and other important supporting technologies.

BUSINESS INTELLIGENCE VERSUS BUSINESS INFORMATION

Obviously, proactive businesses stand to win all the marbles. At the end of the day what separates winning businesses from losing businesses is generally about how effectively one business has acquired and applied business knowledge, or business intelligence.

At the foundation of business intelligence is information about your past, current, and future business activities. The repository for such information is generally considered to be the domain of an organization's information systems. For instance, an ERP system would generally provide information about completed business transactions, whereas a CRM system would provide information about business deals that *did not* convert from a lead or quote into an order.

It has been my experience that what can sell a system's value to upper management is its ability to provide business intelligence through data summarization, trend analysis, and reporting. However, an ERP system alone would not typically provide a rich enough set of analysis tools in order to accomplish this.

Within the past decade, an entirely new breed of software has emerged to help organizations extract information from their existing information systems. This software has also helped to organize and analyze this information in ways not previously considered possible — at least not in an automated fashion. Referred to online analytical processing (OLAP) these software packages extract, transform, and load (ETL) data (also referred to as data mining) into a centralized data warehouse (another software package) that can then be accessed through powerful analysis and reporting software (referred to as business intelligence software).

IT IS NOT ABOUT RETURN ON INVESTMENT

Let us consider again an ERP system. Many believe that an ERP system represents the silver bullet of enterprise information management. Unfortunately, an ERP system alone is generally not the silver bullet of business information and intelligence gathering. Frequently, ERP systems are cost justified based upon a series of financially based, return on investment criteria. In a later chapter, I will cover some of the more common metrics for measuring the value of an ERP system, as well as for some other software packages. For their part, software vendors will likely work their marketing pitches to you using metrics similar to those you will see in this book.

It may come as a surprise to you, but, generally speaking, it is difficult to provide the necessary cost justification desired by management for most software packages. Consider an ERP system. Generally speaking, ERP systems in particular have little, if any, cost justification. At best, an ERP system may reduce some of your overhead associated with maintaining old systems, but really that's about it. If anything, an ERP system may increase your costs. Why is that? Because in addition to the software and initial implementation costs, there may be hardware upgrades and ongoing support costs, such as annual maintenance contracts with the software vendor. So why then are expensive ERP systems so popular?

IT IS ALL ABOUT RETURN ON INFORMATION

Much can be said about information, or knowledge, as power. Businesses that excel in their chosen markets usually do so because they have transformed information into business intelligence and are able to extend and leverage their business knowledge. A far more effective measure of a software package's success is the impact such software has had on an organization's return on information — that is how an organization has been able to leverage information to enhance its shareholder value.

Returning to the case of an ERP system, the real return on investment for an ERP system is related to how the system is set up to gather information and, more important, how this information is subsequently used to alter or enhance current and future business activities. Stopping defects, speeding deliveries, and eliminating process delays are all examples of applying information, as knowledge, in transforming a business process or activity toward shareholder maximization.

One final note about return on information: return on information cannot be measured directly. Return on information must be extrapolated, indirectly through traditional metrics of business performance. It is a cause and effect relationship — as your information gathering improves, this information is subsequently used to improve decision making within the business organization.

Achieving High Levels of Return on Information

A basic tenet of a successful ERP system implementation is that it must provide sound transaction processing attributes that will enable you to deliver your product or service accurately and efficiently. A successful ERP system implementation will achieve high levels of integration and aggregation of information. It will do so across all of the major processing threads or cycles your business has. At the same time, the ERP system must capture details about your business transactions. These details are the activities and materials consumed or needed and in what way they will enhance, or detract from, the value of the product or service that will or has been delivered to your customer.

IT IS ABOUT CORE COMPETENCIES

Quite frankly, more businesses are coming to the realization that building software is not really a part of their core competencies, unless of course they are the software factory. At no time did this realization manifest itself more so than during the recent ramp-up for year 2000 compliance. A record number of businesses adopted packaged software solutions during the late 1990s, casting aside their homegrown, legacy systems in favor of packaged software solutions from software vendors. ERP systems in particular enjoyed enormous success.

Regardless of how hard most businesses may try, the truth of the matter is that they will not create custom applications that ever approach the robustness of a commercially available software package. When a business designs a new product, design for manufacturability is generally an important consideration. When a firm creates software for internal use, design for manufacturability is not a common metric to apply — usually it is cost containment. Sadly, cost containment usually curtails the design for manufacturability attributes in an internal software product. When design for manufacturability attributes are removed, so too is the robustness of the software and its ability to be easily adapted, or retrofitted, to accommodate business change.

SOFTWARE PACKAGE BENEFITS: LONG ON HYPE, SHORT ON RESULTS?

There are as many opponents of packaged software solutions as there are proponents. For instance, opponents suggest that ERP systems are too complex and too general for most businesses. Others will suggest that ERP systems are not robust enough to support complex business processes. Another group of opponents will contend that one ERP system — no matter how good it may be considered — cannot do everything well. As a result, almost any ERP package you select will likely require integration with other software packages and custom applications to fulfill an organization's transaction processing requirements. Out of this thinking, an approach, or strategy, for dealing with software packages has developed.

This approach — using multiple packages from multiple vendors and integrating them — is often referred to as a best of breed approach to software selection and implementation. Special software packages referred to as Enterprise Application Integration (EAI) software have emerged to allow integration between dissimilar software packages. Others contend that a large, complex ERP package cannot be enhanced rapidly enough to keep pace with business needs. For instance, many critics cite the ERP software industry's lack of responsiveness in web-enabling their core software products as such an example. To do business in the e-business world will increasingly require the strength, integration, and flexibility offered by an ERP system.

Sorry, We Are Closed Because Our System Will Not Work

Although this used to sound foolish, it is not so far from the truth any longer. The tragic events of September 11, 2001, in the United States resulted in massive business and economic disruption. It was the dawn of a new era in U.S. business risk management and perhaps for much of the rest of the world as well.

Although the business risks posed by a software package are much different, these risks are nonetheless important issues to consider during the selection and implementation of a software package. This is especially the case when any software failures stand to disrupt your supply chain, or worse, your ability to fulfill customer orders. ERP, and more recently SCM software packages, are bearing the blame at numerous organizations for disrupting business operations and in a few cases are blamed for the failure of the business organization itself.

For instance, you will often hear about the case of FoxMeyer Drugs, the now classic ERP train wreck. FoxMeyer was a multibillion dollar health care products distributor that entered Chapter 11 bankruptcy. This was a result of massive disruptions to its ongoing business processes and supply chain caused by problems reportedly stemming from the implementation of a sophisticated new ERP system. This is an extreme example.

Lesser cases of business disruption — caused by software — have also been reported. Department 56, a gift products distributor, has reported problems with its customer receivables due to a new ERP system. Shoemaker Nike reported that its inventory was disrupted by the implementation of a supply chain management software package. Finally, Hershey Foods attributed inventory and production problems to a new ERP system. Certainly, these were for the most part large organizations that suffered software related business disruption. Smaller and middle market organizations have similar stories, except that their size does not dictate the media attention given to these much larger organizations.

Smaller and middle market organizations can face similar risks of business disruption from software packages. Generally speaking, they can prove equally challenging, even on a smaller scale. Can this happen to your organization? Yes, however, part of the mission of this book is to suggest experience-based best practices that will help you to identify and minimize the business risks associated with the introduction of a new software package into your organization.

If business disruption, or worse, if failure is so close, then why do companies continue to buy and implement ERP or SCM systems? Quite frankly, when properly configured and installed, ERP and SCM systems can and do work. However, if any software package selection or implementation is left to chance, a train wreck is entirely possible.

SOFTWARE PACKAGES: WHY BOTHER?

Much has been written in the trade press about the failure of software packages to deliver on their promises of true business value. Cost overruns, significant gaps, missed deadlines, marginal end results, and little, if any, overall business process improvement make it clear that managing the process of selecting and implementing software packages is a complex feat.

If selecting and implementing software packages is such a complex feat, why then do organizations continue to buy them? Simply put, the costs and risks associated with developing custom business application software is not any better —in many cases it is significantly worse. Indeed, we have come to accept software packages as a necessary part of modern, organizational life.

A case in point is the desktop computer workstation. E-mail packages from companies such as Lotus, Microsoft, and Novell dominate, while office suite software from Corel, Lotus, Microsoft, and Sun dominates. Imagine an organization writing its own e-mail system. Could this be done? Absolutely, but the real question is would an organization want to. The answer is no, for there are far better uses of its capital than building what others have already done for the organization. Of course, the same approach — using software packages — can be applied to virtually all aspects of an organization's business application software requirements.

The selection and implementation of business application software packages generally represents a large-scale investment of both dollar and human capital. Because of their organization-wide scope, the business risks in the typical software package implementation are also significant. Therefore, the defining element in the success or failure of any software package implementation is largely one of project management. Drawing on my own experience, observation, and research of over a dozen years in this field, I have assembled a best practice-based approach or methodology that is widely applicable to the *successful selection and implementation* of business application software packages. Much of this and subsequent chapters will draw on the tenets of this best practice-based approach for software selection and implementation.

WHY PACKAGED SOFTWARE PROJECTS FAIL

Over the course of time, I have seen many packaged software projects fail. However, the reasons for the failure or termination of these projects is usually for one of the following reasons:

- The wrong software package was selected.
- The software package does not work as advertised.
- Too many changes or interfaces were needed (or were attempted) in order for the given software package to work as desired.
- The project lacked executive sponsorship.
- A project plan did not exist, or was not followed.
- Poor or no training — for either or both the software and any business process changes — was provided.
- The project lacked business unit support.
- Insufficient business or technical resources were committed to the project.
- Change management strategies were not instituted from day one in the life of the project.
- A business merger terminates a "work in process".

This book is about providing practical strategies that offer the organization the greatest chance of achieving a successful software package implementation experience. As a launch point for these remaining discussions, the following short list of critical success factors applies to software package selection and implementation:

- Carefully define your specific business requirements.
- Select the right software package for your organization.
- Manage the expectations of your user community.
- Exploit the best business practices built into the software.
- Get the softer side of the implementation right.
- Mitigate project risks.
- Take a holistic, managed approach.

It is also important to discuss early on some of the important realities that an organization will face when implementing a packaged software solution. These realities include:

- The perfect software package *does not exist.*
- No two software package implementations *are ever the same.*
- No software package implementation *is ever perfect.*
- No software package implementation *is ever really complete.*

These realities represent real business risks. Part of the mission of this book is to provide techniques that can be used to mitigate the risks associated with selecting and implementing software packages.

THE NEXT BIG THING FROM ERP

There is an ever-growing community of business pragmatists that favor simplicity over complexity. With an increasing emphasis on supply chain dynamics, the market is clearly telling businesses of all sizes to manage their operations as efficiently and effectively as possible and to strip away nonvalue-adding activities.

At the same time, a countervailing trend is occurring as we increasingly see market models move toward mass customization. In short, the time has arrived when it is necessary for your core business transaction-processing infrastructure to become a quick-change artist. It is about blowing up old business models and starting anew with relationship-driven models that require customer by customer adaptability.

Some contend that with the end of Y2K, the market for ERP software is all but dead. Proponents see the best market for ERP software as yet to come. Why would that be? As business models are reinvented around e-business, the need for ERP system backbones will increase. Furthermore, not every business caught ERP fever during the 1990s. While the largest companies may have ERP systems in place, many smaller and middle market businesses — those with revenues of less than 500 million dollars — do not. That is one of the reasons why this book will actually focus on how business organizations in this size range can leverage software packages to improve their business performance.

As competitive pressure mounts, information system infrastructures, including ERP systems, will move down-market. The small and middle market segment represents a lucrative market for all software package vendors — especially ERP system vendors — going forward. In addition, the market represented by virtually all-new start-up businesses in the years to come will increasingly be built around supply chain or knowledge-based competitive advantages. Again, an ERP system is an important component in the e-business centric information system infrastructure.

The driving force behind business is and always has been change. Although this is not a book about business change, it is about an agent of business change — the business application software package. Generally speaking, software packages represent a robust, out-of-the-box way of automating business processes that can be configured or reconfigured as business needs change and as often as they change.

WHAT IS THE BEST SOFTWARE PACKAGE FOR OUR ORGANIZATION?

Somehow I knew to anticipate that this would be one of your earliest questions. Let me begin by offering some sage advice: selecting and implementing any software package is first and foremost a business imperative; it is not a technology imperative.

Nowadays, it seems that everyone is talking about SAP, i2 Technologies, Oracle, Manugistics, Siebel, Ariba, PeopleSoft, J.D. Edwards, Baan, Navison, QAD, IFS, or Microsoft-Great Plains. Some accounts have glowing praise for a product from one of these vendors, while other accounts will have harsh criticism for the same software package. Who is right? To a certain degree, all of these commentaries likely have an element of truth to them. To determine which software product or possibly mix of products is right for your business will require careful and exhaustive research: first of your requirements, second of the products themselves, and finally, a self assessment of your organization's propensity for and willingness to change.

Only after carefully analyzing and determining your overall business requirements, as well as gaining an understanding of the features and capabilities of the software and your organization's ability to absorb and successfully implement a software package, will you have a complete picture of what is right for you. During the software selection process, every product chosen deserves your full, objective, and unbiased consideration. Once selected, the chosen software package will require your organization's undivided attention if you are going to achieve a successful implementation of the software package within your business organization.

CHAPTER EPILOGUE: SOFTWARE PACKAGES ARE CHANGING THE RULES

A fitting end to this chapter would be to suggest that software packages are changing the way business is done. To a certain extent that is a true statement, but software packages do not deserve all of the credit. There are numerous forces at work. Make no doubt about it, technology enablement is changing the way business is done, and software packages are a large part of that technology enablement. This book is about justifying, selecting, and implementing software packages that have the potential to transform business processes and practices and improve business performance.

2

THE SOFTWARE PACKAGE MARKETPLACE

The intent of this chapter is to provide some pertinent background information about the various types of commercial, off-the-shelf generalized business application software packages available in today's marketplace. It is by no means an exhaustive introduction. In addition, this chapter exposes the reader to some of the business purposes related for each of the software packages introduced. Understanding the business processes served by a software package and how the business process can be transformed or improved by software can represent the impetus for acquiring and implementing a software package.

Software packages fulfill the promise of business process improvement and hence business performance improvement by automating, integrating, and streamlining information flows related to one or more business processes. This chapter discusses, in particular, software packages of interest to distribution, manufacturing and service oriented business concerns. There are a number of other types of specialty software packages in the marketplace as well. These specialty areas are often referred to as vertical markets by software vendors. For instance, health care management systems and association management systems are specialty areas within the service sector.

Although not every category of software package is represented by this chapter, the software package justification, selection, and implementation best practices discussed throughout this book are meant to be universal in application, regardless of the type of software package your organization may need or whatever its specific vertical industry or line of business happens to be.

Although I have many reservations about doing so, from time to time I will mention the names of specific and well-known products, providers, or services. Do not consider such mentions as endorsements; rather treat them simply as representative examples of software packages in particular business application categories. As a consultant, I understand and value objectivity in the selection process; recommendations cannot be forthcoming without an understanding of your business objectives, budget, and processes.

ENTERPRISE RESOURCE PLANNING SYSTEMS

By far, the greatest application of the material in this book will be of use to any organization considering the selection and implementation of an enterprise resource planning (ERP) software package. There are many additional names for this type of software, including enterprise software (ES), enterprise resource management (ERM) software, and extended enterprise resource planning software (ERP-II). Although this type of software has its underpinnings in manufacturing, first with materials requirements planning (MRP) and later with manufacturing resource planning (MRP-II) software, the typical ERP system has grown up.

A Brief History of ERP

ERP systems have been around since the mid-1970s. ERP systems originated to satisfy the information processing requirements in a manufacturing operation. These systems largely grew out of initiatives to support MRP and MRP-II planning and control concepts that were difficult to carry out prior to the commercial availability of computer systems. At that time, such systems ran only on mainframe computers.

Over time, ERP systems have grown in their ability and depth to serve in other organizational business models as well. Today, ERP systems have been adopted for use in virtually every industry or sector of government. Over time, ERP systems migrated from the mainframe to the midrange computer platform and more recently, onto the client/server platform.

ERP has also emerged on the web, especially through the use of information portals that arrange a business organization's various information systems around so-called stakeholder views. These are areas of interest or dealings with the organization divided into a series of related web pages. Stakeholder views enabled by an ERP system or the information within it can include those for customers, suppliers, employees, owners (shareholders), managers, and regulators of the business organization.

What an ERP System Is

The ERP system facilitates the capture, storage, and use of specific information about business transactions that occur within an organization. ERP systems are said to be process oriented.

The ERP system is best viewed as a collection of other, smaller systems. These other systems are often referred to as subsystems or modules of the ERP system within the industry. Each module or subsystem supports the transaction flows specific to a given business process, such as general ledger accounting or inventory control or procurement. The important characteristic underpinning the ERP system is that all of the modules share fundamental information between modules, a concept referred to as integration.

Chapter 5 offers a general business process model, upon which most ERP systems rely. It should be noted that this model assumes a manufacturing orientation and so do most ERP systems. Most ERP systems are readily adaptable to other business models, including the service sector, health care, government, and nonprofit organizations in general. Such major business functions or processing threads are well known and are themselves somewhat generic. So-called best-practice models for many of these major business functions or processing threads have emerged and are widely endorsed and implemented by the ERP software industry.

As an example of the universal appeal of ERP systems both the National Aeronautics and Space Administration and the U.S. Navy are among two government agencies that have recently announced plans to implement ERP systems. In many instances, only certain functions of an ERP system will be useful outside of the manufacturing or distribution arena. For instance, financials, procurement, inventory control and facilities maintenance are examples of functional areas of an ERP system that can be readily applied outside the manufacturing and distribution arena.

As mature systems stretching well beyond their earlier manufacturing heritage, these systems have become complex, integrated, general purpose, and comprehensive back-office support systems that follow fairly generic business process models. They are demarcated by major business functions rather than being dominated by their manufacturing functionality alone.

Today, the starting point for most business organizations seeking to implement a systems strategy relying on software packages will begin with a look at ERP systems as their core, back-office system. Organizations will look at this along with other required business application systems, and even their computer hardware is ultimately being selected based upon the ERP system decision.

What an ERP System Is Not

There is a common misconception about ERP systems and most business application software systems. As a general rule, ERP systems and other business application systems do not automate the business processes themselves. ERP systems and other business application systems do automate information flows related to business processes. Although a subtle difference, some might argue my analysis is nothing more than semantic, but I feel it is an important and frequently misunderstood premise about business application software in general.

The few processes that an ERP system might perhaps automate that today might represent a manual effort in your operation are usually workflow related, such as a credit check, stock availability, or an approval step. To be certain, software is available to effectively automate a business process. Systems that can physically automate business processes are referred to by several names, including factory automation, process automation or real-time systems. As I view the world, a business application system, such as an ERP system, automates the logical or informational flow associated with physical business processes. Even the name — enterprise resource planning system — is somewhat of a misnomer. Most ERP systems do much more than simply provide for the collecting, storing, and facilitating of information or knowledge-based planning.

What Is Happening with ERP Today?

After Y2K, the ERP software vendors have seen a dramatic falloff in new business. Not every business organization replaced aging legacy systems in the pre-Y2K era. Nor did every organization then, or now, that could benefit from the integration and information processing capabilities of an ERP system adopt one. ERP systems or their equivalents remain the cornerstone of any successful business operation. In fact, no matter how ill-fitting or poorly executed the ERP system implementation, it was nonetheless the backbone of the organization's information flow.

While many organizations implemented ERP systems in the pre-Y2K era, few organizations to this day have realized the full potential that an ERP system can offer to their organizations. The adoption of most ERP systems remains a work in progress and is hopefully not viewed as a bottomless money pit, a disaster, or an utter failure by the organization, its management, or its rank and file. To be sure, ERP is a tougher sell in the post Y2K era. This is partly because so many organizations that adopted ERP have yet to see the value or realize the benefits of their lengthy and costly efforts. The fact remains that the potential for process improvement in organizations without an ERP system or a high degree of information integration today remains as great as ever.

Trends That Will Define the Future of ERP

Organizations that have invested substantial sums into an ERP system end up largely with an elaborate new legacy system that the organization is absolutely dependent upon to run their business operations. Because there is so much at stake, ERP providers and customers introduce changes to technology and deployments gradually to avoid costly mistakes. Nonetheless, ERP systems do change, but slowly. It has been my observation that the ERP industry is at least one generation behind the available technology or latest business or software trends.

Today, several important trends are affecting the ERP system. First, the ERP system is reaching forward, into the front office. What this means is that most ERP software vendors are adding customer relationship management (CRM) capabilities into their core software. This does not bode well for the traditional CRM software players. More of these vendors will likely evaporate, as some already have, while others will merge with ERP vendors anxious to add these capabilities into their product family. This is especially good news for smaller and middle market business organizations as the likelihood of being able to do one-stop shopping for software will be more likely.

The second trend affecting the ERP system is that ERP systems are reaching out. These systems are not doing this simply throughout the business organization into other aspects of the business as is the case with CRM, but also outside the organization to customers and suppliers. This is perhaps the most important and fundamental change in ERP software. This is the collision of supply chain management (SCM) and electronic or collaborative commerce with the ERP system.

While offering portals to stakeholders in the form of order taking, status, or activity and delivery inquiries and updates are an important and desirable feature that ERP vendors have recently embraced, more is needed. The future of ERP systems will be defined by a more important trend: the exchange of large amounts of information automatically, especially for product design collaboration and for SCM purposes. Unlike the interactive portal, a pretty face for an ERP system delivered through the Internet, these exchanges will occur behind the scenes. They will occur on an almost constant basis between the systems of customers and suppliers, upstream and downstream, within an entire industry or market segment. The need is for loosely coupled integration between disparate systems.

Obviously, this means that ERP vendors must expose more and more, if not all of their product functionality, through so-called application program interfaces (APIs). Using these APIs, an organization can, through use of enterprise application integration (EAI) middleware packages, initiate, receive, and route messages among disparate systems, customers, and vendors on a near real-time basis across the Internet.

Unfortunately, because ERP vendors are behind in this movement toward collaborative commerce, integrating any two applications is a challenging task. Given the past difficulties that early and deep pocket adopters had in connecting their systems with other applications, the backlash has pushed the ERP industry toward adopting more open and flexible product architectures. Unfortunately, for the immediate future, the benefits are still to come. In general, it is still quite difficult, expensive, and time-consuming to integrate software packages with one another, with legacy systems or across enterprises.

Such major business functions or threads are well known and themselves somewhat generic and include: financial management and planning; human resource planning and administration; procurement; sales order processing; and manufacturing, which is usually further classified by the type of manufacturing operation, such as process, make to stock, or make to order. These packages typically make one or more such major functional demarcations and are applicable to virtually any sector, including non-manufacturing applications and government and nonprofit organizations.

Manufacturing Execution Systems

Manufacturing execution systems (MES) are synonymous with shop floor automation. These systems track both the activities to be performed or completed and their duration. They also track the resources needed or resources used throughout the entire manufacturing process. The manufacturing execution system has traditionally worked closely with an ERP system, primarily by serving as a data collecting mechanism, gathering production related information from the plant floor.

In recent years, MES have become more bidirectional. They extract and send to the plant floor, communications regarding required components, locations, setups, expediting, and order-related characteristics or changes to them to support lean manufacturing and mass customization techniques.

It can be said that MES now connect the plant floor to both the larger organization and outward to interested parties in the supply chain. These systems manage, control, and document the manufacturing process in real time and are instrumental in optimizing production processes.

The importance of MES and automated data collection in general cannot be overemphasized. Data availability and data quality or accuracy remain fundamental principles underpinning the success an organization will have when implementing an ERP system.

Manufacturing Planning and Control

While ERP systems have wide appeal for their ability to automate and integrate back-office information flows for just about any business organization, the primary use of the ERP system remains manufacturing planning and control. Manufacturing or distribution operations performance improvement remains an important reason why these systems are acquired. If an ERP system is to deliver true business value, it must facilitate improvements to the way business decisions on operational issues are orchestrated on a day-to-day basis.

An important part of what an ERP does is to impose a set of rules on an organization. If the business is to be improved through new levels of planning and control via material and manufacturing resources, then the organization must learn a new, more disciplined way of doing business. For an organization that is not already managing itself by planning its work and material acquisitions methodically, this change will be nothing less than a revolution. It will require a completely fresh approach to operating and planning day-to-day business operations. In addition, the potential for success with the planning and control dimension of any ERP system requires heightened levels of an organization's data accuracy, consistency, and documented and systemized business logic.

SUPPLY CHAIN MANAGEMENT (SCM) SYSTEMS

The second most important software package community of interest to most readers of this book will be to automate supply chain processes. As a general rule, supply chain management is more of a management concept than it is a complete system. For supply chain management, in application, to be effected, requires integration between a multitude of specialized internal systems. This includes ERP and other types of systems related to manufacturing planning and execution as well as for demand management and forecasting and for product distribution and transportation. In addition to internal systems, external systems, particularly links with customers and suppliers and other providers, such as common carriers, are crucial.

Defining Supply Chains

A *supply chain* is a network of interconnected entities that perform the functions of procuring raw materials, transforming raw materials into intermediate and end products, and distributing an end product or product family to customers. Supply chains can exist for both manufacturing and service organizations. The complexity of any given end product supply chain will vary greatly from industry to industry and firm to firm.

From a business model perspective, supply chain management is typically viewed to lie between the fully vertically integrated firm, which Henry Ford did at Ford Motor Company's huge River Rouge complex where the entire material flow was owned by a single firm, versus a business model where each channel member operates largely independently of one another. Controlling the supply chain is a daunting task, yet Henry Ford was relatively successful at it in an era when computers did not exist. Unfortunately, times have changed. Sourcing is now global. Manufacturing is increasingly modularized, allowing for mass customization, something that Henry Ford would liken to heresy.

Few organizations since Ford Motor Company's River Rouge efforts have been as successful to the degree that Ford was with vertical integration. In a sense, Ford's River Rouge has been an aberration in the history of business. There are microeconomic forces at play that not only make vertical integration difficult, but perhaps even counterproductive in the long run. These issues include specialization as Adam Smith called it; today we call it core competency. It is hard to be good at everything, so the focus is on what the firm does best, doing only the things that provide competitive advantage or superior returns. The second issue is cost. The question is simply: Can the vertically integrated firm achieve economies of scale? Often times the answer is no. Controlling the supply does not necessarily control costs, for there may be enormous entry costs that must be recouped. This adds burden onto every unit produced. Unless volume is achieved, the results can be less than perfect.

In both of the above cases, the producing organization will turn to a network of suppliers. Each supplier which has achieved specialization and economies of scale within the supplier's product or service offering to achieve an maintain a competitive advantage that is difficult, if not impossible, to overcome.

When vertical integration failed to work, the alternative for large firms became what is known as strategic sourcing. Strategic sourcing provided the microeconomic benefits of vertical integration to the producer but did not completely solve the control issues regarding the source of supply. Multiple suppliers would be used to mitigate the risks of unexpected shortages or delays in material. As producers relied more on outsiders to fulfill their component requirements, quality issues also became a concern.

Traditionally, all of the individual entities involved in the supply chain have operated independently. Each of these individual business organizations has a role within the supply chain, such as marketing, distribution, planning, manufacturing, transportation or purchasing, and each has their own business objectives. More often than not, the business objectives of these individual entities conflict with those of the other entities within the supply chain.

What is the result? A single, integrated plan or vision for the supply chain does not exist, leaving as many plans as there are organizations involved in the supply chain. What is more, such lack of vision and integration contributes to inefficiencies, waste, and added costs throughout the supply chain. Coordination between the various entities within a supply chain is the key to its effective management.

Supply chain management is a business process management strategy that aims squarely at reducing or eliminating inefficiency, waste, and added costs along the supply chain by providing a mechanism through which these different entities can be integrated together. It is important to understand early on that supply chain management is not simply a single piece of software and does not involve a single entity. It is business process strategy — one of collaboration or information sharing, built on mutual trust and gain-sharing. Some industries have been more successful at this than others. One such industry is the commercial aircraft industry. Consider Boeing Corporation for a moment. Boeing today is more an assembler of aircraft than it is a manufacturer, bringing together and assembling large-scale, subassemblies or components from scores of global suppliers into what becomes the end product — a commercial jet airplane.

From a systemic point of view, collaboration and information sharing within a supply chain clearly requires a higher level of system interoperability. This is not merely interoperability between the internal systems of an organization, but between its internal systems and the internal systems of its suppliers and any upstream customers in the case of intermediate goods. Chapter 7 discusses interoperability and extensible markup language (XML), an emerging standard for the exchange of information that can permit such interoperability.

Using Supply Chain Management for Competitive Advantage

Organizations increasingly find themselves being pulled in one direction — by relentless customer demands for cost reductions, faster deliveries or greater customization. At the same time, their stakeholders, who highly value an organization's ability to achieve and maintain consistent levels of profitable growth, are pulling them in an opposite direction. Many organizations have discovered that they can achieve profitable growth by treating supply chain management as a strategic variable. The enlightened organization that views supply chain management as a strategic variable is pursuing tangible outcomes from their supply chain management initiatives, including improved revenue growth, greater asset utilization, and cost reductions.

Supply Chain Excellence

Excellent supply chain management requires an enlightened mindset. What then are the elements that contribute to an enlightened mindset?

First, when an organization does begin to leverage its supply chain, it must think about its supply chain as a whole — a chain of interconnected entities — both internal and external to the organization itself. This chain encompasses all aspects involved in managing the flow of products, services, and information from their suppliers' suppliers to their customers' customers (i.e., channel customers, such as distributors and retailers). It is a trust-based network of unrelated, interdependent parties that must collaborate closely for the common good. The organization must also set explicit objectives for revenue growth, asset utilization, and cost reduction to be achieved by the supply chain management initiative. These efforts must reflect a holistic approach, viewing the supply chain from end to end and orchestrating efforts within so that the overall improvement is achieved. This must be in terms of revenue, cost, and asset utilization targets that together are greater than the sum of the individual parts.

Second, when the benefits are real, it also means sharing both the pain and the gain in managing the supply chain. While manufacturers must necessarily place high demands on suppliers, they should also realize that their supplier-partners must share their goal of reducing costs across the supply chain in order to lower prices in the marketplace and enhance margins. The logical extension of this broad-based thinking required across the supply chain is to engage in gain-sharing arrangements that would ultimately reward every entity that contributes to the greater profitability. Unfortunately, many organizations are not yet ready for such progressive thinking.

Third, if gain sharing is important to supply chain management success, then why do organizations fear them? They are usually not ready for gain-sharing arrangements out of ignorance. These organizations lack a sound knowledge of their costs not only for direct materials, but for just about everything else as well. Fact-based knowledge is an essential foundation for determining the best way of acquiring every kind of material and service the company buys.

It can be said that a critical success factor in achieving supply chain excellence is cost knowledge and control. Such fact-based knowledge is often missing because an organization has an inadequate or inappropriate cost information system today. One costing system or technique that has gained widespread accolades for bringing about needed improvements in cost knowledge to the organization is known as activity-based costing or activity-based management; it is a practice this author strongly endorses.

Fourth, the enlightened organization realizes that excellence in supply chain management is achieved only through a broad-based effort that combines both strategic and tactical process change. This change is within its own organizational framework and extends to its channel partners. Such success relies on a top to bottom analysis of the existing supply chain. The investment in gaining such a perspective is essential to developing any subsequent roadmap for changes to the supply chain.

This top-to-bottom analysis requires a rigorous assessment of the entire supply chain — from supplier relationships to internal operations to the marketplace, including customers, competitors, and the industry as a whole. Current practices must be evaluated against best practices to determine what gaps exist. A cost/benefit analysis can be used to prioritize initiatives, establishing project budget and resource requirements and achieving a complete financial picture of an organization's supply chain before, during, and after implementation of the supply chain management initiative.

A final element of enlightenment is the need for an information technology infrastructure that supports supply chain management. Unfortunately, much of the information that an organization will require to enhance its supply chain will reside outside of its own internal systems. Unfortunately, few organizations have invested in the necessary information technology infrastructure to fully support the "fully informed and collaborative supply chain." More important, organizations must recognize that it is through electronic connectivity wherein the greatest opportunity resides to fundamentally change the supply chain. This change can occur by slashing transaction costs through electronic handling of orders, invoices, and payments to shrinking inventories using vendor-managed inventory programs.

How SCM Differs from ERP

It can be said that SCM and ERP software packages and systems have many overlapping features. In an ERP system, planning for the various materials, capacity, and demand constraints are considered separately, in relative isolation from one another. In SCM products, all the relevant data is considered simultaneously. SCM systems can perform both simulations and schedule adjustments in real time. The traditional ERP system is focused on performing a wider variety of transaction processing tasks relative the narrower role that a SCM solution addresses. Given the dynamic, real-time nature of the SCM planning engines means that planning scenarios occur in seconds, not in minutes or hours from now. This is because planning activities are usually batch processes in the ERP system. Many SCM systems visibly map the entire supply chain, showing where problems are; ERP systems typically do not provide such supply chain maps.

Much like customer relationship management systems, the line between an ERP solution and an SCM solution are beginning to blur. ERP system vendors add SCM capabilities organically or through SCM software acquisitions that are then incorporated into the ERP vendors' mainstream product.

Examples include J.D. Edwards acquisition of Numetrix and PeopleSoft's acquisition of Red Pepper, which were previously standalone, advanced planning and scheduling (APS) systems.

The Dilemma of Enterprise-Wide Integration and the Supply Chain

It seems that one cannot pick up a trade publication or any vendor literature today without some mention of what a product or vendor can do for your organization's supply chain. The reality is these benefits are difficult and costly to achieve. Despite making huge investments in ERP systems, many organizations have found that by merely acquiring and implementing these software packages they have achieved only an internal-facing information technology infrastructure. An external-facing infrastructure is necessary to effectively manage the supply chain. Most of the current enterprise-wide software packages are enterprise-bound. These software packages are unable to share information across the supply chain, except perhaps through electronic data interchange (EDI) transactions — a batch process rather than a real time-process.

Supply chain management requires a higher level of system interoperability. Unfortunately, most such interoperability initiatives, especially by ERP software vendors, are still in their infancy. Generally speaking, this may require that an organization obtains a message brokering software package. This may also mean an upgrade to, replacement of or modifications to an existing ERP or other legacy system in order to accept and initiate supply chain related transactional information. Message brokering for supply chain management relies heavily on XML-based document exchanges. The EDI transactions of the past are being replaced or supplanted by XML-based transactions. In fact, an EDI transaction can be wrapped inside an XML document for compatibility with legacy processes.

Many enterprise-wide software packages — particularly ERP systems — while able to capture reams of transactional data, are usually ill-equipped for translating this information into actionable intelligence that can be used to enhance real-world operations and maximize business performance. Often times, an ERP system will be supplanted by SCM related software. Organizations seeking to improve their supply chains need to build an information technology infrastructure that provides for three essential dimensions of information. The supply chain driven or supply chain focused information technology infrastructure must provide:

- On a short-term basis, the ability to provide for day-to-day transaction processing and electronic commerce across the supply chain. The sharing of this information is used to continuously align supply and demand through daily scheduling. Channel partners must have this short-term information in hand and act upon it if supply chain management success is to prevail. Underscoring this need for a continuous flow of information is that without such, an organization will see its costs, asset levels, and cycle times fall short of the target levels established for supply chain initiative by their business strategy. If the information flow is nothing less than continuous, then the business case for the supply chain initiative will be quickly compromised.

■ On a mid-term basis, the ability to facilitate operational planning and decision-making tasks. This information is used to allocate resources efficiently, providing for demand and shipment planning and master production scheduling.

■ On a long-term basis, the ability to enable strategic analysis. Such a system must provide tools, such as an integrated network model, to synthesize data for use in high-level what-if scenario planning. This kind of information can help the organization evaluate the individual performances and differences over time of manufacturing plants, distribution centers, suppliers, and third-party service alternatives.

Organizations that wish to achieve this supply chain driven or supply chain focused information technology infrastructure will need to rely on enterprise application integration, message brokering, real time Internet based information flows, and XML. Most important, organizations will need to rely on their software package vendors to build into their product architectures native support for these technologies.

Advanced Planning and Scheduling (APS)

The first major category of supply management software is systems for APS. Most important, from the customer service perspective, these systems enable the organization to provide real time, which is available to promise calculation or scenarios. APS is the result of a convergence of technology, evolving management theory and the application of mathematical techniques.

APS uses finite capacity scheduling (FCS) to compensate for the "infinite loading" assumption inherent in the traditional planning logic contained of the traditional MRP/ERP system. Using FCS, the APS system fits a new production order into existing capacity. Material and capacity are planned simultaneously rather than sequentially, ensuring that the resulting plan is within the limitations of available resource and material constraints.

Technologically speaking, APS takes advantage of cheap computer memory. Memory-resident, high-speed scheduling systems are at the core of an APS system. This is a technological advancement, not a conceptual advancement, and employs conventional MRP/ERP logic. Processing speed and memory availability are exploited to accomplish the planning process in seconds rather than in minutes or hours, making simulation or what-if analysis possible. Synquest and ASPROVA are examples of APS systems.

Demand Management

The second major category of SCM software is systems that provide for demand management. The demand management process is largely about consolidating and organizing sales forecast data. These sales forecasts are then translated into production planning and the building of inventory levels to satisfy demand. This is traditionally the domain of the sales and operations planning process within an organization. From the perspective of supply chain management, demand management implies that customers and suppliers collaborate in order to develop and manage a customer-focused requirements forecast.

Requirements, from the suppliers' perspective, represent inventory building. Inventory represents the ability to service a customer order within any given time frame. Ideally, when an order is taken or accepted, the supplier should be able to interrogate existing inventory levels and work in process levels in real time to allow for an intelligent delivery commitment, rather than making a blind promise based upon typical backlogs or turnaround times. The supplier's intelligent delivery commitment can then be "trusted" by customers, who are in turn making their own business or inventory building decisions.

Why the concern about inventory? First, for decades, many organizations covered their lack of planning through inventory — the result was usually too much inventory or too little inventory. In the context of the supply chain, customers and suppliers exchange information about product or component requirements. Second, inventory is costly. By proactively managing inventory levels throughout the supply chain, inventory investment can be driven down. Inventory investments are a major use of working capital for most manufacturers and distributors.

The premise of demand management is that it attempts to project and avert critical shortfalls or excesses in capacity and essential resources. Demand management requires significant interaction between customers and suppliers. Information flows must run both ways in the supply chain. Sales information and forecasts flow into the organization to validate what to produce, while knowledge of inventory availability must flow out to supply chain.

One of the software packages that centers on managing demand and leveraging demand information in the supply chain management and overall manufacturing planning process is Demand Solutions. Developed by Demand Management, Demand Solutions is one such system that focuses on supply chain centric demand management.

Transportation Management

A third category of SCM software is transportation management. A transportation management system (TMS) can assist your organization in planning for the transportation of goods and materials from one geographic location to another. The movement of raw materials, components, and finished products from supplier to the manufacturer and from the distribution center to the customer can represent a significant percentage of the final cost for any product. In addition, knowing the exact location of goods while in transit to a customer is considered an important dimension of world class customer service. It is an increasingly important dimension of overall supply chain management.

There are four areas of major importance in transportation management: route planning, load planning, carrier selection, and shipment tracking. For instance, most transportation management software is able to help an organization:

- Select between carrier alternatives, reducing overall transportation costs.
- Create, plan, and optimize loads to decrease costs and to meet volume shipping commitments with specific carriers.
- Plan and optimize route structures.
- Calculate and apply accurate freight charges to both inbound and outbound shipments.
- Create shipping documents.
- Provide for shipment dispatching and shipment tracking by making order status and shipment information available on a door-to-door basis.

A typical transportation management system defines the process flow that any shipment would follow from the time that a customer order is picked for shipment, until the time that a shipment is delivered to the customer's delivery dock.

Many enterprise system vendors have a complementary transportation management module, while other vendors do not provide this type of software at all. Similar cautions apply to a TMS as for a warehouse management system (WMS); be aware that significant integration is typically required to make a WMS work correctly with an enterprise system.

It is my recommendation to avoid any third-party WMS that does not specifically interface with the selected enterprise software package.

For many organizations, a complete TMS is not necessary. Yet integration of shipment tracking and even delivery status information into an enterprise-wide system is still needed in today's supply chain and customer-conscious world. For instance, carriers such as Federal Express and United Parcel Service make available this information in a format that can be readily introduced into the enterprise system database. This is usually a straightforward customization, available through the software vendor or its implementation partner.

Why integrate carrier information into the enterprise system at all? Simply put, it makes for better customer service. It allows the customer service representative to provide the customer with details about the carrier, shipment date, tracking number, and even a delivery date and recipient. What is more, your organization might consider allowing the customer to use self-service facilities available through its enterprise software that can provide access to this same information — all without referring the customer to the carrier.

Landed Cost Processing

As mentioned earlier, the movement of goods from a supplier to a manufacturer or distributor can represent a significant percentage of the final cost of the product. To determine customer, item, and order level profitability, it is important to properly attach these costs to the goods as received. Such procurement and transportation costs include not only common carrier weight-based shipping charges, but any crating and packing costs, container rentals, demurrage charges, freight forwarder charges, import duties or taxes, and insurance charges that may be incurred. These costs are collectively referred to as *landed costs*.

Generally speaking, enterprise software will support landed cost processing in one of several ways. First, a system may provide for manually entered landed costs associated with an item during goods receipt processing. As a practical matter, although landed costs can be entered manually during goods receipt, such information is not usually available at the point of goods receipt. Also not available are receiving personnel those to whom you may want to assign this responsibility. Second, a system may provide for manually entered landed costs to be recorded during a follow-on process to the goods receipts process. As a general rule, it is preferable to enter landed cost information on a stand-alone basis, as a follow-up process to goods receipt in this manner. Third, many systems support automatic or blind landed cost processing. This means that landed costs are predetermined from tables that your organization would need to build (and maintain) within the enterprise systems' database. This option would relieve your staff from the burden of entering such costs manually. In this scenario, landed costs are typically added onto the goods receipt. Automatic landed cost processing is most suited to items procured in high volumes using predetermined carrier and shipping methods.

Warehouse Management Systems

A fourth category of SCM software is warehouse management. A WMS significantly enhances the control over warehouse operations. This control extends from the receiving and storing items to their retrieval and shipment over what is typically provided for through an enterprise system's basic inventory management capability. In general, the benefits of using a warehouse management system may include improved stock turnover, square footage reductions, quicker fill times, and perhaps even reduced material handling equipment maintenance and fuel costs.

Many enterprise system vendors have a complementary warehouse management module, while other vendors do not provide this type of software at all. Be aware that significant integration is typically required to make a third-party WMS work correctly with an enterprise system. It is my recommendation to avoid any third-party WMS that does not specifically interface with the selected enterprise software package.

While many systems will provide a basic item locator capability, this may not be sufficient in all instances, especially in a large, high-volume distribution center or when shelf life and lot management issues are of concern. As a general rule, if the stock movement and management of your organization can be met through a system's basic item locator capability, then use it. While a WMS does a much better job of controlling stock locations, when simplicity will do, it is best to avoid a WMS implementation. A WMS increases complexity and can potentially add significant layers of transactions onto the daily stock movement process.

Typically, most warehouse management systems are rule-driven. Rules are used to establish parameters for how stock is stored, picked, and replenished. A WMS requires an extensive definition of an organization's stocking locations and the rules that govern the movement of goods to or from these stocking locations as well as item-specific rules regarding storage conditions. These rules can require a significant amount of forethought, planning, setup, and ongoing item maintenance effort. It is important to understand that the WMS redefines the physical warehouse space into a logical model within the system. This implies that any changes in your physical warehouse configuration will require significant reconfiguration of the WMS as well.

The WMS is transaction-based. Warehouse management related transactions are created based upon rules that govern the stocking location from where material is picked or to where it is put away within a warehouse. In general, when a warehouse management system is used, the material transaction flows within the enterprise system are modified so as to generate either picking requests or put away reservations. These requests or reservations are subsequently confirmed through another transaction. In this sense, warehouse management related transactions are best thought as follow-on transactions to selected inventory, manufacturing, purchasing, and sales order processing activities. Depending on the system and how it is set up, these follow-on confirmation transactions can be automatically or manually initiated.

It has been my experience that organizations often encounter difficulties setting up their WMS or struggle to keep it running. Two words of advice apply here: detail and discipline. The WMS requires attention to detail in its initial setup. If you have been thinking about a warehouse redesign, do so in conjunction with, or prior to, implementing the WMS. While the WMS will optimize the ongoing use of physical space, the layout needs to be properly constructed in the first place for maximum benefit. It also requires tremendous discipline to keep it running successfully. With that said, use enabling technologies, such as bar coding and handheld, wireless scanners, to record warehouse movement transactions to aid in the cause.

SERVICE OPERATIONS MANAGEMENT SYSTEMS

Increasingly, organizations are changing some of the fundamental perceptions about what they are all about. Somehow it seems that the total customer experience is increasingly seen as a fundamental tenet of creating both a superior and sustainable competitive advantage. Organizations are now realizing that a large part of the total customer experience is about after sale support, primarily through both the in-warranty and out-of-warranty services provided. Unscheduled downtime, for any reason, is lost production capacity. It goes without saying that customers want high availability. Generally speaking, when we think of service, we think of knowledge-based work, delivered by specially trained technicians and professionals.

While it is true that service delivery is ultimately people-centric and our perceptions about good or bad service center almost exclusively on the people involved, technology has an important, supporting role. Perhaps no one has said it better than did David Vondle in his 1989 book, *Service Management Systems*, remarking that smiling faces and positive attitudes cannot cover an inferior service management system for long.

Increasingly, information technology, and in particular, service operations management (SOM) software, embedded technologies, customer self-service resources, and wireless devices are having a profound impact on service delivery. As a matter of fact, few areas seem to lend themselves to as much integration and synthesis of man and machine, technology, and communication as does a commitment to the total customer experience. A few stellar examples of industry best practices include:

- Incorporating embedded technologies into a manufactured product to provide both prefailure warnings and postfailure diagnostics. In some cases, manufacturers are combining these technologies with other technologies, such as the Internet or wireless communications, to dispatch field service technicians proactively before the customer actually experiences an equipment failure. In other cases, such as with computer equipment where redundant components are feasible, a failing component can be switched out automatically while remaining components take over until servicing or replacement of the failed component has been completed. In other instances, a given piece of equipment is able to call or e-mail a service request for itself.

- Providing customer self-service in a number of ways, including automated voice response systems linked to a fax-back system and through Internet-based, searchable databases of product knowledge and frequently asked questions.

- Building sophisticated artificial intelligence-based systems using fault tree analysis techniques that provide service call takers or the customers with the ability to diagnose equipment problems and recommended service actions.

- Taking service calls verbally or electronically, placing the all-important work order with as few keystrokes as possible and dispatching a qualified technician while most likely using a wireless handheld device to complete the repair, are tasks that all fall within the domain of a leading-edge service operations management system.

- In many ways the SOM system operates quite similarly to a manufacturing resource planning system. Besides providing for the scheduling of the actual service call, the system will also ensure that any required replacement part or special tool is identified and located for the technician prior to making the service call. While in cases, an embedded system may alert or notify the SOM system of a component failure. Before the actual service call is made, the SOM system will then preorder and schedule delivery of the required component that the field service technician may need.

- A wide array of statistics has been captured, stored, and analyzed to predict maintenance actions and to project total cost of ownership.
- The SOM system can be used to cross-sell additional services, such as maintenance contracts or preventive maintenance services, such as a tune-up, cleaning or even to schedule an upcoming major overhaul.

As one can ascertain from the above list, the distinction between different technologies is often so blurred it is difficult to separate them. Such technological interdependency requires an even greater degree of underlying systems integration.

What Is a Service Operations Management System?

For the purposes of this book, an SOM system is a business application software package designed specifically to manage the financial, human, intellectual, and physical capital associated with the completion of project-oriented work. A service management system focuses on the maintenance or installation of physical or tangible items, such as repairing a vehicle, installing or troubleshooting a telephone line, installing a garage door opener or repairing a parking meter.

The Role of the Work Order in the Service Operations Management System

Generally speaking, service type work relies on work orders. The vast majority of service organizations write up a work order or a similarly named transaction to record a customer's request for services to be performed. The work order is then used to initiate and direct all actions necessary to complete the work and fulfill the customer's request. Work orders are also contractual in nature. Sometimes the work order is the sole contract between the customer and the service provider. In other cases, a work order fulfills an obligation under another contractual document, such as an annual maintenance agreement.

Some service-related contracts provide for unlimited quantities, or hours of service, while other contracts may provide for specified quantities of service. For instance, a limitation or cap on the number of hours included in a base agreement, or perhaps services, are provided on a plus materials basis. Not only must work orders be managed, so must contracts, and when necessary, even billing for services rendered or parts needed must be prepared for the customer. Some contracts include an out-of-pocket co-payment or deductible. Service-related payments must be either collected in field, from the customer, or billed to the customer. In some cases the service provider looks to a third party, perhaps an equipment manufacturer or an insurance firm, for payment or reimbursement of amounts not paid or billed directly to the customer.

Often times, the central accounting unit in a service management system is the tangible item itself. Each tangible item or piece of property is tracked, often by a serial number. Regardless of who the current owner may be or what other field service operations center or dealer may have serviced an item previously, the field service agent taking the current call for service can obtain a nearly spontaneous listing of the service history for a particular piece of equipment.

It is often said that a work order-driven business model is among the most difficult to manage, primarily due to the uniqueness of each incoming work request. It is also interesting that as we increasingly shift toward more knowledge-based work, the nature of work, in general, is more work order driven.

Professional Services Automation Systems

Closely related to a service management system is the professional services automation (PSA) system. Generally speaking, a PSA system applies more or less to an organization where intellectual property (products produced through the subject matter expertise of knowledgeable professionals) is the end product of the organization with physical capital playing, at best, only an incidental role. For example, accountants, architects, attorneys, and consultants are more likely to use PSA systems rather than an SOM system. There is a notable exception within the professions.

Some of the types of work performed by engineering firms will often rely on testing equipment, laboratory facilities, and other ancillary supplies necessary to carry out their work. This often involves site surveys and in-field sampling. This would seem to imply that a service management system might be more appropriate for implementation within many engineering firms.

While work orders are the dominant document within the workflow of the service management system, the timesheet, or a similarly named transaction to represent time spent on a client-related matter, is its counterpart in a PSA system. Professional Service Automation Systems focus on client-related projects with each likely representing a separate project file within the context of the professional services firm itself and likewise within the context of the PSA system.

Physical (Plant) Maintenance Management Systems

Another close cousin to the SOM system is a computerized maintenance management (CMM) system. A computerized maintenance management system generally focuses on the management of both preventive maintenance and any necessary service restoration activities should any equipment, machine, vehicle, or portion of a physical system fail. The system also manages any related spare parts inventories used by an organization's internal physical plant and equipment resources. Obvious differences between these two systems are generally related to contract and warranty administration and customer billing features that are required in an SOM system but not necessarily applicable for an internally oriented system.

CUSTOMER RELATIONSHIP MANAGEMENT (CRM) SYSTEMS

CRM has been gaining widespread attention over the last few years. CRM is not simply a set of software applications or tools. Instead, CRM represents a mindset — a way of understanding and doing business with one's customers. CRM requires knowing everything about an organization's customers and putting the customer first. How does a CRM system strengthen the business organization? It builds relationships with customers — one customer at a time. The remaining discussion on CRM systems provides several specific examples.

One-to-One Marketing

The 1980s and 1990s represented the heyday of mass marketing. We have now returned to marketing to the individual; some call it affinity or one-to-one marketing. This means being able to recognize your customers on the phone or over the Internet. Today, companies have many touch points with their customers: call centers, the Internet, in-store sales, customer service, etc. But no matter where, how, or through which channel you make contact with a customer, the customer should have the same experience. If the customer places an order on the Internet, that customer should be able to easily follow-up that order on the phone or in person. This means infomation about the Internet order and the customer is easily accessible to any employee on the phone or in the store or office anywhere in the world. From the point of view of the customer, it can be very frustrating to have to wait for someone to locate the information you are requesting, especially if the customer feels it should be at arm's length. The CRM system should provide the means for the organization to profile its customers or prospects on their buying habits and preferences and anticipate a customers' needs.

Customer Segmentation and Profitability Analysis

Not all customers are alike; some customers are very profitable, while others will cause an organization to lose money. Customer segmentation means grouping customers based on their lifetime value to the organization. Through the use of customer segmentation, organizations can plot strategies to increase sales, reduce costs, improve customer retention, and reduce the risks of customers defecting to one's competitors. A CRM system should allow the organization to segment customers in a number of different ways or categories for future analysis purposes.

To determine the profitability of a customer, you must have a good cost accounting system. It must provide an accurate cost for each of your organization's products and services provided to the customer and for cost of any indirect services provided that benefits the customer. These costs must in turn be allocated to costs of obtaining, selling to, servicing, and maintaining a given customer relationship. Some customer relationships are truly unprofitable and should be abandoned. Do you know which of your customer relationships falls into this category? Perhaps not, for many business organizations still focus on preparing reports about their top customers and not necessarily about their top customers in terms of profitability. A CRM system should combine with an ERP system, perhaps through a business intelligence platform if a natural link between the two does not exist, to provide this type of profitability analysis.

Up Selling, Cross Selling and Down Selling

Organizations must anticipate and not merely react to any given customers' needs in today's competitive world markets. Again, it is a different mindset. It is one that says do not sell customers more than they need or want, or offer something less when it is not appropriate for their needs. The goal is happy, satisfied customers that will not only want to do more business with your organization in the future, but that will also tell others about their good experiences in dealing with your organization.

This way, to win high accolades from customers is to sell them the right product, which may not be what they are requesting. Down selling is telling the customer that an item of interest is inappropriate. This means not selling items that are overkill for a customer's application or that is perhaps completely inappropriate for the customer's use in a given application. It also means suggesting alternate products that are better suited for the customer. Up selling means that when appropriate, selling the customer a better product that has features the customer needs, but may not fully appreciate the reasons why. Cross selling offers the customer complementary products for sale that are related to the item the customer is currently buying, such as ink cartridges along with a printer or shoe polish along with a pair of shoes.

Up selling and cross selling will increase revenue. Down selling will not immediately increase revenue in all cases. Happy customers will more likely return to your organization in the future to buy and will also tell others about their positive experiences with your organization. Down selling also reduces the cost of returns. Up selling, cross selling, and down selling should be done on the Internet, call center, in person, and any other way you sell. CRM systems, through online catalogues and product configurators along with call center management capabilities, provide revenue enhancement potential to all customer contact points.

BUSINESS INTELLIGENCE (BI) SYSTEMS

Many speak today about the 360-degree view of the organization. To achieve this view requires information from a multitude of systems and methods for extracting such information from the universe of disparate systems that the organization may have. Even when systems are integrated, it is usually for labor saving, to prevent redundant entry of data, or for consistency purposes, to prevent the same information from being presented in several different ways. Information analysis is usually not well supported. Business intelligence systems rely on data flowing from disparate systems into a central collection point, usually defined as a data warehouse. From the data warehouse as a hub for the organization's information, all of the data can be related and analyzed in different ways for different purposes when and as needed.

In addition to the data warehouse, business intelligence relies on the ability of a system to extract and analyze information, including patterns and trends in data. This requires employing sophisticated statistical modeling techniques in many such analyses. In other cases, the information need may be less focused on analytics and more focused on the organization and segmentation of data. Reporting, query, and analysis tools from vendors such as Hyperion, Business Objects, SAS, SPSS, and Cognos, are frequently used to provide new insights about the future of the business, relying on past business data and projected business data changes.

Closely related to business intelligence systems are scorecard and dashboard systems. These systems extract and combine key information from a number of underlying systems for real time or near real time for inquiry and analysis purposes. This information is primarily used by organizational managers and knowledge workers, generally on an exception basis, to monitor the organization's performance and plot corrective actions.

These systems often use visual indicators, such as on screen dials, gauges, meters, and graphs to illustrate business performance measures, giving rise to the terms control panel or dashboard. Alerts are issued using a combination of electronic workflow and electronic mail techniques.

Colors or symbols on the dashboard are used to highlight performance areas needing management attention, using management-defined tolerances from normal business metrics to trigger such exceptions. Many of the business intelligence reporting, query, and analysis tool products now incorporate many, if not all, of the features to perform scorecard and dashboard style reporting and alert capabilities.

THE INTERNET AND ELECTRONIC COMMERCE

This book devotes very little specific attention to the Internet. That is because the Internet is no longer the next big thing. It is now simply viewed as an access, entry point, or gateway into software package functionality for trusted individuals. The Internet allows access to software package functionality on an anywhere, anytime basis and places the demand for more real-time abilities onto all software packages. Examples of these access points include a litany of portals, stakeholder self-service web pages, online stores, and catalogues.

The Internet is also a medium of exchange for collaborative commerce between business organizations, through hubs or intermediaries or on a direct business-to-business basis. Collaborative commerce is primarily about system-to-system communications — systems that can be both internal to and external from the organization itself, such as customer and supplier systems. There are many mentions of collaborative commerce and the impact on business processes and software packages throughout this chapter and in this entire book.

KNOWLEDGE MANAGEMENT SYSTEMS

Closely related to CRM and SOM systems are knowledge management systems. These software packages work closely with imaging hardware and electronic publishing software to capture, store, catalog, and organize business information from any source. The knowledge management system then disperses this information, usually through a portal available on a corporate Intranet or through the Internet, to a trusted audience in or outside the organization. Lotus Notes has emerged as a common platform for organizing and managing corporate documents, while Adobe Acrobat has emerged as a common method of electronically publishing information for distribution.

INFORMATION SHARING SYSTEMS

Sharing information is the mantra of the future in the information age. The world is an increasingly smaller and more competitive place. Information in many cases is, or can provide, the competitive advantage, especially when combined with other lean manufacturing practices such as mass customization, just-in-time inventory control and assemble-to-order strategies. More than ever, the reach is extending beyond the myopic "within the four walls" view of the organization that most information system strategies typically had. Strategic partnerships between customers and suppliers and supplier alliances, even among competitors, are being formed at an unprecedented rate.

While some of the early online electronic hubs or marketplaces have failed, there are a few success stories to be told. The greatest future focus is on the supply chain. The supply chain requires above all else, trusted information sharing. While the systems will not build the trust at the foundations of these alliances, they will provide the basis for the information sharing. This information sharing requires four major elements: message brokering software, EAI software, application program interfaces that expose common business processes to fulfill cross enterprise business information processing, and a common business language.

Together these elements form the level of interoperability needed to achieve true supply chain integration. Some of the software packages involved include TIBCO, Saga, and WebMethods in the EAI arena, while IBM MQ Series is a message brokering software package. The Object Management Group, the Supply Chain Council, the Uniform Code Council, the Collaborative Planning, Forecasting and Replenishment Committee, and RosettaNet (an electronics industry consortium), are among the industry and solution provider-sponsored organizations attempting to develop the standards needed to provide the desired level of enterprise interoperability envisioned for the future.

THE SOFTWARE PACKAGE MARKETPLACE: AN EPILOGUE

The emergence of strong, general purpose software packages and specialized software packages for specific industries or types of business organizations has altered the traditional perception of systems that if it was not built here, then it cannot apply to us. In addition, organizations perceive the use of software packages as a method to achieve quicker time to market innovations in their business processes and practices. Software packages also represent "smart sourcing." This allows the organization to focus key resources on extending the core competencies of the business organization, not building systems to facilitate information collection, processing, and analysis.

While software packages automate information flows for specific business activities, they still do not integrate well. The industry is moving toward a plug-and-play software architecture model by relying on EAI software and the use of XML-based software messaging. This will be an easier task when competing vendors in the software industry work together on interoperability standards — a trend that is quickly becoming a reality.

3

BUSINESS PERFORMANCE MEASUREMENT: AN OVERVIEW

This is a brief, but important chapter about organizational performance. Understanding what drives business performance and how to measure performance is an important underpinning of any successful business improvement effort.

This chapter introduces a number of important concepts, including:

- A hierarchy of *needs* for the business organization.
- The *balanced scorecard*, a tool used as barometer of business performance.
- *Benchmarking*, a method of measuring business performance.
- *Best practices*, which are proven business processes that, if adopted, can generally have a positive impact on business performance.

All of these concepts are closely related to business performance and business process improvement.

THE NEEDS OF THE BUSINESS ORGANIZATION

With few exceptions, just about everyone who has ever taken a management theory, organizational development or introductory psychology class is aware of psychologist Abraham Maslow's famous *hierarchy of needs*. Much like how individuals are driven to fulfill certain basic and greater needs, it is my contention that a similar set of needs also exists and applies to any business organization. These basic organizational needs must be fulfilled if the business organization is to prosper and sustain itself.

As a result of my above premise, I have developed a broad-based model based on hierarchy of needs that I contend applies to every business organization. I believe this model is a holistic, need-driven model of the business organization. Figure 3.1 depicts the organizational needs model that I have developed. This model lends itself to another relatively new management practice — the use of a balanced scorecard to measure organizational performance. The balanced scorecard will be further discussed in the next section.

These basic organizational needs are discussed in more detail in the following paragraphs. Note that they are discussed in reverse order, or more precisely, in their order of increasing importance. Note that the highest element in the pyramid is also the greatest need: the need for a successful business organization to sustain itself over time by meeting or exceeding its business objectives. This also implies that an organization must achieve a reasonable balance in each of the underlying elements in order to ultimately move up the pyramid toward achieving its overall business objectives.

Figure 3.1 The Organizational Hierarchy of Needs

Technology

No organization exists without relying on even the slightest thread of technology. However, the technological needs of any given organization vary greatly. The degree and type of technology used will be based upon both the organization's business model and on the industry. For instance, a law firm has completely different technological needs than does an automobile manufacturer, but each employs technology in their work. Technology is not just about computers but represents the whole of applied science that an organization subscribes to. Technology represents physical or tangible investments that a business organization has generated or possesses.

People

No matter how good or advanced the technology, we still have not found a way for technology to be completely self-sustaining. In that regard, technology still requires the knowledge, experience, reasoning, and creative powers of people in order to apply it in any business setting. An organization is only as strong as the people that it employs, enables, and empowers to carry through on its mission. The primary task of management with respect to people is finding the best, brightest, and most diligent to the task at hand. Secondarily, management must enable people and technology through processes. Third, management must empower people to perform, through intelligent and efficient processes that can readily adapt to changing business needs. From the standpoint of technologies, adaptability is not a given. It must be a deliberate plan of management to provide for and to facilitate adaptability — technologies and processes must be adaptable by design.

Process

Applying and using the potential of both technology and people — or process — is often the greatest asset an organization possesses. It represents the organization's reason for being, and usually, their competitive advantage. As industries mature, processes also mature and often become obsolete. To maintain competitive advantage and perhaps an organization's very existence, it must be constantly changing or reinventing itself. This means discarding old technologies, adopting new technologies, changing or abandoning old processes, inventing and adopting new processes, and retraining and deploying people in new or different roles.

Business Knowledge and Intelligence (Know-How)

Most successful business organizations endure over long periods of time. They develop what I call the know-how or simply the momentum to sustain themselves. This force is so strong in a successful business organization that it can and does transcend the individuals, particularly the knowledge workers and managers that are central to the operations in every type and size of organization. How does this momentum perpetuate itself? It is certainly not through osmosis. Rather, it is through business knowledge and intelligence. It is also through custom or tradition. When an organization does not formalize its business knowledge by reducing it to a published form, it is transferred through the spoken word; this is what I call custom or tradition.

The concept of the holistic, need-driven model of the business organization relies squarely on business knowledge and intelligence. If knowledge sharing between the generations of knowledge workers and managers who pass through the doors of any organization were to cease, so would the business itself. With that said, every organization must have a process for knowledge transfer at every level and technologies to capture, store, and organize business knowledge and intelligence for reuse and revision as the organization grows and changes.

The knowledge and business intelligence element of the model recognizes the importance of capturing how the business operates, meaning how people, process, and technology come together and perform a service or produce a product. Knowledge represents the intangible investments that a business organization has generated or possesses. A good example in this case happens to also be a famous one as well: the secret recipe that we have heard about from Colonel Sanders' Kentucky Fried Chicken restaurants for so many years.

Management

I like to view management's role in a largely facilitative role for the modern enterprise. I define the modern enterprise as one that is an agile, team centered, self directed, learning organization. In their role as facilitators, management establishes, in conjunction with stakeholders, the mission and vision for the organization through measurable goals and objectives. This is increasingly done through the use of a balanced scorecard — that includes both financial and nonfinancial metrics. More will be said on the balanced scorecard later in this chapter.

Management is also the guardian of the stakeholder's interest. In this capacity, management serves as both the business controller and as the agent of business change. Management orchestrates how people, process, and technology come together and perform. Management must develop and execute both short- and long-term strategies that move the overall business operation continually toward its goals and objectives or desired business results.

The world of business is swift and is constantly changing. Management requires information about the performances of people, process, technology, and itself in order to be successful in achieving the desired business results. Management requires an *early warning system* — a performance monitoring system that helps management continuously fine tune the combination of people, process, and technology toward achieving those desired business results. It is this need that ultimately defines the underlying role of business information systems in the modern business organization.

Information technology has two significant roles to play in an enlightened organization. First, information technology can be used to enable the organization to be responsive — to in effect conduct its business at the speed of change. Second, information technology can be used to manage the organization by wire — to provide business results in real time and to adjust key business variables quickly, continuously, and to the extent that it is practical, automatically.

Results

The greatest need a business organization must fulfill is the need to demonstrate results to its stakeholders. Stakeholders expect results. These results are achieved through meeting or exceeding the measurable goals and objectives that the organization has established in conjunction with its management. Many smaller and middle market businesses are family owned, not publicly held megacorporations. The stakeholder audience may be more concentrated. Their desires for the business to achieve sustainable, profitable growth and a suitable return on investment are no different than those for any publicly held corporation.

THE BALANCED SCORECARD: AN INTRODUCTION

As I mentioned in the preceding section, the balanced scorecard is a relatively new performance measurement tool for organizations. Robert Kaplan and David Norton, authors of *The Balanced Scorecard*, are widely regarded as the originators of the need for this different, more complete, and more holistic manner to measure corporate performance and to report the results of these measurements to stakeholders. The concept of the balanced scorecard stems from their research in the area of corporate performance measurement conducted over an extended period of time involving a number of companies.

When I think of maximizing business performance, as the title of this book suggests can be done through software packages, I am also inclined to visualize the measures of business performance through the use of a balanced scorecard. When I think of the balanced scorecard, I am immediately reminded of a quote that is often attributed to Peter Drucker, "If you can't measure it, you can't manage it." Although I do not know the source or context in which Drucker purportedly made this remark, I would suspect that Drucker, as is often the case in management theory, was simply ahead of his time in postulating perhaps what is the fundamental purpose of the balanced scorecard — organizational performance measurement and measurement for the sake of organizational improvement.

I would contend that any discussion about maximizing business performance should include a discussion of the balanced scorecard as the preferred tool for measuring business performance. With that said, I would like to discuss what a balanced scorecard is all about and why it is relevant to the content of this book.

The Balanced Scorecard: How It Works

Traditionally, businesses have defined performance measures usually only in financial terms. The balanced scorecard approach complements or balances financial metrics with other nonfinancial performance measures. The premise of Kaplan and Norton's work is that a causal relationship exists between these nonfinancial performance measures and an organization's financial performance or business results, thereby taking to task the old adage that sometimes a business is successful in spite of itself.

The authors consider the balanced scorecard plays a role somewhat akin to that of a storyteller. This involves telling a story of an organization's business strategy through a series of interlinked cause-and-effect relationships between business measures — demonstrated through scorecard values — and the underlying drivers that influence an organization's performance. It can be said that a balanced scorecard links an organization's strategic goals and objectives, or vision, to the organization's actual business performance. Most important, by linking business strategy with both financial and nonfinancial metrics, the organization leverages all of its activities toward achieving its strategic vision or objectives.

The balanced scorecard presentation is made using stakeholder perspectives. Each stakeholder perspective is comprised of core measures. Each of the core measure of performance, target, or threshold values is established; these are often referred to as benchmarks. Organizations usually benchmark themselves against any number of criteria for each of the stakeholder perspectives. Performance is measured through a comparison to actual results. The root cause of business performance is the business initiatives or drivers that are undertaken by the organization. Kaplan and Norton's extensive research indicates there are four of these primary perspectives that a balanced scorecard should minimally include:

- A *financial* perspective focused on business owners or shareholders.
- A *client* perspective focused on customers of the business organization.
- An *internal business process* perspective focused on an organization's supply chain, including its internal business units and external suppliers.
- A *learning and growth* perspective focused on the organization and its resources, particularly on its human resources and management.

The next few paragraphs briefly review each of the perspectives. Although others might suggest that additional perspectives are necessary, Kaplan and Norton contend that these four perspectives are generally sufficient. Figure 3.2 illustrates the concepts discussed in this section that build out the definition and use of the balanced scorecard.

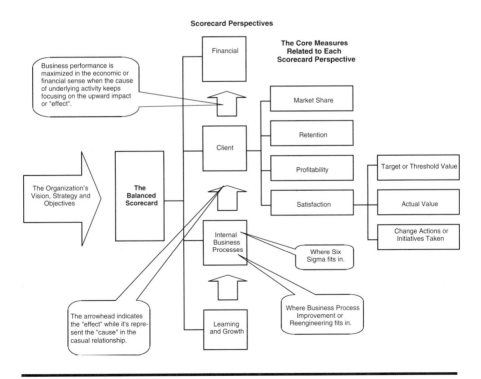

Figure 3.2 Building the Organization's Balanced Scorecard

The Financial Perspective

As previously mentioned, the financial perspective is the traditional method of analyzing business performance. In the not so distant past at the height of the dot-com era, one would have thought that traditional financial performance measures had been all but abandoned. Both the economy and the financial markets are going through a gut-wrenching reality check as this manuscript is being written and financial performance measures are once again very much in vogue. With that said, most business owners and business investors follow what is generally referred to as a value-driven or fundamental analysis of the business organization. Although Benjamin Graham and David Dodd first described these analysis techniques many years ago, they remain as relevant today as when they were first described. A complete discussion of financial performance analysis techniques is beyond the scope of this book, but suffice to say that stakeholders are generally interested in several major dimensions of financial performance that include:

- Return on investment
- Capital appreciation
- Earnings quality

Return on investment is defined as the amount earned on the invested capital provided by the business and is usually expressed as a percentage. Return on investment rewards the business owner for taking on the risks of investing in the business organization. To succeed, most business organizations must exhibit a pattern of growth in revenues and in earnings. Earnings quality is an increasingly important measure to stakeholders. Every business organization will have its ups and downs, but mistakes and surprises are not kindly regarded; they usually are indicative of poor underlying management quality.

With the most recent wave of accounting industry, investment research and corporate governance lapses in judgment, conflicts of interest, self-dealings, and wrongdoings, increasing attention and likely additional regulations covering financial performance reporting will emerge. The pressure is on to improve financial performance reporting and the underlying generally accepted accounting principles that today govern corporate accounting and financial performance reporting.

The Client Perspective

The client or customer perspective is important to any organization in a market-driven economy. It stands to reason that when a business organization understands its products and services through the eyes of the customer, the organization will have a much sharper perspective on how to obtain, satisfy, and keep its customers. The customer, generally speaking, has the following concerns about a supplier:

- Performance as requested. The customer expects on-time deliveries of products or completion of services. In addition, the customer expects the product or service has been completed or delivered to the highest standards of quality.
- Ease of doing business. The customer has to feel good about doing business with your organization. One or two bad customer experiences and the customer will go somewhere else, regardless of how favorable other factors of the existing relationship have been. It is very much a what have you done for me lately attitude. Simply put, do not take your customers for granted. Customer relationships are not entitlements; they are earned in each and every business dealing between the supplier and its customer. Perhaps Jan Carlzon said it best when he so appropriately called such customer interactions moments of truth. When something does go wrong, the response must be immediate and direct. The attitude must be one of whoever took the call, owns the problem.
- Fairness in pricing. The customer expects value from the products or services provided by the supplier. The customer is willing to pay for such value, but no more than the going rate or market price for similar products or services.

Client or customer focused performance measures are an important part of the story that must be told. In fact, tighter supply chain management elevates the importance of performance measures to a way of doing business with a group of stakeholders that has been far too often taken for granted — the customer.

The Internal Business Process Perspective

An organization cannot succeed unless it has a predisposition to achieve a competitive advantage or unique value proposition. This requires hard work and involves not only being good at what it does, but staying that way, and continuously. This constant, relentless process innovation effort is another name for continuous improvement. It is also a tenet of good management practice.

Continuous improvement is largely centered around business cost reduction, by making an inefficient or an ineffective process — referred to as waste — efficient or effective or by making unnecessary aspects of a process simply go away. This is usually what is referred to as a nonvalue-adding activity. Whatever you call it — business change, business process improvement, business transformation, process innovation, or reengineering — the results should be the same. They are measurable process improvements that improve efficiency or effectiveness and lower operating costs.

The continuous reinvention of processes occurs through business process reengineering. Business process reengineering relies heavily on process simplification and automation to achieve new levels of process efficiency. Software packages are often at the foundation of an organization's business process reengineering efforts.

How Six Sigma Fits in the Picture

It is noteworthy to mention that an organization that has already adopted a Six Sigma philosophy has embraced the type of continuous improvement effort that links business strategy, business results, and business process improvement. Six Sigma should be viewed as more than just another quality improvement program. The methodologies of Six Sigma should be an integral part of the operations and measurements within the organization.

Furthermore, Six Sigma is also an integral part of the overall business strategy; the results of the Six Sigma program itself should be measured under the learning and growth perspective on the balanced scorecard. A Six Sigma business strategy should lead to process improvements, often times through reengineering projects centered around process simplification and automation. As previously mentioned, such initiatives will often use business application software packages to achieve such process improvements.

Linking Business Process Improvement, Performance Measures, and Investment Decisions

What does a good process-related performance measure look like? Table 3.1 links business processes and functions to performance measures. When an organization seeks justification for process improvements, particularly for capital outlays, such as software packages, the incremental change or affect in a process measure is said to be a benefit to the organization. Such benefits can be a one-time event or a recurring event having a positive impact over an extended period of time, which is sometimes referred to as the benefit cycle. The key to the cost justification of capital investment projects, such as a software package acquisition and implementation, is to dollarize these benefits and weigh them against the costs an organization will incur to effect such process improvements.

Table 3.1 serves as an important guide to understanding the drivers of business performance. Associated with any given driver is one or more metrics. A metric in turn relates to business performance. If the software package positively influences a driver, a metric value should change and that metric can be monetarized to show financial benefits of a business process improvement. There is a causal relationship between business drivers and business performance.

The Learning and Growth Perspective

Organizations can and do grow stagnant or complacent. Such a condition is not only dangerous, but when left unchecked, can be fatal to an organization. Product innovation is the lifeblood in the growth industry, while process innovation is the lifeblood of the mature industry. If your organization is not innovating along one of these two dimensions, then you are likely not keeping up with your competition. Learning and growing are two traits every organization must exhibit. It is about a commitment to a continuous, lifelong learning process by the organization and for its staff. More important, it is about accepting the challenge to achieve internal, organic growth through continuous product and process innovation.

Small and Middle Businesses and the Balanced Scorecard

The balanced scorecard is a particularly powerful tool for small and middle market businesses that are constantly struggling with growing the business. How is this? The balanced scorecard helps these organizations answer these fundamental questions:

- How do clients perceive the organization?
- How does an organization improve upon its past success and create further value?
- What must an organization excel at?

While many small and middle market businesses are privately held, an increasing number are publicly held. In such cases, the balanced scorecard also assists an organization with the question of how an organization appears to the investment community.

Linking Scorecard Perspectives and Software Packages

It is interesting to note that Kaplan and Norton's scorecard perspectives can be linked to categories of software packages. When it comes to the change actions or initiatives taken, software package implementation may well support any one of these perspectives. Table 3.2 summarizes the

Table 3.1 Linking Business Processes and Functions to Performance Measures

Business Function	Business Processes or Drivers	Performance Measures Associated with Drivers
Manufacturing planning, control and execution	Planning and scheduling Resource management Production management Process monitoring and control	Predictability for on-time deliveries Reduced overhead costs Reduced material costs Improved quality Resulted in faster throughput Increased use of subcontractors and contract manufacturing
	Maintenance	Increased equipment availability and equipment life
	Quality management/Six Sigma	Reduced in-field failure and rework rates
Logistics and distribution	Distribution planning Inventory management	Reduced warehousing costs Improved on-time delivery Utilized vendor managed inventory to reduce stockroom control expenses and average inventory investment
	Trade management	Reduced import/export time/cost
	Transportation management	Reduced delivery costs
	Warehouse management	Improved space utilization and reduced picking times
Finance and administration	Accounts payable	Minimized cash outflow
	Accounts receivable	Reduced credit losses/sales outstanding
	Asset management	Increased utilization/output
	Costing	Used activity based costing
	Planning and budgeting	Improved customer profitability management
	Financial reporting	Used balanced scorecard reporting
Sales and marketing	Customer demand management	Improved forecast accuracy
	Price and promotion management	Improved price and promotion strategy
	Client information systems	Improved customer specific expectations

Function	Process	Benefit
Sales and marketing (continued)	Sales force management	Improved productivity/effectiveness
	Configuration management	Improved on-line accuracy
	Sales order entry	Improved accuracy/fill rate and on-time delivery
	Business development and marketing	Improved ratios of bids versus closes
		Improved retention of customers
		Improved penetration of market
		Increased sales revenues per customer
Engineering and product development	Product development	Increased product configurability; mass customization
	Product rationalization and simplification	Used Faster time to market
		Improved manufacturability
		Used target costing/pricing
		Used fewer parts
		Resulted in common or shared components and platforms; used fewer stock keeping units and used kits
Purchasing and supplier management	Quote/contract management	Improved terms and conditions
	Purchase order management	Decreased procurement costs
	Receiving and stockroom	Reduced handling/storage costs
	Invoice verification	Used evaluated receipt settlement processing
	Product performance management	Reduced performance variability
	Vendor performance management	Improved vendor contracting
	Supply chain management	Lowered overall inventory levels
		Lowered lead times for critical components
Human resource management	Self-service benefits	Lowered benefit administration costs
	Compliance management	Provided flexible benefit programs to help retain employees
	Workplace health and safety	Provided for Occupational Safety and Health Administration, Equal Employment Opportunity Commission, and workers' compensation Reporting
		Resulted in reduction in reportable incidents and lost work days through safety training, audits and environment sampling

Table 3.2 Linking the Balanced Scorecard and Software Packages

Scorecard Perspective	A Sampling of Applicable or Related Business Application Software Packages
Financial	Activity-based costing and activity-based management software; balanced scorecard or digital dashboard software; budgeting and financial modeling software; expense management software; manage the enterprise process model functionality in an enterprise resource planning system
Client	Call center software; collaboration software; customer relationship management software; data warehouse and data mining software; design to build process model functionality in an enterprise resource planning system; enterprise information portal software; online analytical processing software; quote and bid software; services operations management software; supply chain management software; Web site and store front software
Internal business processes	Advanced planning and scheduling software; business process management software; demand management software; e-procurement software; manufacturing execution software; order to cash, procure to pay and plan to make process model functionality in an enterprise resource planning software system; professional services automation software; transportation management software; warehouse management software; workflow management software

Table 3.2 Linking the Balanced Scorecard and Software Packages

Scorecard Perspective	A Sampling of Applicable or Related Business Application Software Packages
Learning and growth	Collaboration software; design to build process model functionality in an enterprise resource planning system; document management software; e-learning software; electronic publishing software; enterprise information portal software; human resource management software; knowledge management software; process modeling software; project management software

relationship between the scorecard perspective and the change actions or initiatives taken. This table links the various perspectives of the balanced scorecard with various business application software packages. It serves as a fitting end to the introduction of the balanced scorecard along with its role in maximizing business performance.

BEST PRACTICES AND BENCHMARKING: AN INTRODUCTION

There are numerous mentions of two topics throughout this book — best practices and benchmarking. An understanding of these two concepts is important and requires formal introduction. They have particular relevance to an organization interested in justifying, selecting, and implementing a business application software package.

What Is a Best Practice?

A *best practice* is a business strategy or tactic that has been proven, through application and demonstrable results, to be highly effective. Other companies can emulate these companies and use the strategies and tactics as a benchmark for comparison to determine how well they are doing. Best practices are established for a process regardless of industry.

Generally speaking, best practices are, at least at first, considered as a unique or innovative approach to a particular business challenge. A best practice offers a unique value proposition or solution. Best practices are typically documented in the form of case studies and white papers. Such best practices and their results are frequently highly documented or referenced — to the point where one could argue that such promulgation leads what was once considered a best practice to common practice.

Best practices typically emanate from organizations that are well followed and highly admired. In recent years, Dell Computer is one such example of a highly admired company that has received accolades for a business model that minimizes inventory and represents mass customization. General Electric is another company that is well followed and highly admired for many aspects of its business model. But of course, a few best practices here or there does not make an organization best-in-class in every aspect of its business. As an example, recent news reports have suggested shortcomings in after-the-sale customer service at the often mentioned poster child of best practices — Dell Computer.

Most important is what drives this quest for best practices. Quite simply, it is usually competitive forces at work. Most best practices have been implemented and honed to such an extent that they raise the stature of the practitioner to that of a formidable, widely admired and highly profitable competitor. This is why so many other organizations wish to adopt and emulate the best practices or secrets of success that are employed by an industry-leading organization.

What Is Benchmarking?

The most common method for determining what best practices are right for an organization to pursue is to benchmark the organization against known best practices that are prevalent in the organization's industry and throughout the larger business community. Generally speaking, each example of a best practice for benchmarking purposes should illustrate the best practice in place at a company highly regarded for its capabilities in this area. This should be preferably in an organization's own industry or one that has a similar business model.

By assembling a list of best practices, an organization can then subsequently perform a gap analysis between the practices of their organization, identifying what opportunities exist for adoption and then prioritizing those best practices for adoption. Benchmarking is also frequently a prelude to and becomes an integral part of adopting the balanced scorecard performance reporting mechanism. It also behooves an organization to determine what industry peers have adopted a balanced scorecard and how they are measuring themselves using their scorecards.

Linking Business Process Improvement and Business Performance

Recall that Table 3.1 illustrates how business functions and processes are linked to their underlying drivers and ultimately to metrics. These links are vitally important. They are usually identified during the process audit, and are an integral part of any business process reengineering initiative, or during the management audit process that precedes business process reengineering. What happens during a process is said to drive business performance. The process is known as the driver of business performance. The performance is measured by processing goals or outcomes. A process results in a completed deliverable or deliverables — an output or end product or some form of service or activity.

As a part of the process auditing or modeling that occurs in a business improvement initiative, the suppliers, inputs, processes, outputs, and customers (SIPOC) model identifies process or system "outputs." The SIPOC process model is discussed in Chapter 5, but suffice to say the model and technique elicits and documents a set of "outputs" and "customers" for those outputs. It should be understood that a customer has requirements or specifications that represent minimum acceptable performance levels or characteristics that apply to the product or service. The result of any given process is that the product or service right or working as desired or intended. This applies equally to any internal or external customers or products provided or services rendered from a given processing sequence.

Best Practices Fuel Business Cases

Typically, organizations that adopt best business practices must rely to some extent on business application software technology. In many instances, the adoption of certain best business practices are facilitated or supported only through software package architectures or features. When recommending the adoption of best business practices relies on software package architectures or features, their costs and benefits to the organization should be quantified and used as a part of the business case to acquire a software package.

Any prepared list of best practices should also include reference to what metrics illustrate the benefits — or economic value — of the best practice. Once an organization employs best practices it can then readily benchmark its performance using these metrics against peer organizations.

Where Can Information Be Obtained Regarding Best Practices?

An extensive amount of research has been done regarding best business practices. Try an Internet search on a subject area of interest first. It is best to look at case studies for ideas. Even if they are vendor-sponsored sales documents, they can still nonetheless be the source of inspiration.

For example, try an advanced search on a search engine site like AltaVista or Google. As an example, look for inventory cycle counting if that is a specific practice of interest. A more generic search example might be inventory improvement. Simply put, you never know what you may find.

Some of the most common best practice models include the Supply Chain Council's Supply Chain Operations Reference Model (SCOR) and the ABCD Checklist for Manufacturing Excellence, a product of Oliver Wight and Associates. SCOR has been available for many years and has undergone numerous revisions over time. Many other consulting firms create their own databases of best practices, which are usually culled from client projects and their own research into best practices.

There are research houses that seek out and compose databases of best practices, usually by industry or for a given function within the organizational context. Examples of two such research services that offer databases of best practices, on a paid subscriber-basis, include Best Practices' website (www.best-in-class.com) and Best Practices' Best Practice Database, (www.bestpracticedatabase.com). How prevalent are best practice databases? Even the United Nations sponsors a best practices database on humanity.

The popular business media, including publications such as *Business Week*, *Fortune*, and *The Wall Street Journal* will occasionally feature case studies of best practices and other emerging business trends as they are sometimes called. Finally, trade groups, such as the American Production and Inventory Control Society, and trade publications, such as *Industry Week* and *Materials Handling and Equipment*, focus on gathering best practices from the field. They report on best business practices, typically through case studies of a particular firm or industry. So what does a best practice look or read like? A well-known best practice is presented as an example in the next section.

Evaluated Receipt Settlement: Illustrating America's Best Known Best Practice

Perhaps I am being a little presumptuous about the notoriety of evaluated receipt settlement (ERS). But make no mistake that this is one of the best known and most frequently cited best practice examples.

> ERS is widely credited to Ford Motor Company. Prior to adopting ERS, Ford paid their bills much like any other industrial company; a clerical staff (and as one can imagine in the case of Ford, this was a large staff) matched purchase orders and receipts to the invoices received from their vendors.

But Ford had a better idea. Why not skip this entire matching step? Why not simply pay for what was noted as received? The payment could be made based on the unit price from the purchase order and the quantity received off the receiving ticket. Of course some heads at Ford were raised in dismay. They would ask, "But why? We have always done it this way." and "What will the auditors think?"

However, others within Ford pressed, "What value was this matching really adding?" Given the price of the goods were negotiated through a long-term contract, price variances were not the issue. In most cases, scheduling agreements had all but eliminated routine purchase orders, so verifying existence of an order was not an issue. If the count was accurate to the packing list, it stands to reason the vendor's invoice would be the same quantity as well, so a quantity variance was not the issue either. What more was needed or possible through a match? Ultimately, these ambitious value seekers won their case. An entire process was rendered obsolete, replaced by a much simpler, less labor-intensive process.

For Ford in particular, the cost savings were tremendous. An army of highly paid clerical personnel had previously spent their every working hour poring over and matching invoices, purchase orders, and receipts. Not having to perform this step saved Ford hundreds of thousands of dollars.

This example is simply for illustrative purposes and provides some insights to what a best practice is. It also shows how a radically different best practice enhances or streamlines an existing, well-known business process.

EPILOGUE: BUSINESS PERFORMANCE MEASUREMENT

This chapter was about organizational performance. The chapter introduced the needs that a business organization has and the need for identifying both the drivers and measures of business performance. It also presented several important concepts germane to business performance measurement and business performance improvement, including the balanced scorecard, benchmarking, and best practices.

Of all the points raised in this chapter, perhaps the most important is the need to identify specific process-related metrics. Table 3.1 illustrated some representative process-related metrics. Such knowledge is essential in building the business case for process improvement and ultimately for the software package. When a business metric can be influenced, it can usually be monetarized. It can then provide economic benefit to the organization and some degree of business performance improvement.

4

DETERMINING BUSINESS NEEDS THROUGH DISCOVERY

This chapter represents the starting point of a journey. The purpose of this journey comes about in many different forms. Many times, the journey begins in a moment of inspiration. An executive or manager has made a connection between process improvement and technology. Knowing that you have a journey in mind is helpful, but, that is not always clear. In fact, business process automation is not always desirable or necessary. Automating processes that should not exist in the first place does not improve business performance. Nor does automation alone improve bad processes and business performance.

This journey is equally likely to spring forth from a moment of desperation when an executive blurts out, "Why don't I have the information I need?", during an important, yet frustrating meeting. The remarks are usually made in a heated moment because a desired set of key facts or figures is simply not available. The executive is frustrated because the information needed to make an important business decision either does not exist or is not readily accessible.

Many organizations already have good information systems in place. Yet, the information within these systems is not linked to the business as a whole. In short, the organization is data rich and information poor. In other cases, an organization fails to capture vital information about its processes. Often times existing systems can capture such information — that is only if existing systems are properly used. Using good systems will not necessarily improve upon an organization's bad practices or processes.

THE SOFTWARE PACKAGE LIFE CYCLE CONCEPT

In case one has not guessed by now, this journey I am referring to is the justification for, selection of, and use of software packages to improve both business operational and decision-making processes. I have chosen to name this journey the Software Package Life Cycle (SPLC). This chapter is about making the journey an easier and more manageable process.

In addition to my work with software packages, over the years I have been involved with numerous software development efforts and other forms of project work. This work has ranged from building new operating facilities to launching new products and services. The concept of a life cycle is certainly not a new one, especially in most forms of project work. Although the concept is well known and almost universally understood, little, if any, application of the life cycle concept to software packages seems to exist. Part of the reason why the idea of a software package life cycle has received so little attention is that often times the steps comprising this process itself are treated as independent entities when, in fact, they are closely linked. This chapter provides an introduction to the SPLC concept or model as I envision it and to its early stages.

The Software Package Life Cycle: An Overview

The SPLC model provides an overall roadmap for the justification, selection, and implementation of a business application software package. This model is illustrated in Figure 4.1. Each stage of this model will be briefly

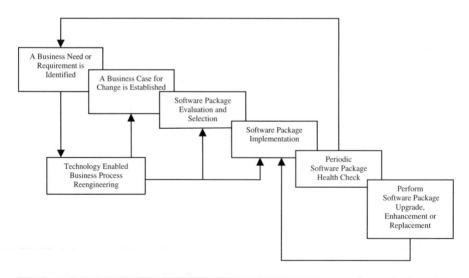

Figure 4.1 The Software Package Life Cycle Model

introduced in this section. Before introducing each stage of the life cycle, there are several important attributes or characteristics of the model worth mentioning.

The first attribute of this model is that it links what are traditionally viewed as separate initiatives into a single, comprehensive life cycle approach. Most of the time we view a business process improvement initiative as a project, the selection of a software package as another project, and the software implementation as yet a third project. By linking these separate initiatives into an overall process or model, synergies between stages can be built into the overall process. Linking these stages together and building in synergies can lower an organization's overall cost, effort, and duration. It also serves to maintain momentum and focus during the initial roll out of the software package's functionality and over the life of the software package.

The second attribute of this model is that it represents a closed-loop system suggesting that while a near-term milestone may exist — the implementation of the software package — a longer-term view is needed. The software package implementation is not the destination. Continuous business process improvement and overall business performance maximization represents the destination, the software package is only an enabler. Thus, the software package configuration will evolve over time as the business itself changes.

The third attribute of this model is that it purports that a software package has a useful life. This is not simply a book or accounting life, but an economic or value-add life to the organization. At some point in time, the software package will become obsolete for business processing or technical reasons and will require replacement. Replacement of a software package can occur on several dimensions. This will include upgrading to the latest version of the same software package or replacing it. A replacement will start the entire life cycle over again, searching for a suitable successor to the software package that is already installed and running.

Discovery: The Early Stages

The early stages in the SPLC are collectively referred to as discovery. Figure 4.2 illustrates the steps in discovery. Discovery is an important part of the SPLC. These early stages suggest and provide for discovery and investigation of business issues. It is during this stage of the SPLC that an agenda for and the urgency of business change should be established. For instance, the first stage represents a call to action. In this stage, a business need or requirement is identified. This identification can be a reactive or a proactive response and subsequent action. I suggest and recommend they be proactive responses.

From this call to action the organization then pursues measurable business process improvements that link to business drivers. From these drivers, metrics are identified and monetarized, building the business case for change and ultimately for business improvement. Figure 4.2 illustrates these early stages of discovery, measurement, and improvement. It also illustrates the business case for technology enabled business process reengineering through the embrace, selection, and adoption of a software package as business operating strategy supporting business process improvement.

The management audit is the starting point in a proactive business process improvement strategy. The management audit is an operational or business process audit and should not to be confused with an annual financial audit. While the management audit raises awareness of the underlying business issues requiring action or the compelling reasons to change, the audit process deliverable is not a blueprint for change.

The next step is to develop such a blueprint for change, through what I refer to as the development of a process vision. The process vision emerges after reaching a deep and thoughtful understanding of an organization's business processes and their simplification. Sometimes simplification actions are completed independently of any further steps, as processes or steps within a given process, or may be abandoned or eliminated. At other times, such simplification is not achieved without some form of automation, such as through the use of a software package.

To suggest that business process improvement will occur also suggests that some form of measurement or benchmarking has occurred that demonstrates improvement. Benchmarking is the name commonly associated with determining, establishing, and using metrics to measure business process performance. When measurement occurs, the nucleus of a business case for change is also established. A business case for change is established by dollarizing or monetarizing the business process improvement.

CHANGE AS THE DRIVER

A number of years ago I came to recognize that the business world is a sea of uncertainty. Such business uncertainty also seems to magnify in intensity with each passing year. Paradoxically, at the same time, I concluded that the one constant that we can rely on in business is change. The organization that can navigate this sea of uncertainty and leverage change, much as a sailor does when taking advantage of prevailing wind pattern, stands the greatest chance of continuous business success. Given this view, it should come as little surprise that when I chose a name for

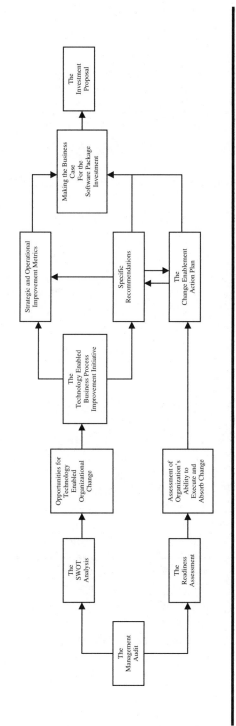

Figure 4.2 Building The Business Case For The Software Package

my consulting practice, Tradewinds Group, that it too needed to reflect this same perspective.

So how does an organization navigate within this sea of uncertainty and deal with business change? First, we can navigate an uncertain business environment through effective short- and long-term planning and control — or management — of the organization. Second, we can harness and exploit change, not simply react to it. Third, through preparedness, although we cannot eliminate uncertainty, we can often mitigate certain business risks.

THE MANAGEMENT AUDIT: AN OVERVIEW

How can the uncertainties and changes that an organization must deal with be identified? They can be identified through a periodic assessment process. The process or technique that I have found most effective in understanding both the state of the business and the prevailing climate the business operates within is the management audit. At this point you may be thinking, "I have never heard of a management audit before. What is it?" I will offer this definition: The management audit is a *multiple purpose business assessment technique*. The technique most often will critique an organization's performance by analyzing key facts, figures, and other information gained through a structured analysis process.

Early on I should also point out that other names are frequently given to this type of management auditing process or technique, including business audit, effectiveness review, and organizational assessment. My strong preference is for the term management audit. There are several good reasons for this, which will be revealed in this section through a more thorough discussion of the scope and purpose of a management audit.

Most important, I believe the management audit is an important preamble to the success of any software package initiative. In the software package initiative, the management audit or organizational assessment will actually play multiple roles. The role of a management audit can be expanded or reduced through its breadth or the scope of the assessment conducted. In fact, the management audit itself can be adapted to a single project or for a given business unit as well as fitted to the entire organization.

Do not confuse a management audit with a financial audit. The management audit is distinctly different from the annual financial audit. A financial audit is an analysis of a firm's past and current financial position. It is designed to verify and evaluate the effectiveness of a firm's financial controls and the integrity of its financial statements. The management audit reviews a much broader array of operating and strategic issues. In addition, management specialists, not accounting specialists, typically conduct the management audit.

As a prelude to *any* organizational change, the management audit is an invaluable tool. It has several major dimensions. The first dimension is what I shall refer to as the discovery dimension, while the second dimension is a readiness assessment dimension; some might equate this latter role to a climate survey. I want to quickly point out that the content of a full-scale management audit is much more than a climate survey.

Although management audits are often undertaken to detect and overcome any operational deficiencies or problems in ongoing operations, especially when there is a sense that something is amiss, the management audit need not be relegated to such a narrow role. When conducted properly, the management audit should look not only at what is wrong, but also at what is right with an organization. The management audit should be a positive, forward-looking experience and should serve as an instrument of self-renewal for the organization and a nucleus for process improvement or innovation.

Unlike the financial audit, which must be conducted annually, there is no such requirement for management audits. In fact, management audits are completely discretionary and need not ever be performed. That is certainly not my recommendation. When an organization follows a regular management audit program, it is constantly assessing its overall organizational health; that is simply a good thing to do.

This idea of a regular checkup or audit program of the organization's effectiveness and efficiency is not a new or unique concept, nor do I stand alone in making this recommendation. Noted author, consultant, and educator Peter Drucker proposed that a business or management audit should be conducted every few years. For some organizations, even this may be insufficient if significant industry or internal changes are occurring. Management audits are also frequently done when top management or ownership changes, when a significant change occurs in an organization's corporate mission or strategy, or when an organization has made a major business acquisition.

The focus of the traditional management audit evaluates how well management accomplishes its stated organizational objectives; how effective management is in planning, organizing, directing, and controlling the organization's activities; and how appropriate management's decisions are for reaching stated organization objectives. The management audit is a comprehensive and constructive examination of the organizational structure. This includes its components, such as divisions, departments, ventures, plans, and policies; its financial and administrative control systems; its method of operation; and its appropriate use of financial, human, physical, and technical resources, including business application software.

The Management Audit: Is It Necessary?

Although one could argue that if an organization already has some form of total quality management program, particularly a Six Sigma program, an activity-based management initiative, or a Balanced Scorecard, that it is continuously monitoring itself. These initiatives will trigger any corrections or improvements as needed, rendering management audits as obsolete exercises.

Although I will not dispute the value that any one of the previously mentioned initiatives can bring to an organization, I still believe there is room for the management audit. Peter Drucker once commented that cost control is not a one-time event, it must be an ongoing process. The same can be said for business process reengineering. Consider this question: How does an organization know if the continuous improvement programs it has instituted are working as intended and are adding value to the organization? Simply put, my answer is through a management audit of those processes.

The management audit is often an unpopular activity that an organization will engage in. Part of the problem may lie in the use of the word audit. To many, the management audit, in particular, is similar to some other unpleasant and unpopular organizational concepts. This may include reengineering, scientific management (time and motion studies), reorganization, flattening the organization, running lean, and downsizing. To these charges, the answer is guilty as charged. The recommendations in a management audit will often lead to any one of these activities as a follow-on organizational imperative — even to technology-enabled business process change using a software package.

The Management Audit as a Discovery Instrument

In the discovery role, the management audit provides an assessment of an organization's strengths, weaknesses, opportunities, and threats, known as a SWOT analysis. The management audit assesses the degree of effectiveness in the execution of business and operating plans. The management audit also reviews the effectiveness and efficiency of operations. It just happens that operational activities are traditionally the parts of the organization's business model that are most affected by an organization's information model, and ultimately, by its business application systems or software packages.

Building a Business Case Using the Management Audit

Forget about justifying technology for the sake of technology alone. In the post-Y2K world, corporate managers, especially information technology (IT) managers, are finding that argument is no longer an acceptable one to justify software expenditures that can easily swell into hundreds of thousands of dollars, if not more. Instead, justify technology for business reasons. The reality is that any major software investment requires a financially responsible business case to be made for its acquisition. The management audit can provide, through the SWOT analysis, the underpinnings necessary to build a business case for technology-enabled business process change, particularly for software packages and complementary technologies.

Management Audits: Who Should Conduct Them?

As a general rule, management audits are most often conducted by consulting firms. Internal auditors, business analysts, and industrial engineers have the requisite backgrounds, if not the time, to also build and conduct a management audit. The disadvantages of using internal resources is less objectivity, fear of being perceived as critical of the organization, and perhaps undue influence by management.

The advantage of using consultants is that they often bring ready-made management audit templates and a formal process or workplan. The disadvantage of using consultants includes cost and the learning curve needed for the consultant to understand your business model. An experienced consultant will usually be able to grasp your business model and any issues with relative ease. Just be sure the consulting firm does not pitch with team A, then sends team B in to complete the work.

THE MANAGEMENT AUDIT: FROM CONCEPT TO DELIVERABLE

Now that I have introduced the management audit in conceptual terms, it is now time to understand the specific contents of the management audit deliverable and the process of constructing that deliverable. A typical functional or organizationally based management audit is divided into a half dozen or more major sections. Each major section considers one operating or administrative function within the enterprise. For instance, the typical functionally based management audit in the manufacturing environment will contain reviews of the following areas:

- Financial administration
- Procurement and supply chain management
- Operations and manufacturing
- Presales marketing and support
- Postsales support

- Product development and management
- Human resources administration
- Information technology

In a nonmanufacturing environment the review areas will vary. For instance, a professional services firm likely does not need to review procurement and supply chain management practices. That review might simply be combined with the financial administration review. A university or hospital would not develop new products *per se*, but would be interested in reviewing professional standards, staff development, and the adoption of leading-edge techniques. On the other hand, all organizations conduct business by delivering a product or service. So, although it may not be called distribution or manufacturing, it is an operations function or delivery as it is often called in the professional services business. All organizations have a sales and marketing function of some kind.

This leads to the next area of concern: "What specific inquiry areas should a management audit address?" There are many books and publications that provide business assessment checklists or guidelines. Unfortunately, few of these publications combine this information into a single, comprehensive, immediately usable management audit template. For instance, I have had to develop the series of templates that I use as starting points in conducting management audits. Every situation is somewhat unique, and the person, or team, conducting a management audit will need to be creative in their approach in developing the actual assessment criteria or list of questions. The information presented here provides only some well-traveled guidelines, not specifics.

Before providing some general assessment questions, a starting point is needed. In other words, within each review area the question to answer is, What should be the focus of the audit process? The starting point for the overall assessment is through what I refer to as assessment categories. The assessment categories I typically use to answer the question, "What does the management audit look at?", are:

- Strategy
- Organization
- Process
- Controls
- People
- Technology

The assessment categories do not typically vary by review area. For instance, financial administration, postsales support, or operations and manufacturing would all include these assessment categories, with appropriate assessment criteria being established for each review area in each assessment category.

Assessment Criteria

The next and most important consideration is the actual assessment. The assessment should be a series of introspective, deeply probing questions. The assessment should be from the top down. The questions must be frank. They should question the organization's vision, objectives, leadership, structure, and processes. Those responding — usually executives and managers — should be frank with their answers. In that vein, amnesty and anonymity should be the hallmark of a management audit.

Within each assessment area are a number of important questions that must be addressed. Every organization will develop and use different questions as the basis of its assignment. It is this bank of questions used that will limit or can expand the scope of the overall management audit. Auditing is about posing a series of *probing questions* that are answered through observation, interrogation or interview, and subsequent analysis. Most important, the questions must focus on determining and evaluating the key drivers in each assessment area. To illustrate this concept, consider this sample question:

> Do production materials appear to be standing around or piled up unnecessarily?

The word "appear" suggests this question must be answered through visual observation. If the auditor answers yes, then the auditor has an obligation to follow up. The auditor will then query the production supervisor about the stockpile. The response might be any one of the following:

- "Assembly was halted on those units due to parts shortages."
- "Those units are awaiting rework."
- "Those units are awaiting movement into the next assembly area."

Notice that any one of these responses will (or should) lead to further questions, but not necessarily scripted questions. The scripted questions or assessment criteria only define the scope of work for the overall audit. They do not define completely the level of detail that an auditor must operate at in order to be satisfied in hearing every detail about a subject. When the auditor does reach that level of understanding, the auditor can then make an assessment as to the impact the observation has on the organization's overall efficiency and effectiveness. Consider how the auditor might report this observation as an audit finding:

> *We observed what appeared to be an excessive amount of materials piling up in the production department. Upon further analysis, we determined the stockpile was work in process inventory that had built up due to a parts shortage. This appears to be a significant, recurring event and suggests to us that safety stocks on critical materials must be reviewed.*

The above finding is only one possible explanation. It does not necessarily lead to the conclusion that a system is needed. It only suggests that an existing system is not likely being used correctly. This observation could also lead to a starkly different finding as noted in the following example:

> *We observed what appeared to be an excessive amount of materials piling up in the production department. Upon further analysis, we determined the stockpile was work in process inventory that had built up due to a parts shortage. This appears to be a significant, recurring event. Our analysis indicates it is caused largely by the manual inventory controls that are in place today that use an arbitrary safety stock quantity of bin size. This does not necessarily relate to material flow volume through the production process.*

In this finding one can find cause to suggest or recommend that a computerized inventory control system would help to solve some of the firm's work in process inventory stockpiling issues. Another issue that is likely operating in this scenario is the early or premature release of the production work order or request to the plant floor — before all materials have arrived. Again, a computerized production planning and control system might prove to be the recommendation.

It is also entirely appropriate to seek out the opinions of those questioned on what recommendations that a given individual has regarding how an observed issue or problem can be remedied. At the same time ask them, "How would you back up your claim?" Again, this gives the auditor a possible lead to follow in determining the underlying business driver or drivers of an identified business issue or problem.

When developing assessment questions, my concern is with developing penetrating, thought-provoking questions. Again, I develop questions around organizational functions (i.e., production, finance) and themes or what I call assessment areas (i.e., strategy, controls). I prefer to use two types of questions. The first type of question requires only a yes or no reply; this is often times the first question and serves as groundbreaker into a new area. The second type of question is a confidence-rating question. Many surveys use these; they usually appear as, "On a scale of...how would you rate the following?" Forget numeric rankings — people respond better to words, such as poor, good, or excellent. Words can always be associated with numeric values behind the scenes.

As I noted earlier, there are numerous resources available that provide what are usually checklists of dos or don'ts and best practices. Just about any business related book in any subject area has these types of lists. Unfortunately, it is beyond the scope of this book to present a model management audit.

On a final note, assessments are qualitative in nature and represent opinion, not fact. The auditor must identify metrics and must relate qualitative assessments with cold, hard facts — numbers. Do not attempt to improve upon something until causal relationships can be determined that tie to one or more business metrics. These are metrics that can be monetarized and tied to a business organization's bottom line. The assessments must lead to the metrics or drivers associated with the overall performance of the organization.

The SWOT Analysis Deliverable

The SWOT analysis is the management audit deliverable. This document summarizes the results of the management audit by assessment category for each review area. Figure 4.3 illustrates the management audit deliverable format. The results of a management audit are typically referred to as findings. Findings can be classified as major or minor. Major findings are typically those items requiring immediate, corrective action, while a minor finding is of less cause for concern. As mentioned previously, the management audit does not simply find fault. By design, it should also highlight positive findings. This SWOT analysis template is a part of the author's template collection. Consult Appendix A for more information about these templates.

I have seen management audits that offer a quantitative dimension to each finding, usually rating each criterion on a scale of 1 to 5 or 1 to 10. Other formats provide a visual indicator of finding severity, such as the use of full, half-full, or empty glass; a fuel gauge-like instrument, or a stoplight with red, yellow, and green indicators. Without the benefit of a color printer, stoplights do not reproduce well, but they remain my preferred visual indicator.

CHANGE MANAGEMENT: AN OVERVIEW

While the management audit's SWOT analysis provides recommendations regarding potential change or improvement activities, it does not address how such change should be implemented. As previously mentioned,

Management Audit Report of Findings
Prepared for ABC Manufacturing Company by Tradewinds Group, Incorporated

TradewindsGroup

Review/Assessment Area	Strengths	Weaknesses	Opportunities	Threats	Recommendations
Financial Administration					
• Strategy	Has implemented a three-year strategic planning and budgeting process.				Implement a balanced scorecard reporting mechanism to complement existing strategic planning process.
• Organization			Disbursements made at outlying facilities could be managed centrally.		Implement shared services model for Accounts Payable.
• Process		Month end closing is largely a manual process. Accounts payable processing is an extensive manual effort today.			Implement a new financial system. A new financial system would significantly streamline month end and closing process.
• Control		Inventory swings in excess of $10,000 on a monthly basis.		Current system audit trails do not drill down to transactions.	A new financial system could provide downstream and upstream audit trails using "drill down" capabilities from ledger to detail or detail to ledger. A perpetual inventory control system, a "closed" storeroom and the adoption of cycle counting practices would substantially reduce inventory swings.
• People		High turnover. The department has an average turnover in clerical personnel of 35% and in professional staff of 43%.			A new financial system would significantly streamline month-end closings and reduce burden on staff to work long hours for several weeks each month.
• Technology			Manual budgeting process. Manual invoice verification.		A new financial system would provide online budgeting. An ERP system could allow for automated invoice verification and electronic receipt settlement, plus would provide both financial, inventory control and procurement integration.

Figure 4.3 The SWOT Analysis Matrix: The Management Audit Deliverable

people do not embrace change and often fear it. Moreover, most organizations are ill-equipped for change. As processes and procedures become institutionalized, they too provide convenient barriers to change.

There have been numerous articles and reports suggesting widespread disappointment with software packages. In addition, these articles and reports often cite that a significant number of software package implementations are failures. It has been my experience and observation that a good number of software implementations fail not because of bad software, but because of bad ways. Sloppy business practices and procedures will not improve with new software. An organization's lack of discipline, preparation, and ability to follow through can stall or thwart an implementation. Simply put, no two tools and techniques will better prepare your organization for this journey that I have chosen to call the SPLC than will change management and project management. If your organization is not good at either, hire someone who is. In the long run, it will be money well spent.

In some areas of an organization, change can have disruptive and wide-ranging impact. It is common to find that even change management is frequently and rightly institutionalized. If you are an IT professional, consider how important design freezes, scope control, software version control, and configuration management are to a smoothly running operation. An engineering or product manager is usually well aware or has even designed the engineering change management or the engineering change notification process for the organization. The manufacturing operations manager always favors preventive maintenance and scheduled downtime to prevent unplanned production line disruptions and stoppages.

When implementing business process improvements of any kind, including new software packages, the same degree of, if not more, change control must be exercised. It is a process generically called organizational change management. Every project, no matter how large or small, should include a change management dimension. I have found that many project managers and administrators usually, and naively so, limit change management to scope control or expectations management. Scope control is not the only of kind of change management needed when business changes, especially ones with far reaching or organization-wide impact, are being made.

On numerous occasions I have encountered individuals who simply have a bad taste in their mouth for change of any kind. They are usually able to cite fairly lucid, strongly opinionated evidence, in the form of stories from within their own organizations, about the good, the bad, and the ugly of change. Sometimes these stories are indeed accurate, while at other times they tend to be organizational folklore.

Humans are change-adverse. We talk a good game about change, but if left to our own devices, we quickly erect barriers to resist change. To be successful at change, the organization must make a strong commitment to carefully managing change, including commitments to change education, communication, and experimentation. As a prelude to any organizational change, I strongly recommend conducting a formal assessment of the organization's readiness or propensity to absorb high degrees or levels of process change.

The Readiness Assessment: What Is It?

The purpose of a readiness assessment is to understand the organization's capacity to execute change. It is one thing to make a recommendation of change; it is quite another to successfully execute business change. Virtually all established organizations already have a track record with change — good or bad. The readiness assessment reviews in part the organization's history with change. The idea is to understand where and how an organization succeeded with change in the past and to incorporate or leverage that knowledge into the proposed change initiative.

Organizational change is difficult. Understanding how change works or should be done may require skilled facilitation. If your business improvement or audit team is uncomfortable with this subject matter, there are consultants available whose expertise is in this area.

The Readiness Assessment: What Should It Look Like?

The readiness assessment is another high-level assessment, somewhat akin to a management audit, but with a different goal or perspective separate and apart of the management audit. If you felt the management audit was a radical concept, then buckle up as the readiness assessment stands to spark even more controversy. The readiness assessment is intended to be a critical assessment of the organization's ability to propose and execute change. The purpose is to help identify who has or can bring about change in the organization and what elements will be necessary for success at change from the viewpoint of an organization's staff.

The readiness assessment should focus on three dimensions of change. The first dimension of change is the organization's change management track record. The second dimension should be an assessment of an organization's change leadership. Who has led change in the past? Why or why not have they been successful? The third should be an assessment of the individuals who will be the subjects of change. How do they perceive change? What will make them more comfortable with or receptive to change? The following list provides a series of questions intended to elicit some information about the organization's change capacity and change history.

■ Change History

What has been the most significant and positive change that has occurred in this organization since your tenure began? Why do you feel this way?

What has been the most significant and negative change that has occurred in this organization since your tenure began? Why do you feel this way? What perhaps would you have done differently?

Name an executive you feel has vision — the ability to see into the future. Can you cite an example?

When things must change in this organization, in general, how would rate the organization's speed of response? Why do you feel this way?

■ Change Leadership

Name an executive that you feel has vision — the ability to see into the future. Can you cite an example?

Name a senior manager you feel has vision — the ability to see into the future. Can you cite an example?

Name one of your colleagues or peers you feel has vision — the ability to see into the future. Can you cite an example?

Name an executive you feel exhibits leadership — the ability to make things happen and to get others rallied behind a cause. Can you cite an example?

Name a senior manager you feel exhibits leadership — the ability to make things happen and to get others rallied behind a cause. Can you cite an example?

Name one of your colleagues or peers you feel exhibits leadership — the ability to make things happen and to get others rallied behind a cause. Can you cite an example?

Whom have you seen lead a change in the past? What was the change? Were they successful? Can you cite one thing that they might have been done differently?

■ Change Personalization

How do you perceive change?

What makes you more comfortable with change?

If an organizational change were to affect you personally, what three things would you expect from the organization in terms of support? Which is the most important and the least important?

What has been the most significant change in your life? What did you learn from this experience? How has this experience changed your life?

Questions related to organizational change are not easy and are in fact downright sensitive. Most organizations fear upsetting the apple cart or starting rumors by assessing the organization's climate or attitudes; this is especially true when change is considered. For instance, I try to dispel such notions at the onset of the change assessment interview. Here is a typical opening sequence to such an assessment interview:

> I've been asked to review the business processes and practices of this organization and to determine if there are areas where improvements might be helpful to your organization's business strategy or operations. For instance, many types of business improvements, such as implementing a new software package, require a significant amount of change in an organization. I'm trying to understand how this organization and its leadership has executed change in the past; what lessons can be learned; and how individuals, such as yourself, perceive change. I have a series of questions about change I would like to review with you at this time. Do you have any questions about our purpose in meeting? May we proceed to my questions for you now?

Here are some final notes on change assessment. First, it is helpful to ask a cross section of individuals (i.e., executives, managers, supervisors, senior staffers, office and line personnel) from an organization's staff about change. Second, it is helpful to ask these questions of both relatively new (6 months or more) and seasoned veterans in the organization. Third, if your organization has hostile labor relations, it may be inappropriate to survey labor. Finally, in a union shop, it may be inappropriate to approach unionized workers with this survey unless it is first discussed with the union representative.

The Guiding Principles of Change Management

There are numerous examples of organizational change. While some of these changes succeed, others fail. What is clear from both the successes and failures in this area is the need for a comprehensive change management plan. It is the readiness assessment that leads to construction of a change enablement action plan, or simply put, the organization's overall change management plan.

The readiness assessment is the starting point in building the successful change management plan. While no change will ever be perfect, there are specific steps that can be taken to manage the impact of change on the organization. The goal of change management is twofold; first, it must minimize the disruptive effects of change, and second, it must manage change toward achieving the full benefit of the proposed change. With that in mind, some guiding principles govern effective change management:

- Change must be viewed as constructive.
- Change must be viewed as a positive force.
- Executive sponsorship is a critical, first step. Complete sponsorship, from the highest to the lowest levels within an organization's management hierarchy is necessary.
- When it comes to change, stakeholder buy-in is a work in process. Until the changes are complete and the situation is stabilized, they will remain so.
- Resistance to change must be actively managed.
- A shared vision of change must be established and communicated to all stakeholders.
- Change is not easy. For change to have any chance of success, education is an essential ingredient.
- Change behaviors must be reinforced. Prior to change implementation, practice the important changes to everyday behaviors. Upon postimplementation, stand ready to answer any question and reinforce infrequently used behaviors.
- When any aspect of change runs amiss, it must be addressed quickly.
- Awareness is key. When everyone is aware of the facts surrounding change, rumors are meaningless.
- The buy-in is also important. One way to elicit buy-in is to include process owners and stakeholders in the discussions regarding the current state and the desired outcomes of their processes.

At times, change can be a delicate matter. When jobs are on the line and the livelihoods of people are at risk, emotions will run high. Job loss is usually the highest fear the average individual has when it comes to organizational change. The next section speaks to these concerns.

Change and the Human Dimension

The business world has become an unstable one. The unwritten "job for life" employment contract forged over the past 100 or so years between the business organization and the modern worker has also changed. As an example, my father-in-law worked for one company his entire adult life, from high school until retirement — a span of more than 40 years. In my case, I have had three separate careers and five employers over a 25-year span and have been the victim of downsizing, outsourcing, and bankruptcy liquidation. Furthermore, I still have another 20 or more years before I reach my normal retirement age as defined under current social security laws. Suffice to say my roller coaster ride in the new era's job market is far from over. These are the very changes we as humans fear most — the fear of insecurity in an uncertain world. As we age, we are less willing, and in many cases, less able to change.

Unfortunately, much of this fear is well founded after countless bouts of downsizing and the seemingly unending flow of good-paying and skilled jobs moving offshore. Remember, anyone could be the unwilling victim of organization change, including ourselves, a co-worker, a long-time colleague, friend, mentor, or neighbor. My only suggestion is that an organization should avoid job losses to the greatest extent possible when making changes. However, when they must occur, transitioning personnel to new careers inside or outside of the organization, or perhaps into an early retirement, are the costs of the change that must be weighed against the benefits of that change.

Though I wish I could argue against job loss in all cases, there are times when business performance will be maximized by reducing the size or scope of operations or in moving processes offshore or to an outsourcer. I must quickly add that the kind of change we are talking about in this book — technology-enabled business process change primarily using software packages — as a general rule does not reduce headcount. The management audit that precludes any such change will undoubtedly reveal related process improvements that may impact the current organizational structure and may adversely impact headcount. There are several areas in which headcount is usually most impacted by technology-enabled business process change:

- Information technology
- Data administration
- Clerical processing
- Materials handling and movement

If an organization has an existing, complex IT infrastructure and its technologies are dated, it will likely have too many programmers on staff. In the future the organization will most likely rely on a single, integrated system.

Moreover, the current programming staff may be ill-equipped to deal with the new technologies behind the latest generation client server based, object oriented integrated systems. Configurable, enterprise-wide, integrated systems require strong networking and performance tuning skills and often less programming skills. When changes or modifications are needed to these systems, they are usually a more difficult task than with traditional legacy systems. Many software package vendors, especially those peddling enterprise-wide enterprise resource planning (ERP) systems, will bill their products as user configurable or allow end users to fulfill their own reporting needs. Do not be too quick to believe this completely. Be aware that even the reports of programmable report writers are usually more technical than can be abosorbed and applied easily by most staff typical of a business organization unless it is a skill they will use on an almost daily basis.

Expect significant retraining costs and the impact of a learning curve for those who will remain to support the new technology. At the same time, an enterprise-wide, integrated system requires internal support expertise. Do not assume that all IT personnel may be candidates for such a role. When system changes or modifications are needed, they must closely follow the vendor's established guidelines for making and integrating code changes. Cowboy coders should not apply or even be considered as top candidates to support a complex, enterprise-wide integrated system. Remember that cowboy coders are the ones who built those previous, nearly unmaintainable legacy systems.

The Change Enablement Action Plan

The deliverable from the readiness assessment process is a change enablement action plan. This document should summarize both the change assessment survey results and the guiding principles of change noted previously into a plan of action. The change enablement action plan is an important part of the business case. The business case for any process improvements will not be complete without the change enablement action plan. The change enablement action plan answers several important questions related to project risk:

- When will the business improvement benefits begin to take effect? (Usually they can't begin until the changes are operational.)
- Have we taken into account all that is necessary to ensure benefits from this project will be forthcoming?
- What are the steps that will lead to a smooth implementation of the proposed changes?

Every project has risks. Business improvement projects tend to have a greater degree of risk. This is because the organization could be disrupted if the changes are not implemented in a controlled, deliberate, and verifiable manner. A plan of action is necessary to avoid undue business risks as a result of the business changes to come. The change enablement action plan should minimally address the following areas:

- Who will be the sponsors of the changes?
- What provides the impetus for change?

- What demonstrable results are envisioned as result of these changes?
- How will the need for change be communicated?
- How, when, and by whom will the specific changes be communicated? Consider this a plan for change-related education.
- What must change?
- What processes or functions will be impacted?
- How will the process or function change? (i.e., altered, eliminated, automated)
- What job positions will be impacted? At this point, such identification is usually only by job position or role, not by individual.
- How will these job positions be impacted? For instance, will holders of this position be retrained for this position, redeployed into other roles within the organization, or displaced (i.e., the positions are eliminated)?
- How, when, and by whom will any adverse job action be made?
- What steps will be taken to prevent or minimize business disruption?
- Who will monitor the change rollout for effectiveness (accuracy, completeness) and how will they measure it?
- How quickly will processes be stabilized or normalized after changes are introduced?
- How will customers and/or suppliers be impacted?
- How, when, and by whom will customers and/or suppliers be notified? (Consider any dealers and distributors as your customers.)
- Customers and/or suppliers to facilitate the proposed changes will incur what costs?
- Should/must the organization absorb, rebate, or credit these customer/supplier costs to facilitate these proposed changes?
- What specific risks are posed to the business by these changes? How will these risks be identified? Have contingencies been devised to overcome each of these risks?
- How will the project scope be controlled? If processing gaps are identified, what will be the process to determine their severity and the course of action to act upon any such gaps? When will a gap be considered so significant as to stop the project from moving forward or the implementation from occurring?

There are certainly other aspects of change management that do not appear on this list. They are primarily technical changes to the software, the hardware, and the software operating and network environments. These technical changes should be part of the project management infrastructure. The last two questions should also consider the impact of such technical issues.

Changing the Way Business Is Done: It Is about Learning the New Way

A software package or system does not necessarily make processes better or more efficient. Software and systems are simply information processing tools. An important part of the change enablement action plan is to address how the software will be utilized in the business processes and how the software will improve these processes. To be certain, some tasks, usually transactions and document routings will be automated. These are the easiest to identify and accommodate in terms of change management — they are "hard" changes. The tougher changes to identify and manage are the "soft" changes. Soft changes are those that improve the process only when information from the new system is leveraged or used to make better, more informed, or timely business decisions. Learning how to interpret, use, and respond to the data from a materials requirements planning run is one such example of a soft change. The types of education these changes require are very difficult. As with all business training, I suggest using case studies or examples drawn from your real world business environment. Try to show examples in both a before and after context.

Communicating Change

The need to communicate about significant business change is not a one-time event. Change management requires periodic updates about the progress toward the implementation of any previously announced changes. This information must be given to all those who will lead or be impacted by the changes. The change management action plan should parallel and become an integral part of the overall business improvement project or the software package implementation project plan.

Change management does not come free, nor can these costs be avoided or shortchanged if the desired business changes are to be successful. Every task in the plan has a price tag and very real benefits to the overall project. The costs associated with change management must be considered as an integral part of the overall cost and benefit analysis when making the business case for a proposed business process improvement or software package acquisition and implementation.

BUSINESS PROCESS IMPROVEMENT: DOING IT RIGHT

To be successful with business process improvement or reengineering, it has to be done correctly. As previously stated, the organization must, above all else, understand both its readiness for change and its propensity to change. If the organization is not ready or in a position to embark upon or embrace change, then the status quo may be better than undertaking a change that could be chaotic, disruptive, and even worse, counterproductive.

An important, and some would argue the most important element to the success, in any business process reengineering effort is minimizing or removing the barriers to change that usually permeate an organization. Change, no matter what you call it, breeds doubts, fears, and uncertainty in the minds of the workforce — these are the barriers to change as I perceive them. These fears strike the hearts of everyone in an organization set to embark on great change — the young or old, a new or senior worker, a hardhat from the plant floor, or a pinstripe on mahogany row.

The organization must deal effectively with removing these barriers to change. Otherwise, it risks failure in achieving any meaningful results or finds that such changes are counterproductive. Some of the ways to reduce these barriers to change include:

- Participation, to the extent possible, in making any process changes or recommendations for change.
- Education about why the changes are necessary, in addition to ample education and reinforcement of new or differing work-related responsibilities.
- Developing an appreciation, or buy-in, in every worker for change as instrumental to the organization's continued success as a whole.
- Continuity and transition planning for the business itself and for the individuals that make up the business.

One question that invariably arises is, "What will happen to me in this time of transition"? The consequences of business change are not always pleasant. Yes, sometimes certain work and its associated workers will be displaced. The concept of continuity and transition planning is meant to address and alleviate these concerns. Business continuity and transition planning should be important aspects of the change enablement action plan.

THE POSTIMPLEMENTATION MANAGEMENT AUDIT

The use of a management audit has another role with respect to software packages. As you will recall, I suggested that management audits are something that should be done regularly. It is also a flexible technique that has wide-ranging applications in the organization and can be applied to many business scenarios.

Within the context of this book lies another practical use of management audits. The management audit can serve as a postimplementation deliverable that is completed on a periodic basis throughout the life of the software package. This was previously introduced as the SPLC. Others refer to such a postimplementation management audit as a health check or postproject physical. As a postimplementation diagnostic tool, the management audit is used to assess if both the software package and the organization are meeting the expectations for effectiveness and efficiency that were set forth for both in the business case used to initiate the software package investment.

For instance, in this role, the management audit might also reveal that an existing software package is not being fully utilized, an all too typical finding. In other cases, it might reveal that major parts of an existing software package are either turned off postimplementation, or left off during implementation. There are numerous reasons why this can occur. Perhaps it is because the software was considered inadequate, inappropriate, or not fit for use at that time.

Often, speed of implementation meant that portions of a system were initially left off. Unfortunately, many organizations never seem to get around to wrapping up or restarting the stalled or postponed implementation or the second or subsequent phases as they are often called. When a software package fails to achieve its complete vision, it usually also fails to accomplish the business case upon which the decision was based.

More often than not, education and training surface as significant postimplementation issues during such audits. This leads to several conclusions. The first conclusion is the need for adequate education. This does not just encompass software product knowledge, but also business process understanding as well. I have found often times that many organizations do not have significant experience in a given area of process change.

The application of manufacturing resource planning is representative of such a business process improvement. Do not believe for a minute that every organization today is using or will even understand completely what manufacturing resource planning (MRP-II) is all about. What I have found in practice is that because the process is misunderstood, its application to an organization's business practices are also failing. The software — in this case an ERP system — becomes an easy, nonhuman target. It receives the blame for much, if not all, of an organization's woes for failing to achieve business results using MRP-II related best practices.

A more careful analysis usually suggests that such blame is often unjustified. I have encountered multiple instances where software features are left off or turned off because of such process ignorance. The root cause is often that an organization did not prepare itself for the onslaught of business change precipitated by the software package. Sadly, process ignorance can become a major source of discontent with both software packages and new processes; any benefits that might have been originally envisioned as having for an organization are quickly thwarted. This analysis leads directly to my second conclusion — to be proactive at the earliest stage in any technology-enabled change project. This involves conducting the readiness assessment and the resulting change enablement action plan and why I have stressed such in this chapter.

WHAT THE MANAGEMENT AUDIT IS NOT

The management audit is not a detail-level undertaking. While the audit process may identify specific opportunities and weaknesses, it does not go into elaborate detail. Additional exploratory work is necessary to fully justify the implementation of a specific recommendation within the context of a business case for a software package. This is usually done through process auditing, which is usually a part of any business process improvement or reengineering process. Process auditing and business process improvement and reengineering will be discussed in Chapter 5.

AN EPILOGUE: WHY BOTHER WITH MANAGEMENT AUDITS?

Remember what your cause is — organizational improvement, or more simply put, maximum business performance. In that vein, the management audit is intended as a review to discover an organization's innermost strengths, weaknesses, opportunities, and threats and to recommend actions the organization should take that will:

- Leverage its strengths.
- Overcome any weaknesses.
- Exploit the opportunities.
- Avoid or mitigate business risks due to real or perceived internal or external threats.

The management audit provides the impetus for business change. While at first glance a management audit may seem to be an unorthodox approach toward building a case for a software package, it is not. First, buying and implementing a software package must solve real business problems, facilitate fulfillment of unrealized opportunities, or leverage the strengths of the business organization. Second, not all of an organization's business strengths, weaknesses, opportunities, or threats will benefit from new software alone. Recall my discussion of the organization's hierarchy of needs in the preceding chapter; technology plays a role, but also combines with other factors to achieve business results.

5

LINKING BUSINESS PROCESS IMPROVEMENT AND SOFTWARE PACKAGES

Chapter 4 presented the management audit process as a discovery vehicle to uncover areas where improvement is needed. This management auditing process and the deliverables produced by it represented a call to action for business process improvement. This chapter is a discussion of the techniques for business process modeling and improvement that is centered around the use of technology, particularly business application software packages, to improve business processes.

This chapter will present arguments for conducting business process modeling and improvement prior to software package selection. This is also considered a somewhat controversial position and the reasons why it will be discussed. This chapter also discusses and illustrates a specific business process modeling technique appropriate to software package implementation, often called technology-enabled business process reengineering.

RETURN ON INFORMATION AND BUSINESS IMPROVEMENT

Chapter 1 introduced the concept of return on information versus return on investment. First, please understand that return on investment will, as a general rule, always determine which capital projects an organization will invest in. On the other hand, Return on Information should be used to determine where and how to apply technology to the business organization in order to maximize business performance. This is usually done primarily through operational improvements and efficiencies, such as maintaining lower levels of inventory, experiencing fewer customer returns, or performing less rework.

It can be said that any business information system has the following primary goals:

- Record information about an organization's current business activity.
- Analyze trends present in both current and past business activity.
- Aid in planning an organization's future business activity.
- Serve as the organization's early warning indicator, providing management alerts that something is amiss or not going according to plan.
- To keep score of how the business is doing based upon current, past, and projected (future) business activity.

If your current information systems are not providing all these goals, then those systems are failing your organization. It can be said that they are failing to provide an acceptable or optimal level of return on information.

No organization simply collects information without at least some purpose (or at least it should not be collecting such information). Unfortunately, most information systems are not fully leveraged. This usually means that the two outer goals from the above list are served well but that the inner three goals are usually not met completely; in some cases they are not met at all. When all five of these goals are met, the organization has fully leveraged information and is achieving high, if not optimal, levels of return on information.

A software package or system does not necessarily make processes better or more efficient. Software and systems are simply information processing tools. In that sense, the software or system is only an enabler or facilitator of both process improvement and ongoing levels of acceptable performance. Information processing is all about capturing, analyzing, and providing the essential information relevant to decision making or process completion in a timely manner to the place or person where the information is best acted on.

I use a fairly simple series of questions to demonstrate how information-literate an organization is. My information literacy test consists of the following questions:

- Where are the bottlenecks — the problems — in your business operation today?
- How do you know that these are your real bottlenecks or problems?
- What hard evidence exists to substantiate that the cited problems exist?

- How would you go about quantifying the effect or impact of these bottlenecks or problems?
- What known business issues confront your organization today?
- Are these isolated cases or do they represent a trend?
- What hard evidence exists to substantiate or disprove that this is a trend or pattern?
- How do you quantify the effect or impact these issues are having on your business?
- What information or knowledge are you lacking about your business operations today?
- If you had this information, how do you envision using it?
- Cite at least three examples of how such information could have been leveraged to improve your overall business performance.
- How would you go about quantifying the effect or impact such information had or would have had on your business performance?

It is not unusual to encounter organizations that already have enterprise resource planning (ERP) systems installed and to hear of their frustrations with the system. Usually, these complaints are that the new system has not made any substantial improvements to the way that business is done, the organization is unhappy with the amount of time it took to install the system, or the price tag for the system was too high, given the benefits achieved.

Does this mean such an organization has selected the wrong system? Perhaps that may or may not be the case. Sometimes organizations fail to realize the full benefit of an automation project because the organization itself has fallen short. — For example, an organization can fall short by failing to place enough value on information, lacking confidence in a new system, not educating itself on a new way of doing business, or by failing to discipline itself to follow a new process. It is for these reasons that I previously stressed the need to prepare for and achieve a readiness to accept and embrace change or business process improvement. It is also important to learn how business should be done the new way — through the system instead of around the system as it so often happens.

For instance, customer relationship management (CRM) system implementations, which are all the rage today, are often cited as having high failure rates. Upon careful analysis, the reason why so many of these efforts fail is the inability of the organization to adapt its selling process to the disciplined, activity-driven model that accompanies the adoption of a CRM system. In this case, the system has not failed, but the process itself has.

I have also encountered a number of organizations — both large and small — that have implemented ERP systems, but not in their entirety.

Ironically, it is the most important aspect of these systems — the resource planning functionality — that is usually not being tapped, with the materials requirements planning (MRP/CRP) portions of these systems not being used. In some cases, these systems are being used as nothing more than a simple production work order system used to backflush component inventories and book an end product that can be shipped.

In these cases, the common thread is generally a lack of education and related experience using automated planning techniques as the root cause. In other instances, there have been some early failures or disappointments using new processes or techniques — sometimes these are high profile incidents — and the organization has abandoned, for instance, the use of CRP/MRP before the problems can be corrected. What happens then? Often these earlier failures seem to live in infamy within the organization, and it never gets around to implementing the rest of a planning system and never fully realizes the true value of its system investments. Yes, it is true that when not properly understood and used appropriately, MRP stands for many reams of paper, but this is not how it should be.

The lessons to be learned from these examples is simply that business process improvement is about developing a synergy, through the effective combination of people, process, technology, management, and organization structure. This combination will reduce costs or enhance revenue potential while sustaining or improving business results; it is never simply about new technology alone.

Selecting and Applying Business Performance Metrics

The management audit discussed in the previous chapter represents a commentary or summary about the performance of the business on an overall basis. The management audit also identifies the drivers of business performance. Usually these drivers can be thought of in terms of measures or metrics that can demonstrate the value of any organizational change or improvement. At the same time, it is an actionable document, calling attention to significant business issues and significant deviations in business performance from what is desired or expected.

These performance related metrics — actually the *anticipated or projected changes or improvements demonstrated* in business performance as measured by these — will then become the tangible, quantifiable benefits used in making the business case for change. The biggest problem by far, with best practices and with business process reengineering in general, is determining and applying an appropriate set of metrics that can demonstrate a clear cause-and-effect relationship between the business change undertaken and the bottom-line impact such changes have. Making this connection is an integral part of the business process improvement effort. Without such, it is difficult, if not impossible, to demonstrate a business case for the proposed business improvement recommendations.

BUSINESS PROCESS IMPROVEMENT

Finding the root causes of operational bottlenecks and problems of business issues is the essence of business process improvement. Although modern day authors such as James Champy, Thomas Davenport, and Michael Hammer are credited with kindling the current interest in business process reengineering, the ideas are largely rooted in industrial engineering or scientific management concepts. These concepts were first devised around the turn of the last century by Frederick W. Taylor. There are several common names given to business process improvement, including business process change, business process reengineering, and business process transformation. All of these terms can be used interchangeably. I have attempted to be consistent in my usage and, where practical, limit my usage to the term business process improvement.

In general, reengineering presumes improvement will take place by critically reviewing and reconstructing processes, generally from the ground up. There are several approaches that can be taken with respect to executing business process improvement and both will be described in this section. The first business process reengineering approach is referred to as the clean sheet approach, while the second is referred to as the technology-enabled approach. One of these approaches in particular, technology-enabled business process improvement, is more germane to business change or improvement using software packages. The starting point for business process improvement is usually the process audit, which presumes a process orientation; both will be discussed in this section.

The Importance of a Process Orientation

One of the important contributions of the business process reengineering movement has been the reemergence of a process focus. This is something industrial engineers have been practicing on the plant floor for decades. Over time, the process focus gave way to organizational structure. Unfortunately, organizational structure often times placed unnatural barriers or constraints on process flows and a source of waste or nonvalue-adding activity.

Fortunately, Champy, Davenport, and Hammer helped to place process at the center point of business activities once again, through the so-called business process-reengineering revolution. When processes are reengineered, instead of processes flowing through or aligned to organizational structures, the organizational structures are aligned to the processes — or at least the organizational structure should not impede the process flow in any way. It should come as no surprise to learn that most software packages employ a process orientation. In fact, many of these packages now incorporate business rule driven work flows. These work flows further drive forward a process orientation such that it can route or move information through a traditional organizational structure. A generic process model for a manufacturing organization is illustrated in Figure 5.1.

The Clean Sheet Approach

In the clean sheet approach to business process reengineering, the presumption is you are starting over with a clean sheet of paper when designing or reengineering a given business process. The clean sheet approach is often times called radical reengineering. This approach assumes that there are no barriers to the amount of business process change that can be proposed or undertaken. This was the often controversial type of business process reengineering espoused in the early 1990s by Hammer and Champy in particular.

The clean sheet approach largely ignores the constraints of available technologies and what capabilities or enablers of change may exist. A clean sheet or radical reengineering project can result in recommendations to replace some or all of an organization's existing business application software. It is important to understand the role of software packages in the clean sheet approach. If a software package can enable the changes envisioned by the clean sheet approach, so be it. Otherwise

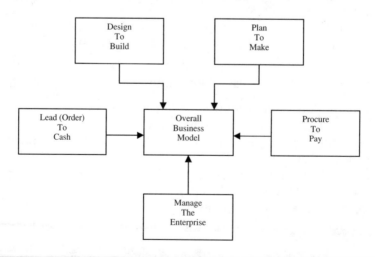

Figure 5.1 The Manufacturing Organization: A Generic Business Model

the reengineered solution is largely a custom software undertaking. This type of reengineering project is executed exclusive of software package selection.

Unfortunately, the results in the corporate world from many radical reengineering projects have been mixed, at best. In addition, while the clean sheet approach may suit the large multinational corporation, it has not suited smaller and middle market business organizations; the second approach, technology-enabled business process reengineering, has proved more popular. Smaller and middle market business organizations that have budget realities to deal with have learned that this is the best way to reengineer their businesses. Figure 5.2 illustrates the clean sheet business process-reengineering model described by this author.

The Technology-Enabled Approach

The second approach to business process change is referred to as technology-enabled business process change. The impetus driving business process change is new technology and for purposes of this discussion, it

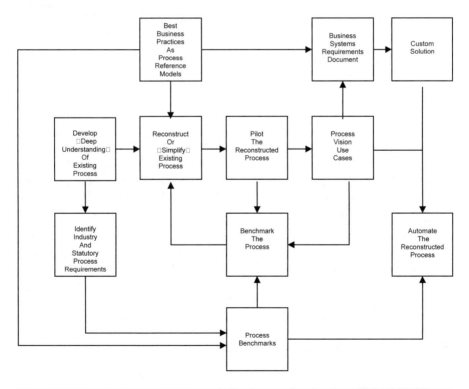

Figure 5.2 Clean Sheet Business Process Reengineering: A Generic Model

is a business application software package. Existing business processes are abandoned, changed, or replaced by new processes that exist through or as a result of the technology adopted. Think of the commercial off-the-shelf software package as an agent of business change. When an organization buys a business application software package — virtually any package — that organization will undergo some degree of business process change or transformation. (Even if the organization does not want any process changes!)

Although one might feel that the difference between these two approaches is largely one of semantics, that is not entirely true. A clean sheet approach does not presuppose what the end solution for automating the process will be; it could just as easily require a completely custom solution or it could make use of a commercial off-the-shelf software package. Under the technology-enabled approach, it is squarely the adoption of specific hardware or software technology that is driving business process change. Figure 5.3 illustrates the technology-enabled business process-reengineering model prescribed by this author.

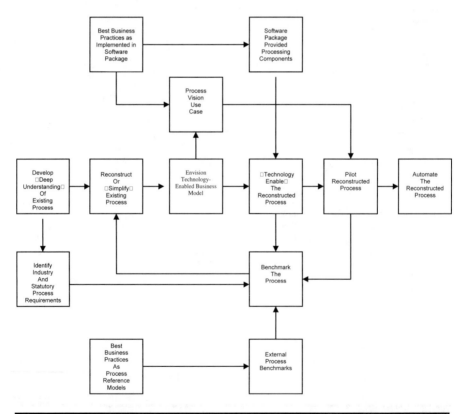

Figure 5.3 Technology-Enabled Business Process Reengineering: A Generic Model

Technology-Enabled Change versus Radical Change

These models, along with the basis of my approach and details regarding each step will be discussed throughout the remainder of this chapter. Please note that since this book focuses on software packages, it should come as little surprise that the emphasis here is on technology-enabled business process reengineering.

Why bother going to the time, effort, and expense of acquiring and implementing any software package unless the intent is to accomplish at least some technology-enabled business process improvement using that software? A new software package should not simply provide or represent, as my friend and former colleague, William C. Walker, once remarked, "a new way to do exactly what was done before." No process benefits will accrue if such an attitude prevails. Many software packages purchased and installed to address Y2K issues were done so with this attitude. Maybe that is why studies and surveys show such wide dissatisfaction with the results achieved, especially from ERP systems.

It must be readily accepted that the adoption of any new technologies into the workplace will, to a certain degree, change existing business practices or processes. Such changes may not represent radical change from the organization's present-day conditions or processes. This is especially true when legacy systems exist that may already automate part or all of an existing business process, but do not provide integration to the level desired. Achieving dramatic improvements in supply chain management is such an example.

Nonetheless, both a rethinking and retrofitting of all affected business processes is necessary in order to move forward with the implementation of new technology. That is why it is referred to as technology-enabled business process change. It should be well understood that when business process change is technology-driven, for instance by a commercial off-the-shelf package, it means that the organization has made a conscious decision to adjust its old ways of doing business. It is simply not good enough to replace an old system with a new system and not attempt to gain at least some order of magnitude business improvements at the same time. If this is not the case, then why bother with a new system at all?

My Way or No Way!

In the case of any commercial off-the-shelf software package, included with the package is an out-of-the-box way of doing business. What is important to understand here is that the software package vendor's view on the way of doing business may be different from yours. In fact, it may be so different a perspective that it is counter to the best interests of your business operations. This is also why it is crucial to model existing business processes before selecting a software package. The availability of such business process models can be used as the basis for building software demonstration scenarios that will allow an organization to compare and contrast the vendor's way of doing business versus its existing process.

ORCHESTRATING BUSINESS PROCESS IMPROVEMENT

Several years ago, I was inspired and moved by what I consider an elegant, simple, and common sense-based strategy for business process reengineering. This strategy is referred to as the USA principle and is the brainchild of Karl M. Kapp. Kapp first described this model in an August 1996 article, "The USA Principle" from *Manufacturing Systems* (now MSI) magazine. Kapp suggested a three-stage strategy to business process reengineering:

- Understand processes
- Simplify processes
- Automate processes

Kapp contends in this article, which based upon my experience I believe is well founded, that processes should not be automated until they are first understood and simplified. I have chosen to build my approach for conducting business process reengineering work around this strategy and have found in practice that is quite effective. What is more, this strategy applies equally to either clean sheet business process reengineering or technology-enabled business process reengineering.

The Process Audit: Finding the Waste

If the management audit represents the view from the top down then the process audit represents the view from the ground up. The process audit is the method or approach used to gain a deep understanding of business processes and particularly seeks to identify any process inefficiency or waste. The process audit leads to recommendations or a process vision for redesigned, streamlined, or simplified processes. The process vision makes the call regarding whether the process redesign is a candidate for automation. In turn, it is this process vision that represents the detail that will drive both the selection and implementation of any software package. This is in the technology-enabled business process-reengineering approach or in building custom system specifications using the clean sheet business process reengineering approach.

With that said, it is important to understand that typically a business process improvement project is not just about reengineering a particular business process or function. It is generally about reengineering or over-hauling the entire business; it is a corporate-wide reengineering project. Certainly an enterprise-wide system undertaking, such as an ERP system selection and implementation, will demand this type of extensive review. In the case of a process audit that is conducted in concert with a technology-enabled business process improvement, a collective or enter-prise-wide process vision should be the objective. The enterprise-wide process vision will, in turn, lead to the automation of business processes and practices through the ERP system.

The process audit would follow any given business transaction on a cradle to grave basis throughout its life cycle across the entire organization. The lifeblood of any for-profit or nonprofit is arguably the same — the provision of some good or service that is desired, needed, or wanted by other entities or individuals. If the deliverables, the products, or services the organization provides to customers can be identified, then so too can the processing threads (although perhaps with different names) that acquire or build components or end products and provision them to customers. The major processing threads in a typical manufacturing orga-nization are defined as:

- The lead to cash (also called the quote to cash or order to cash) process
- The procure to pay process
- The design to build process
- The plan to make process
- The enterprise asset management (or the manage the enterprise) process

These processing threads were illustrated in Figure 5.1, which repre-sents a generic business process model for a manufacturing organization. Although the process audit may be described from a singular perspective, it is important to understand that process auditing is an iterative process. It concludes when all of business processes have been understood and reconstructed or simplified in this manner.

While Figure 5.1 suggested a process view of the manufacturing organization, the organization can also be viewed as a systemic process. This process consists of a series of linked acquisition, conversion, and delivery processes that require both inputs and outputs through inter-action between internal processes and the customers and suppliers to the organization. Figure 5.4 illustrates such a systemic view of the organization. Often times, each process is usually considered a subsystem within the overall systemic view of the organization. This alternative, systemic view of business processes and of the organization itself is also

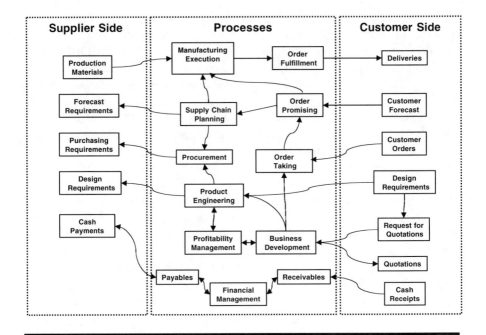

Figure 5.4 The Systemic View of the Organization

the basis for a specific process modeling technique, referred to as the suppliers, inputs, processes, outputs, and customers (SIPOC; pronounced sye-pahk) method. The SIPOC process modeling technique will be described later in this chapter.

Process Reference Models

Another approach to conducting a process audit is to use a process reference model. Process reference models are usually industry related and are generally sponsored by trade groups or associations. These groups are usually comprised of industry suppliers and customers, educators, and solution providers, including software vendors and consultants.

The Supply Chain Council, an example of one such industry group, has published a popular reference model. It is referred to as the Supply Chain Operations Reference (SCOR) model. This model has four orientations:

- Plan
- Source
- Make
- Deliver

The process reference model has two important roles in business process improvement and reengineering projects. First, industry sponsored process reference models, such as the SCOR model, are usually followed by the major software vendors. One drawback in most process reference models is that the exact implementation of a process is usually not specified by the reference model. The interpretation or implementation of a reference model may vary widely between software packages. Second, these models are considered composites of best practices. This is where the value lies during the process audit; the reference model is used as a benchmark for business process improvement. The final process adopted or recommended should embrace the best practices of the reference model.

Understanding Processes

Before attempting to radically alter a business process or overlay a current process onto a new technology, it is imperative to gain a deep understanding of the current process. This means what steps are done and why each step is completed. The deep understanding needed is gained primarily through an interviewing and write-up technique that I previously referred to as the SIPOC method. Note that the SIPOC method is part of an overall work flow that I follow. It is this work flow that is illustrated here. This work flow and technique both work for this author. In particular, I have found the work flow and techniques presented here to be efficient when time is short and the reengineering effort, in general, is focused around systemic possibilities. Other authors, business analysts, and consultants will have varying techniques for fulfilling their requirements of gaining this deep understanding that is necessary to fulfill the analysis and redesign of any given business process.

Do Not Overlook the Frontline Staff's Role in Process Improvement

It can be said that the organization's own staff will know more about their day-to-day work than anyone else. In fact, these individuals will likely already have a mental list of several ways they can improve their job or a given process. It can be said that the line worker's role as a subject matter expert is every bit as important as the manager or knowledge worker when undertaking process improvement.

The organization must minimally encourage the articulation, if not the implementation, of employee suggestions for work improvements. The consulting or internal process audit team should certainly seek to learn any of the frontline staff's ideas about ways to improve processes. Being able to make one's work more productive or meaningful to the organization can be viewed as another form of job enrichment. In addition, buy in to process change will be stronger when the frontline staff has been involved and are able to see their own ideas implemented.

Business Process Maps: The Starting Point

The starting point for process understanding is a roadmap of the business process formed through business process maps. The business process map is largely a process identification or inventory technique, usually conducted with the subject matter experts for a given business function. This document identifies the what and when of the business process or business function. This is an iterative step and must be repeated for each function or processing thread considered in scope for the purpose of the reengineering effort.

Using the Business Process Map, the goal is to identify all sub-processes conducted or performed within each business process on a routine and nonroutine basis. When they exist and if they are current, departmental policy and procedure manuals are sometimes helpful in constructing these maps. The process map format consists of a series of up to six columns: daily, weekly, monthly, quarterly, annual, and as-needed processes. Note that as needed processes can be classified as daily processes, since technically, they can occur on any given business day. An example business process map is illustrated in Figure 5.5.

SIPOC Business Models: The Core Component

The next step is modeling each of the specific business processes noted on the process map. As was done with the business process map, this is also an iterative process that is completed once all of the processes on the process map have been reviewed and modeled. The technique used to document or model each business process is referred to as the SIPOC technique; it is best viewed as an interviewing, write-up, and modeling technique all in one.

From the process map, a SIPOC process model is produced for each of the identified processes. This document describes or identifies the who, what, where, how, and why of the business process. Recall the earlier suggestion that the organization of a business organization and its business processes can be represented or viewed systematically. In fact, this is the underlying assumption behind the SIPOC modeling technique. The SIPOC technique identifies the suppliers, inputs, processes, outputs, and customers of every candidate process to form what is called an AS-IS or current state process model. The SIPOC AS-IS model becomes the important deliverable in this stage of a business process improvement or reengineering initiative.

Client	ABC Manufacturing
Document Number	STKCTLMAP
Overall Business Process	Stock Item Inventory Control
Process State	Future (To Be)

Daily*	Weekly**	Monthly	Quarterly	Annually
For stockroom items, an issue slip is completed. The issue slip indicates the quantity taken from stock, item number and purpose. If the purpose is not production related, the account code and/or project code is also noted.	For non-stockroom controlled items, print count sheet by master planning family.

Blackout out period for stock subject to count begins at this time. (No receipts or stockroom issues during this time.) | | The physical inventory is planned.

Blackout out period for all stock begins at this time. (No receipts or stockroom issues during this time.) | |
The stockroom attendant enters the issue slip into the system.	Count stock on hand; forward count sheet to stockroom attendant.		Print count sheets for all stock controlled items.	
A teardown (customer return) is performed. Stock is returned to the stockroom. The returned stock is adjusted into inventory.	Stockroom attendant enters shop floor adjustment into system.		Count the stock on hand.	
A return to vendor is created (negative purchase order). When			Accounting enters the quarter-end adjustment into system.	

Daily*	Weekly**	Monthly	Quarterly	Annually
shipment is made to a vendor; a negative receipt is entered into the system.				
For scrapped (damaged) stock an issue is made against a scrap account,				
For obsolete or value-impaired stock, a zero dollar value adjustment is made against the on-hand quantity (stock is revalued to zero dollars).				

Notes

* Performed daily or as needed.
** Performed weekly or as needed.

Assumptions

- Requires custom report "count sheet" easily created using the Software Package Report Writer.
- During "blackout" period no purchase order receipts are entered into the system.
- An Excel worksheet can be used to calculate the adjustment quantity. Download "count sheet" information into Excel.

Figure 5.5 The Business Process Map Document: An Example

When practical, I attempt to complete the business process map and the SIPOC business models related to that map in one or two working meetings or interviews with the process owners, each lasting several hours. Once the business process map is completed, work can begin on the SIPOC process model. Invariably, during the SIPOC modeling, previously unmentioned business processes will emerge and must be added to the business process map. These processes are then candidates for a subsequent SIPOC process model.

Sometimes additional meetings are needed if not all of the functional business areas, or so called process co-owners, were represented in the interviews, but have been identified as participants in a given process flow. Their role in the process must be fully understood, as must any specific requirements they have for inbound outputs from the process being reviewed.

The SIPOC Method: How It Works

The SIPOC method relies on a cradle to grave review of the business process under review. Usually this is a structured interview session built around the SIPOC process modeling document format with those who are intimately involved with the process. The process works as follows: First, the group is asked to identify the outputs (and customers) from the process, then about the inputs (and suppliers) needed by the process. Finally, the discussion shifts to the conversion process, focusing on how the inputs are transformed through processes and procedures into outputs. Sample documents are gathered or requested at this time to construct a simple data model corresponding to the process.

When I model business processes, I like to focus on addressing a series of process-related questions. For this purpose, I have constructed a process interview checklist. I use this as both an agenda and as an instrument for quality assurance checkpoint for my overall understanding of a client's given business process. This process interview checklist template is a part of the author's template collection. Consult Appendix A for more information about these templates.

It is best to record working session notes on a flip chart, attaching each flip chart sheet to the wall as the meeting progresses. It is a good way to confirm (and add to) discussion items made on a continuing basis. As an added advantage, the facilitator will not need a note taker in attendance as these flip chart pages can then be used to construct the formal SIPOC process model write-up document, illustrated in Figure 5.6.

Note that 3M Corporation makes a portable easel pad with Post-It note style paper, available through most office supply merchants. This paper provides an excellent medium for note taking during these process

SIPOC Business Process Model

TradewindsGroup

Client	ABC Manufacturing
SIPOC Number	AP030
Process Title	Accounts Payable – Contract Manufacturing Payments
Process Description	XYZ Assemblies produces a product line for ABC Manufacturing. Customer shipments are made directly from XYZ Assemblies and billed to ABC Manufacturing.
Process Owner	Accounting Department
Process Frequency	Daily
Process State	Current (As-Is)

Supplier	Input	Process	Output	Customer
ABC Manufacturing Customer Service	Customer Order	1. An order is placed with ABC Manufacturing for a direct ship item (manufactured by XYZ Assemblies).	Direct Ship Order	Purchasing
Purchasing	Direct Ship Order	2. A purchase order is prepared and sent to XYZ Assemblies.	Purchase Order	XYZ Assemblies
XYZ Assemblies	Purchase Order	3. The purchase order is received; products are produced and shipped against the order.	Shipment of Goods	ABC Manufacturing Customer
XYZ Assemblies	Shipment of Goods	4. An invoice is prepared and mailed.	Invoice	Accounts Payable (ABC Manufacturing)
Accounts Payable	Invoice	5. The invoice is vouchered into the current accounting system.	Voucher	Accounts Payable
Accounts Payable	Voucher	6. Vouchered invoices are copied and forwarded to XYZ Assemblies for payment.	Vouchered Invoices	Accounts Payable (XYZ Assemblies)
Accounts Payable (XYZ Assemblies)	Vouchered Invoice	7. The invoice is "paid" by XYZ Assemblies through an inter-company charge to ABC Manufacturing.	inter-company charge	ABC Manufacturing

Printed on 08/01/02   - Proprietary and Confidential -   Page 1 of 2

Figure 5.6 The SIPOC Process Model Document: An Example *(continued)*

TradewindsGroup

SIPOC Business Process Model

Supplier	Input	Process	Output	Customer
General Ledger Accounting	inter-company charge	8. The inter-company charge must journalized in the current accounting system.	Journal Entry	General Ledger Accounting

Comments/Observations

ABC Manufacturing is a subsidiary of XYZ Assemblies.

Directions/Legend

- SIPOC Number - Two Characters for the major business process (e.g. AC for Accounting), two characters for the sub-process (e.g. AP for Accounts Payables), followed by three digit sequential number (initially assign in increments of 5 or 10).
- Process Title – Title given to the process.
- Process Owner – The business unit name responsible for the process.
- Process Description – A brief description of the process that includes special scenarios or background.
- Supplier – The name or function that provides the input item(s) necessary to perform this process.
- Input – The item(s)used in the process to achieve the listed outputs.
- Process – A list of steps that describes how the input items are converted to the output items. The step must be action oriented and descriptively detailed enough that an individual unfamiliar with a current or proposed system, or the client process, can understand the steps involved. The name or title of the person who executes the process should precede the action.
- Output – The item(s)representing the outcome of the process.
- Customer – The name or function that receives the output item(s) of this process.

Figure 5.6 (continued) The SIPOC Process Model Document: An Example

interview sessions. I attach each page to the wall as it is filled, so everything said can be reviewed throughout the session. I then use these notes when preparing my formal documentation.

As a general rule, it is best that the sessions are conducted with two facilitators present; the additional analyst or consultant can ask relevant business questions that the first person might not have addressed. This is especially true when the first person is working outside his or her usual area of expertise.

Many individuals prefer to model business processes through visuals by preparing diagrams. My preference favors a narrative format, but that is not to say that I do not also produce process-related diagrams. The fact is that some individuals understand a process visually, so they are a necessary deliverable from the overall modeling process. Also, the process chart is an excellent way to guide a review meeting and confirm the completed or documented process model with the original working session attendees.

My preference is to prepare process diagrams (actually flowchart style process diagrams) using a flowcharting software product called allCLEAR (www.allclear.com). I have been using this product for well over a decade now, and it has stood the test of time and user interest by surviving at least three separate ownership changes. I like this product because I spend little time preparing the visual models. First, I simply copy the processing steps from the SIPOC document that I have prepared. Second, I paste this list of processing steps into the allCLEAR program, which instantly creates a process-oriented flow chart. I find this technique can save lots of time, especially for the dozens of SIPOC process models that I need to create.

Finally, if the organization prefers to adopt a formal, visual approach to business process modeling, there are a number of visually based business process modeling tools available. Some examples include the ARIS Toolset from IDS Scheer (www.ids-scheer.com), Corporate Modeler from Casewise (www.casewise.com), and Process Modeler from Scitor (www.scitor.com). Other methods are certainly doable. For instance, virtually all of the diagrams in this book were prepared using Microsoft Word. I also use Microsoft PowerPoint in a similar capacity. In both instances, I have used the AutoShapes feature from the Drawing toolbar in these products. Two other popular flowcharting tools that can be used to illustrate business process flows include Microsoft Visio and Micrographx's ABC FlowCharter.

Use Cases and the UML: An Alternative Method

An alternative to using the SIPOC method is to prepare a use case. Use cases and the closely related visual modeling language known as the unified modeling language (UML) are popular techniques for describing software system specifications. The UML has been billed as a standard or universal method for describing and translating user requirements into software design specifications, particularly for today's object-oriented software systems. There is nothing to say that use cases and the UML cannot be used to document and model business processes for purposes other than software development. The major difference between the use case based method and the SIPOC method is that use cases can best be described as dialog based and are therefore particularly adept at detailing the dialogue between a user and the system.

UML diagrams are typically prepared using a special visual tool or workbench that is geared toward the software engineer. The UML defines or specifies a series of standard design diagrams to be produced by software engineers. With a little bit of creativity and energy, several of the UML diagrams are particularly applicable to process reengineering work. The UML workbench products can produce these diagrams with a minimal amount of information and effort. The UML notation is included as a template set in some flowcharting software packages. UML diagrams can be produced in these flowcharting packages, but generally not as easily as through a UML workbench. In addition, these workbench products have other features that are germane only to the software engineer. Three such workbench products include: GD Pro from Advanced Software Technologies (www.advancedsw.com), Rose from Rational Software (www.rational.com), and TogetherJ from TogetherSoft (www.togethersoft.com).

Using SIPOC versus Use Case Models

Although use cases can be illustrated visually through these tools, my preferred technique and the one that I feel works best for technology-enabled business process improvement is a narrative format. I have developed a formal template set and a set of techniques for building narrative use cases for such purposes. As a general rule, I still advocate the SIPOC method over use cases for process modeling. There is one situation I have found where the use case format excels. This is when it is used for the development of a detailed business process scenario or script that is referenced for software demonstration purposes during the software package selection process. Consult Chapter 9 for a further discussion of the narrative format use case and an actual illustration of how it is applied to a product demonstration scenario.

System Problems and Business Issues

Often times we will hear that the system is to blame for a given business problem or issue; usually it is prompted by a phone call we make and we are hearing the excuse, "Your order was late due to a system problem." In fact, I have heard this far too often and perhaps you have as well. Most of the time, this stock answer is a mask for other shortcomings an organization may have. Simply put, it is often not the system at fault at all. In my experience, process failure and human error are more significant factors when measuring an organization or any given system's shortcomings.

Systems are far too anal and binary to fail; they require a lot of help — usually the human kind — in order to fail. This is not to say that systems are defect free. Most system failures are the result of weak designs (human error no less). They are so poorly designed from a technical or infrastructure perspective that the system is not functioning or workable in its delivered state; usually these are performance or volume issues (again human errors) more so than anything else. With that said, the process auditor must be certain the system is really the root cause of an ineffective process and must understand why it is so.

Reconstructing Processes

Once the as is models of the business processes are completed, the process of analyzing these processes and making specific changes, simplifications, or recommendations can be completed. This analysis process will result in a series of TO-BE or future state business process models. In the case of a clean sheet change approach, one would recommend ways to streamline processes, and where applicable, suggest best practices, benchmarks, and standards to be adopted. Ultimately this would produce a business system requirements document to automate the redesigned process. The format for such a document is beyond the scope of this book, but a similar process (and document) is needed for software package software customization, a topic discussed in Chapter 8. A business system requirements document template is a part of the author's template collection. Consult Appendix A for more information about these templates.

Recall that the clean sheet approach considers the future state modeling without any consideration or regard for the practical implications of technological support of the new process. The presumption is that the organization will do what it takes to make the process changes happen. I submit this is often a naive, if not dangerous position. It is also why, in my estimation, that some attempts at business process reengineering fail outright or produce little, if any, of their desired benefits. One can't simply assume that technology enablement is practical or even feasible.

Developing a Process Vision

In the case of technology-enabled business process improvement, instead of a set way of doing the process, a process vision should emerge. This process vision is then used as a way of benchmarking off-the-shelf technology that will be used to implement business process improvements or changes. This requires understanding the technologies that are available and how they specifically facilitate automation of business processes. Strive for objectivity in the process design, not bias toward any one system. Do not let current or past systems experience limit the vision. Identify and specifically note any industry-specific processes or requirements where possible.

One of the problems an organization will have is envisioning or imagining the future state when it has little or no exposure to the software technologies it wishes to exploit. In such instances, most reputable software package consultants can help an organization develop this process vision. Understand that most consultants will have some biases toward particular software packages. As a general rule, consultants cannot possibly know all the intricate details, designs, and inner workings of the literally hundreds of packages that are available. Consultants tend to specialize, usually based upon their experiences with specific software packages. Consultants who have experience with multiple packages are indeed best. Their multiple package experiences should help them produce a more generalized process vision.

The process vision should be constructed in terms of a cradle to grave vision or business transaction scenario for the major or business critical transactions or processing threads of the organization. Recall that Figure 5.1 illustrates the major processing threads for a typical manufacturing organization. These process visions form the nucleus for the business process scenarios (described in Chapter 9) and are a centerpiece in the software evaluation and selection stage of the Software Package Life Cycle (SPLC). In terms of software package selection, the process vision represents a benchmark for determining if proof of concept or proof of process vision is achieved. Such proof of concept emanates from product demonstrations, an integral part of the software selection process.

I have previously mentioned that use cases are an ideal format for presenting such process visions. An example of such a process vision based use case appears as a product demonstration scenario in Figure 9.3. A product demonstration scenario is nothing more than this process vision supplemented by sample business data.

During the software evaluation and selection stage of the SPLC, your organization will evaluate the goodness of fit between the process vision and the software features of each software package as demonstrated by the software vendor or reseller. The procedure is done by benchmarking or comparing the process vision versus the software features that fulfill or perform the envisioned business process. Differences between the software package feature set and the process vision represent functionality gaps. These gaps must be carefully considered in forming the final recommendations that support your desired technology enablement goals, including software package selection.

Documentation Leverage: Cheat to Win through Reuse and Adaptation

It is my contention that any deliverable produced during business process reengineering should be useful and relevant throughout all aspects of the SPLC. For instance, if use cases are used to document a process vision, by merely adding sample business data they are transformed into product demonstration scenarios.

As another example, AS-IS or current state SIPOC process models represent the starting point in creating a SIPOC model for the TO-BE or future state. This is done by reworking or transitioning the model documents from one state to another during the brainstorming and innovation that occurs when revamping processes. The business process maps are then reworked in this same manner to reflect how processing threads will change on an overall basis.

Another example of document leverage occurs when business process maps and SIPOC process models are used to transition into business process proposal documents during system implementation. The business process proposal documents translate the organization's business processes into the specific software package features and functions used to automate the business process. Although a business process proposal will rely heavily on the SIPOC process model, an intimate understanding of the software package is also a prerequisite.

The business process proposal documents are then further leveraged in terms of constructing training materials. For instance, training exercise guides that formalize transaction scenarios into step-by-step exercises conducted on the system may be desired. These exercise guides are usually necessary for larger implementations, but are not necessarily needed for smaller implementations where training might be conducted on a one-on-one basis.

The business process proposal documents are also instrumental when building quick reference cards. These cards are summaries, usually a one- or two-page laminated card that highlights the system menu paths corresponding to job related or departmental processing (i.e., accounts payable, receiving, storeroom) functions. These are something that I would put together for any size implementation. They usually serve as good memory joggers, especially for infrequently or little used system functions.

One thing I try to do is to avoid rewriting the software package documentation that is provided by the software vendor. One of the reasons for buying a software package is to outsource software development, including the development of any detailed documentation. The documentation I propose here is held to a minimum. The focus is on what your organization does with the software (i.e., exercises) and when and what features apply to your business process. There is a second reason why an organization should not spend enormous sums on documentation: it has been my experience that after training, most of the documentation becomes reference material and will be used infrequently. Generally speaking, the training exercises and quick references represent about all that is needed to supplement the vendor's materials. Sometimes vendors will provide exercise guides that are usable as is, so all that may be needed in those cases are data sheets that are germane to your business organization.

There are times when more elaborate documentation is needed, particularly for complex functionality or when the vendor's documentation is of poor quality (usually it is simply unclear or is not logically presented) for any given process. To ensure that your organization is not buying into a significant writing task, it is a good idea to review documentation for each of the major business processing threads as a part of the overall software evaluation process. Be particularly careful with software that is developed in the non-English-speaking countries, (which is happening more and more) and is then adapted to English. The documentation is often of poor quality and may require lots of rewriting to be particularly useful in the future.

Eliminate Redundancies in Process Documentation

Sometimes there may be some redundancies between processes. For instance, any number of departments might identify a processing step of "check inventory balances." At some point, preferably before preparing business process proposals during the software implementation process, it will be desirable to inventory all business process steps. It is important to identify common steps so they are only documented once in terms of how they should be implemented within the software package.

Pilot the Process Changes

Once agreement or consensus is reached on what the business process will look like, as portrayed through the TO-BE or future state model, it is time to step through the process change in terms of a conference room pilot. The purpose of this step is to validate the appropriateness and feasibility, from a practical standpoint, of the proposed process change. This is done by process simulation.

Some of the business process modeling tools can simulate processes, but in a very narrow sense. Their simulation is usually cost or throughput (time) based; this action alone does not visually prototype or simulate the complete business transaction or process as this step implies. In no way do I want to imply that cost and throughput simulation is not a valuable exercise; it is simply not sufficient. What I propose must be done is a far more extensive simulation.

The prototype simulation should step through the business transaction from beginning to end. Recreating a prior, verifiable business transaction using the proposed processing steps completes the simulation. This recreation of a prior transaction uses the business data from that prior business transaction, in the proposed process or system, as if it were now real. This allows for the comparison and verification of results between the real and simulated transaction. Each different transaction that is to be demonstrated or prototyped requires a scripted business transaction scenario. Again, review Figure 9.3, which illustrates a use case based product demonstration scenario.

In the case of a technology-enabled change approach, this would involve setting up the process in the software and completing the relevant software-based transactions. Usually this is done by a vendor or reseller in terms of a software package product demonstration. It is limited to the more critical business processes as represented by one or more business transaction scenarios contained in the request for proposal document sent to vendors.

Although it would be desirable to see every aspect of a software package before it is acquired, that is usually not practical. Although process auditing may yield dozens of business process models, only the most significant transactions — usually a half dozen or less are the core business transactions — would be reviewed in terms of the product demonstration. The remaining business process models would be held for prototyping during the actual software package implementation. Many times, these additional transaction scenarios are variants of the core transaction scenarios. Usually, more complex transaction scenarios are chosen for demonstration purposes.

For a complex business process to be undertaken by a software system, sometimes visual representations, in the form of screen mock-ups, are essential to reaching consensus and a complete understanding on the overall processing requirements. This is usually a mandatory step when designing and developing a custom business application software system, perhaps when engaging in a clean slate business reengineering project. However, it is an uncommon step when dealing with software package requirements.

The technique does have relevance to software package selection and implementation in two areas. First, I find this a particularly useful technique for illustrating how a complicated business process, such as a product configuration feature, might be expected to work in terms of a software package. Second, this is a helpful technique for visually prototyping any software customizing requirements that will be needed to fill in any gaps between your requirements and the software package.

My technique is to sketch out the process vision in terms of the user interface view of the software-enabled business process or transaction flow. I prefer to use a storyboard approach. In recent years, I have typically used PowerPoint for this purpose. Each PowerPoint slide animates a different step or feature in the software-enabled transaction or process flow. Again, this technique is also an excellent way to visually prototype a reengineered or reconstructed business process when taking the clean sheet business process reengineering approach. This technique serves as a springboard to defining the underlying process automation requirements.

Process Benchmarking: Calculating the Worth of Business Performance Improvement

Recall from Chapter 3 that business performance is closely associated with process efficiency. In fact, it is measured by the success of process outputs in meeting or exceeding the specific performance requirements or product characteristics of customers. Assuming the SIPOC models of processes are complete, the next step is linking processes or drivers to metrics. The first step is to identify specific output requirements or characteristics — criteria that each process or system output must achieve. Do this for each output listed in the SIPOC model. The second step is to determine how often these requirements are met on the first attempt without requiring any further work or rework. Such output requirements or characteristics are examples of the kinds of business metrics affected by the drivers or underlying processes and processing actions and by any process improvements.

The third and final step is to calculate the cost of failure — the cost to rework the output when the first attempt fails. Each successive percentage point improvement should demonstrate savings equal to the marginal cost of the rework that has been avoided. This represents a cost savings to the organization that can be monetarized for cost and benefit analysis purposes.

Automating Processes

Only after the business process has been rationalized, or as Kapp suggests, "simplified," does the process become a candidate for automation. The logic here is simple enough; if you should not be doing something in the first place, why bother automating it? To do so only perpetuates process waste. Not only does the automation of business processes provide labor savings potential, it also provides a scalable solution. As the business grows, the scalable process is one that will not quickly become a major bottleneck in the overall business operation. For smaller and middle market business organizations, scalability to accommodate anticipated, future growth is often a major reason to adopt automated processes.

In a technology-enabled business process reengineering effort, software packages are usually involved as the engine of process automation. Most software packages have some very real limitations. In the case of an ERP system, many organizations will find that it is unlikely a single ERP system from among the hundreds that are currently in existence will automate all of their business processes in the exact manner desired. All organizations are further advised to establish a process automation agenda that represents a set of priorities for their immediate task automation initiatives.

If a package cannot meet the most critical or most essential of your process automation requirements, usually deemed to be 80% or better, the software package is likely not a good fit for your organization; business reengineering goals will not be accomplished. To knowingly accept an inferior software package solution that requires extensive and costly customization or modification is a risky business proposition. If your organization does not have a good track record on meeting its business system requirements today through its existing software development infrastructure, the software package as an additional variable will not make the situation better and may worsen it.

Buying Features for the Future

While automation is clearly the best long-term alternative for most business processes, realize that not all processes are immediate candidates for automation. It is important to buy for the future in terms of any software package, since it has an average 5- to 10-year life span. Make sure any package can support automation of as many processes as possible, even if they will not be features of the software package that are deployed immediately. Good future feature need examples related to ERP might include multiplant processing and foreign currency processing.

AT WHAT POINT SHOULD BUSINESS PROCESS REENGINEERING BE DONE?

This author believes the organization is best served by completing the business process understanding and reengineering process prior to software package selection. The reasoning here revolves around Kapp's USA principle — that business processes should not be automated until processes are understood and simplified. Also, selecting the wrong software package in terms of an organization's business model will prove to be a bad, if not a terrible, business decision.

How then does process understanding and modeling help with software selection? The reason is simply that from the modeling process will emerge the business processing scenarios that can be used as software package demonstration and evaluation scripts. In addition, the business process models can be used to build a list of required software features or functions necessary to fulfill the organization's specific processing requirements. Business process understanding and modeling is critical to successful business process reengineering and software package implementation.

The Case for Just in Time Business Process Reengineering

Others will contend that reengineering — in advance of software implementation — is an unnecessary or wasteful exercise. The view presumes that software packages are considered as a special case of reengineering. The new business process model is, practically speaking, based squarely on what the selected software package will allow.

Another argument against any preimplementation reengineering is that software packages are largely commodity buys. Also, as a general rule, they are already full of best business practices. Why bother with a reengineering of the business if the software will natively do so using these best practices? It is simply a matter of transitioning the organization to the new ways of the software package.

In practice, I have also found resistance, if not reluctance, to engage in any formal business process reengineering. Though I do not necessarily recommend or condone either the no or the deferred reengineering view, from a practical standpoint, I understand the cost and time constraints that often dictate otherwise in many smaller and middle market organizations and require a consolidation of effort. In practice, this happens more frequently than I would prefer. This means that software packages are selected without any advance process modeling being done, or at least not by this author, prior to being engaged to provide assistance during a software implementation. Therefore, these situations have forced me to improvise an alternative work flow strategy.

When I wrote *Implementing J.D. Edwards OneWorld*, I coined use of the phrase, "just in time business process reengineering." This is the implicit reengineering that must occur with the adoption of a specific software package. (In the case of that book, it so happened to be J.D. Edwards OneWorld.) Other terms I considered using to describe this implicit reengineering process was "organic" or "native" business process reengineering. Although both seemed a better a fit, neither took into account exactly when I usually needed to perform the reengineering effort, which was during software implementation and where the idea of using just in time sprang forth.

The way this alternative work flow works is as follows: The AS-IS modeling is completed *during* implementation, using the standard techniques proposed in this chapter. A future state or TO-BE modeling process (the reengineering step) is not done. Instead, using the current state or AS-IS model, future state business process maps and business process proposals (by definition these are forward looking) are then prepared by retrofitting the organization's business processes and practices to what the software package has to offer.

The organization's business processes are natively or naturally reengineered to the software package's organic business process model. The implementation model proposed in Chapter 12 and illustrated in Figure 12.2 actually embodies this alternative work flow. In addition, Figure 12.6, an illustration of the early stage work flow of the implementation, further illustrates the alternative work flow in practice.

As a final note on this matter, this type of alternate reengineering arrangement works best for a relatively small, unsophisticated single plant or single facility based organization desiring a rapid or fast track implementation. This is where few bells and whistles are wanted or needed and customization is not on the table as an option.

BUSINESS PROCESS IMPROVEMENT: AN EPILOGUE

This chapter presented a perspective on how to conduct business process reengineering as it relates to software packages. The focus has been on technology-enabled business process change, in which case the software package is considered the centerpiece of an organization's business process improvement objectives.

This author contends that business process reengineering should precede software selection. Also improvements to processes as measured through business process related metrics or benchmarks can be monetarized. This provides the requisite financial justification needed for reengineering processes through automated techniques, particularly using software packages and complementary technologies.

6

BUILDING THE BUSINESS CASE FOR A SOFTWARE PACKAGE

The title of this book suggests that business performance can be *positively impacted* through business application software packages. Buying and implementing a software package is not an off-the-shelf, instant energy boost for an anemic organization. To make matters worse, although rare, there are some widely reported cases where buying and implementing a software package — usually an enterprise-wide enterprise resource planning (ERP) system — has actually been cited as the cause of an organization's failure. I cannot guarantee that after selecting and implementing a new software package I will not read about your organization in the financial news headlines. I do believe by following the advice and recommendations presented in this book that your organization's chances of success are much better.

Buying and implementing any software package is not a simple task. It is a significant business investment involving intellectual and monetary capital and often extends to involving the goodwill of an organization's customers and suppliers. In short, there are many business issues that can pose very real and significant business risks when buying and implementing any software package. The focus of this chapter is said to be *business case driven*. Business cases are widely viewed as an effective technique for reducing business risks, primarily by quantifying expected results or outcomes of capital investment decisions. This chapter will answer the following questions:

- What is a business case?
- Why is a business case needed?
- How is the business case made?

Most important, this chapter will provide a practical, step-by-step approach to building a business case for acquiring and implementing a business application software package.

TAKE YOUR PULSE, THE 1990s ARE OVER

Not too long ago, in the years immediately prior to the Y2K rollover, during almost a decade-long period of economic prosperity, there was an unparalleled interest in technology. The 1990s was truly a period of high energy and an economy in overdrive — when worn-out legacy systems needed replacement and Internet-mania was in full stride. It seemed that little, if any, attention was being paid to technology project costs, benefits, and in many cases, project failures and budget overruns.

To many observers, it seemed that during this period, technology projects were given virtually a free ride through the executive offices or the boardroom. This was especially true during the latter half of the decade and especially so for technology related spending when about all stakeholder groups needed to hear were the words "Y2K compliance." Most information technology related projects simply moved to the head of the line, often in front of projects that had greater tangible benefits. The questions asked were when and how fast, not how much and why. It was the era of the blank check to just get it done. Those days, for the most part, are gone.

We have moved from the spending spree mentality of the 1990s to the realities of measurement madness in the new millennium. Not only have boardrooms tired of major technology expenditures, they are also now expecting a complete justification for the expenditure —a financially sound and compelling business case. The business unit or technology manager making the business case for a software package must now approach this task with this new frame of reference in mind.

In general, a sound business case comes from presenting the software package acquisition and implementation as a true business investment, not merely as another expense or cost of doing business. In fact, projects that are only cost savings as benefits will likely be regarded more or less as marginal. Consider the case of using the software package as the centerpiece of a business improvement or reengineering project. The same benefits underlying the need to engage in the business improvement project are also the benefits achieved from automating the business process and perhaps more. The business case should present metrics that quantify the expected benefits of the software package investment to the organization — a concept called return on investment (ROI). Ironically, the title from a 1990s' movie is a fitting characterization of this new mantra: "Show me the money."

TAKING RISKS, MAKING CHANGES: IT IS WHAT A BUSINESS DOES

Business is largely about taking calculated risks. Indeed one of the most frequently heard questions in business, regardless of the underlying issue, is "What is the impact of...on our business?" The basis for such questions is largely rooted in risk analysis. We seek information in order to reduce risks. The majority of us are risk adverse by nature. Not only are humans largely adverse to risk, but they are also adverse to change. In fact, change itself is a risk. Also, taking risks usually involves making changes. It can be said that these two concepts — change and risk — are both related and largely interchangeable.

Buying and implementing a software package is one example of what can generally be referred to as a calculated business risk. Other examples of a calculated business risk include adding a new production line, replacing a production machine, or developing a new product or service. It has been my experience that most business organizations are risk adverse or change resistant. The basic question or frame of reference driving their decision making usually is: Do the benefits outweigh both the costs and risks involved by *not acting* on a given proposal to change the business in some way?

WHY ARE BUSINESS DECISIONS SO DIFFICULT?

Every organization has a purpose or mission for which it has been chartered. The business organization, regardless of its stated business purpose or the products or services it offers, has a profit motive — to achieve profitability. Consider this narrative model or purpose of a business organization:

> To generate revenue, the business organization manufactures or distributes products or provides services. In generating revenue, the business organization incurs numerous operating expenses or costs, such as manufacturing and distribution expenses, research and development expenses, and selling and general administrative expenses. Subtracting costs from revenues yields what is known as operating income or net operating profit of the business organization.

At the same time, every business organization operates under a framework of limited cash resources. A major function of an organization's senior and executive management team is to efficiently manage both the cash requirements and the overall profitability or financial structure of the business organization. In short, their ultimate goal is to maximize business performance, as measured through ROI. Making business decisions would be much easier if management did not need to concern itself with achieving profitability or operating under this framework of a limited supply of cash.

Business investment decisions are further complicated by the wants and needs of stakeholders. From a financial perspective, the stakeholders in the business are generally limited to either business owners or shareholders and debt holders. Business owners who have invested cash into the business are said to have provided equity to the business, while other providers of cash usually provide so in the form of borrowed money or debt.

Most businesses rely on a combination of debt and equity. There is a strong predisposition to finance a business through debt rather than through equity, a concept generally known as leverage. The intelligent use of debt minimizes the business owner's cash risk in the business. The concept of leverage then implies that every dollar of earnings will further increase the owner's rate of return on their investments. Business decision makers are, generally speaking, the elected or appointed representatives of the organizations' business owners or shareholders. They have a primary obligation to weigh heavily the business owner or shareholder interests in deciding on capital investments.

With nonprofit organizations, the purpose is albeit slightly different, but similar forces still exist. The mission may be a civic, charitable, educational, life-sustaining, or social need, but the nonprofit organization still has that limited supply of cash along with a different management challenge. The challenge is avoiding deficit spending if not producing an operating surplus — the equivalent of profitability in the for-profit business context. Virtually all the same rules that apply to a for-profit business organization can be applied in a nearly identical fashion to nonprofit organizations. Although much of this discussion in this chapter may focus on business case development in the for-profit context, the concepts can be readily applied to the nonprofit organization as well.

Management of the enterprise in its simplest form can be construed as a cash balancing or allocation activity — an activity that has both short and long term implications for the organization. To put this into perspective, consider how cash is both generated and consumed by the business organization. Cash can be provided or consumed by one of the balancing or allocation activities in a business organization. These include investments, usually made by business owners or stockholders; financing, usually by debt holders such as commercial banks, insurance companies, investment banks and finance companies; and the day-to-day operations of the business enterprise. Refer to Figure 6.1, which illustrates the sources and uses of business cash.

As can be seen from Figure 6.1, one use of business cash is the making of capital investments. Some examples of business investments include adding plant machinery and equipment, developing and launching a new product, buying a new delivery vehicle, licensing the rights to manufacture a product from its inventor, replacing an aging copier machine, or opening a new sales office. More often than not, the capital investment has a continuing impact on the business and particularly on operations. In fact, most business investments have an economic life that exceeds one year and may last any number of years into the future. A software package is an example of such a capital investment.

Most important, capital investments represent long-term business or economic decisions, and more often than not they involve large sums of cash. Because of their sheer size and long-term impact, most of these decisions require considerable analysis and understanding. Given the limitations on the amount of business cash available, the business decision makers must weigh the use of business cash for one purpose versus the use of cash for other purposes. In effect, investments or uses of cash compete with one another for funding. Generally speaking, if all things are equal, only business investments providing a ROI that is at least equal to or greater than the organization's cost of capital or hurdle rate, a value which is usually an amount in excess of an organization's cost of capital, will typically be authorized or funded.

What compels an organization to invest in new technology, such as a software package or equipment? The answer to this question lies within the business case. A business case must be established for any new technology investment, including any business application software package and the incremental hardware and software infrastructure to effectively use that software. It is important to note that buying software packages is generally not the highest priority investment for a business organization, nor in most cases should it be the highest priority. There are sound business reasons, generally found in the form of operating benefits that are measured, financially speaking, through operating cost reductions and increased revenue potential. The business case must make a compelling case for the investment based upon a quantification of these operating cost reductions and revenue-generating potential.

It is quite important to understand that a business case must make a persuasive and compelling argument for accepting a given business investment proposal. The most effective and widely regarded method for doing

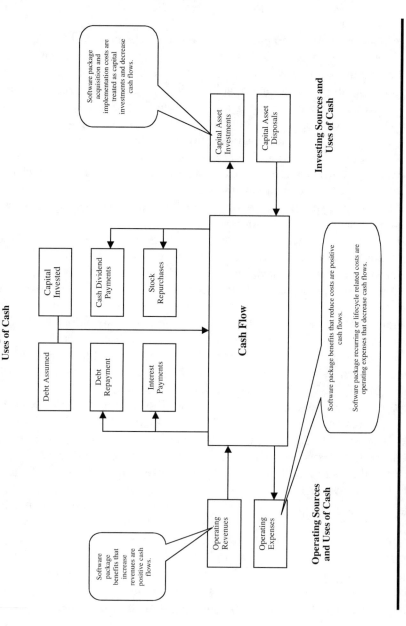

Figure 6.1 The Sources and Uses of Business Cash

so is through the use of metrics or numbers. While numbers are important, they do not tell the whole story. In fact, that is why there is so much more than a mere presentation of numbers or financial analysis that must be presented in terms of making a business case. Some projects have arguably neutral financial impact, but for a variety of other nonfinancial reasons, make good business sense. In other cases, projects have decidedly negative financial impact, but if not undertaken, have potentially dire consequences for the business. For instance, Y2K related software remediation spending fell largely into this category, as does the replacement of a leaky roof.

Projects that have a concrete, positive financial impact are the easiest to act upon. Unfortunately, it usually is not that easy, and this is especially the case for most software package investments. Unlike adding plant capacity or new product development, which can both link directly to forecasted sales revenue increases, software packages do not provide similar, direct financial benefits to an organization. This is not to say that such projects do not have benefit. It is just that the financial benefits are indirect — the result of using a software package or really the information contained within it to improve in some way, the day-to-day operations or business processes of the organization. Finding and projecting indirect benefits is a difficult, time-consuming, and very necessary task in making the business case for a software package investment. The rest of this chapter is focused on how to construct well-purposed business cases related to software package investments.

WHAT IS A BUSINESS CASE?

The term business case is relatively new. In my formal education in finance and accounting I cannot recall having heard the term — we called them capital budgeting decisions. Business case is quite an appropriate term and implies process, which is never a bad idea, especially when we are dealing with financial matters.

With that said, let me introduce the business case as an action document. The business case often takes the form of a proposal; my personal preference is to refer to a business case document as an investment proposal. It is a proposal to make an investment in a capital-intensive project. In this case it is the purchase and implementation of a business application software package and the myriad of other hardware, software, and services necessary to prepare for and implement the software package. The business case is best perceived as a tool used to facilitate organizational planning, capital budgeting, and decision making. It is important to understand that a business case must make a persuasive and compelling argument for accepting what is proposed.

An important aspect of the business case document concerns itself with answering the question, "What will be the financial consequences if we choose to proceed with this proposal?" A business case represents the quantitative assessment of an investment decision. The well-scripted business case must show the expected *cash flow* consequences of the proposed investment over time. The financial impact portion of the business case should present both a detailed statement of the costs and benefits or cash flow and a financial analysis of those cash flows. The financial analysis usually consists of one or more common ROI-related metrics, which will be discussed later in this chapter.

Through its business case presentation an investment proposal document will reveal the risks, costs, and benefits of a project along with other relevant information to support the investment decision. Good, bad, or indifferent, the deciding factor governing most investment decisions at the upper level in an organization is typically the underlying financial metrics for reasons stated previously. It behooves the authors of the investment proposal to prepare a financially oriented, sound business case.

WHO CAN HELP IN PREPARING A BUSINESS CASE?

For organizations that do not have any existing business case guidelines, the remainder of this chapter will be particularly useful. It will provide numerous guidelines in a formal investment proposal document's content and format. This chapter is based upon my experience at putting together business-related investment proposals not only for software, but in the areas of new product development and business expansion as well. I have found that while larger organizations have a fairly rigid process, smaller organizations often do not.

A cautionary note is in order. While this book can provide guidelines, it cannot provide specific guidance. That is not the intent. For instance, the cost of business capital plays an important role in assessing the financial impact of any given proposal. Every organization has a unique financial structure that weighs heavily on the cost of business capital. It is beyond the scope of this book to provide anything more than a relatively generic and simplistic procedure for determining the cost of capital related to an investment proposal evaluation.

In addition to the guidelines provided here, assistance is available in the form of templates. The investment proposal document and related worksheets presented in this chapter are also available as Microsoft Office templates from the author. Please consult Appendix A for information about how to obtain these templates.

Internal Guidelines

Many organizations already have formal specifications as to what an investment proposal document should look like. Therefore, many points raised in this chapter will already be covered or supplanted by their existing guidelines. Usually the chief financial officer (CFO) is responsible for developing the guidelines related to capital budgeting requests. In some cases, an organization's existing guidelines may be limited to guidelines for the financial presentation of a business case. The remainder of this chapter should help fill in any such void for you.

Software Tools

Software tools are also available to support the development of business cases. One such software tool is CaseView. CaseView is a Microsoft Windows-based computer program used to build financially based business cases. CaseView uses a wizard-like approach toward building the business case. The program resembles income tax return preparation software by asking questions. In this case, the questions are about the proposed investment's costs and benefits rather than an individual's income and expenses. For those unfamiliar with financial budgeting and capital decision-making processes or with Microsoft Excel, this type of software removes some of the fear, uncertainty, doubt, and sheer drudgery preparing the financials portion of a business case. CaseView is available from HMC International (www.hclintl.com). An Excel spreadsheet template is a part of the author's template collection. Consult Appendix A for more information.

Consultants

Consultants may assist an organization to identify business improvement issues through a management audit-like process or help with software package selection. They will also be capable of assisting the client organization in developing a business case in relation to their work and recommendations. In addition, some consulting organizations specialize or have practices that specialize in helping organizations develop business cases.

WHO WILL COMPRISE THE AUDIENCE FOR THE BUSINESS CASE?

A good first rule in most professional presentation, teaching, or writing situations is to understand who your audience will be. The audience that one presents or writes to determines the content, formality, depth, and the level of preparation necessary. As alluded to earlier, capital investment decisions are usually made at the highest levels in the organization: the president, the CFO, and other senior operating and administrative executives. Depending on the organization's size or project value, the board of directors may have final authority. It also holds true that before an investment proposal ever reaches the executive or board level that one or more middle management reviews may need to be cleared as well. Thus, business case must be prepared and presented to senior managers, executives, and possibly even to the board of directors before a final decision is made. Ultimately, the capital investment decision will be reached only after carefully weighing the impact of the investment decision on the organization, particularly on the cash position and profitability impact.

WHAT ARE THE STEPS INVOLVED IN MAKING A BUSINESS CASE?

The business case is typically a formal, written proposal type of document. I tend to refer to business case documents as investment proposals and have used the two terms interchangeably throughout this chapter. The first step is to identify the information needed to prepare the investment proposal document. The second step is to prepare the formal document. I should caution that this second step is an iterative process; expect to add, subtract, and modify content. Once the business case document has been prepared, it is usually summarized into a slideshow presentation. At this point, the business case is considered a draft document and is ready for an initial review by management.

The third step is likely a review meeting with senior, nonexecutive level managers. Changes are likely recommended and may sometimes be wholesale changes. Do not become disenchanted. Once the changes are made a revised draft document is circulated for final review. Assuming it is a go, it is time for the main event — the formal presentation of the proposal to a group of decision makers.

The main event in the life of most investment proposals within most organizations is usually a date on executive management committee's calendar. My first word of advice: expect that the investment proposal will need to be distributed in advance to each member of the committee. I have found that in most organizations I have worked with that this committee convenes and conducts itself with the rigor of a seemingly religious-like event; in many ways this committee is akin to the supreme court of the business organization. With that in mind, such committees are usually steeped with egos, while face time, or what little of it that you will have with this esteemed group is usually considered a privilege.

Some have equated the experience to interviewing for their original job, while others have sought sanctuary in other organizations.

Have I scared the living daylights out of you yet? Sorry about that, but there is a point to all of this. Yes, the future of the investment proposal does hang in the balance and although your job may not, your career aspirations might. Making a professional, well-rehearsed presentation to the boss is never a bad idea. Also, it may be more appropriate to wear that dusty Brooks Brothers suit instead of Dockers on this particular day. Consider that the executive management committee is comprised of the top leaders of an organization who are all well versed, intelligent, and accomplished. They will likely ask challenging questions. Be ready for them. They will perhaps seem distant or disinterested in the proposal. Regardless of the outcome, their job is done when the verdict is reached. If the verdict was a positive one, your job may just be starting.

As a final note on this subject, one additional step may be needed. Depending on the value of the proposal or the size of your organization, it may be necessary to appear in front of the board of directors. Again, this involves presenting the proposal largely under the same conditions and pressures relevant to the first audience — the executive management committee. It is hoped the outcome will be the same.

On Being a Good Presenter

A good proposal is often made better or worse by the way it is presented to decision makers. It requires that the presenter anticipate untold pressure during the presentation. The presenter must remain clear, concise, positive, and calm. Be prepared — actually over prepared is best. Anticipate questions and develop answers for them ahead of time. Certainly refer to the business case presentation in answering questions. Do not make up answers to questions you do not know. Instead, offer to provide an answer as a follow-up. Sometimes the unanswered question will simply go away; other times it will not. Have someone assist you in the presentation. Make this person responsible for keeping you organized, have him make notes about questions and concerns that are raised during the process. Try to get help from a coach or mentor. This could be someone who has previously presented to the executive committee and can provide some pointers and critique the presentation.

WHEN SHOULD THE BUSINESS CASE BE MADE?

The capital budgeting or funding process will vary in every organization. For instance, I find that many organizations wrongly require up-front funding commitments for an entire project. These up-front requests will invariably miss the mark because too little is known about the overall business requirements. There is also little known about software package costs; required hardware, software, or networking infrastructure requirements; and training, consulting ,and any customization costs.

To overcome the uncertainties of up-front project budgets, I advocate funding business improvement and software package projects as a series of funding stages. These funding requests or stages largely parallel the stages of the Software Package Life Cycle. The first funding request would be for a discovery project. The request would cover the costs associated with the management audit. The completion and presentation of the management audit would serve as the first checkpoint.

A second funding request would then be made to implement the recommendations of the management audit. This is accomplished by completing the requisite business process reengineering activities up to the point of business process automation. The completion and presentation of the current and future state business process models and process vision would then serve as the second checkpoint.

The third funding request would cover the costs of selecting a software package solution that will enact the process vision. The funding for this stage would cover the costs of formalizing the requirements, conducting the software evaluation, and making the final business case. This is based on gathering up all the costs and benefits and making the formal investment proposal discussed in this chapter. Upon completion of the software evaluation and final solution cost negotiations, a checkpoint review would be held. This review finalizes the software package purchase and authorizes the full amount of the implementation budget.

A fourth checkpoint review should be conducted during the implementation project. This should occur at the conclusion of the solution prototype. It would be at this point that any significant technical or performance gaps would be known, prioritized, and funded. The fifth and final checkpoint review would occur at the conclusion of the production readiness stage during implementation. At this point a substantial amount of the project costs have occurred. The remaining costs are end user education and the go live or deployment and support team related costs. Also included are any project closing costs, such as knowledge transfer between the implementation consultants and the internal staff.

At this point the reader may ask, "Is this chapter out of sequence with the rest of the book? The answer is no. Understanding the contents of the business case now will help one to write the request for proposal (RFP) document. The RFP document is used to gather necessary costs and other economic information from vendors. It is instrumental in making the business case that will decide the implementation budget.

CAPITAL BUDGETING: A QUICK OVERVIEW

Before diving into the details of preparing the investment proposal document, some background information on capital budgeting is necessary. If the reader already has a corporate accounting or finance background, this material may be old hat, while for others it will likely be new ground. The analysis of a capital investment relies on what are called capital budgeting techniques.

Capital budgeting is different from the types of budgeting that most business unit managers would typically be accustomed to. Although the business case may contain elements that are usually associated with an organization's budgets or financial reporting statements, the business case is simply not another budgeting or financial report. This section presents what this author considers as the most important or distinguishing characteristics of capital budgeting.

Make the Right Analysis

The corporate financial community long ago developed and adopted well-known quantitative techniques to facilitate so-called capital budgeting or capital investment project decision making. Generally speaking, there are two types of presentations of data that must be made in the investment proposal document.

The first presentation is of project costs and benefits or cash flows. This presentation is an accounting-like assembly of cost and benefit information. The second presentation is the financial analysis. It is a presentation of the results using one or more of the quantitative analysis or modeling techniques — simply put, calculations. These calculations rely on the project's underlying cost and benefit information, along with certain capital budgeting-related assumptions.

The Business Case Is Cash Flow Driven

Capital budgeting techniques *focus on cash flows,* not on profits or profit and loss impact. Investment decisions represent a change in the financial makeup of the business organization and therefore are based on cash flow. Earlier in the chapter, the profit motive of the business organization was presented along with a problem that every business organization faces — a limited supply of cash.

In producing revenues, a business organization not only incurs operating expenses, but it also must invest dollars into property, plant and equipment, and working capital to sustain its business activities. In addition, the business organization must pay income taxes on its earnings. The cash that remains after funding these investments and paying taxes is known as the organization's free cash flow. Investment decisions are based upon the availability of cash — essentially the free cash flows — that can fund investment proposals. Capital budgeting decisions both consume and generate free cash flows.

The Business Case is Time Driven

Nothing lasts forever. In the case of business investments, every investment will have a limited life span — the economic life of the investment — during which the investment provides utility or has value to the organization. A time line based approach to identifying and detailing the investment's costs and benefits is the accepted method of presentation. This is generally referred to as the investment's proposed useful life. In the case of software, the rule of thumb is generally a life span between 5 and 15 years.

Understand that this rule of thumb does not necessarily represent the depreciable life of the software package under generally accepted accounting principles (GAAP) or under Internal Revenue Service (IRS) depreciation guidelines. It is also important to understand that depreciation is not a cash flow. Only the income tax impact of a depreciation tax deduction has any impact in the capital budgeting decision-making process.

The Financial Impact Is Incremental

It is true that capital investments have wide ranging implications for an organization's entire financial structure and ultimately its financial performance. That impact is considered an incremental or marginal change from the present-day financial structure or performance exhibited by the organization. As a general rule, incremental values are usually the accepted presentation choice for capital budgeting purposes.

Dollars Today Are More Valuable Than Dollars Tomorrow

A dollar received today has much greater value than a dollar received in the future. If it were in hand today, it could be conceivably invested now and worth that much more in the future. This concept is known as the time value of money. The time value of money and the investor's required rate of return work closely with one another to influence both the analysis and undertaking of business-related capital investments.

DEPRECIATING SOFTWARE FOR TAX PURPOSES

Depreciation is an important and complicating consideration to the analysis of cash flows related to business asset investments. First, here is a little background on depreciation. Under GAAP, when we capitalize a business asset, the initial investment costs are not charged against operations all at once. Instead, the initial investment costs are allocated to operations on a periodic basis. This allocation is usually based upon the investment's projected economic useful life. The business asset is said to depreciate over time. Also it is necessary to match the cost of the asset itself to the usefulness of the asset to the business organization within a given accounting or time period.

With an understanding of depreciation in hand, the focus can change to cash flows and depreciation charges. When analyzing capital investments, accounting or book (GAAP) depreciation is ignored. The reason for this is depreciation charges or allocations are considered a noncash expense and at the same time, financial analysis is cash flow driven. Since there is not any cash involved, book or GAAP depreciation has no relevancy. However, depreciation does have relevancy for tax purposes.

Both the IRS and GAAP require the depreciation of business assets over time. As an expense or cost of doing business, business income is reduced by the amount of the depreciation expense and lowers the organization's income tax. Any new business asset stands to lower the corporation's income tax bill by the amount of the depreciation charges. The tax benefit provided by depreciation benefits must be included in the financial analysis of a capital investment under consideration. All of this accounting and tax talk must sound complicated. I promise that it is a relatively straightforward adjustment to the investment's proposed cash flow, given the right information. The right information means an understanding of how the IRS treats or qualifies your property for depreciation purposes that determine the timing of the depreciation charges and tax benefits.

The IRS considers software an intangible for depreciation purposes. The primary issue here is your software investment will not count toward the section 179 expense instead of depreciation election. It is hoped that your organization spends at least $20,000 on other qualified property under the current IRS guidelines. From time to time, Congress has authorized investment tax credits. Generally they apply only to qualified property and not to software. Most computer hardware qualifies as 5-year property under current IRS guidelines.

Under current IRS guidelines, off-the-shelf computer software purchased after August 10, 1993, must be amortized over a period of 36 months from the date of purchase. Customized software purchased after that date must be amortized over a 15-year period. Consult with your organization's CFO or accounting firm to determine how to characterize the software line items in your investment proposal.

The Cost of Capital

Financial analysis techniques assume that investment capital is not free. Business owners and debt holders assume they will be repaid in time, the amount of their invested capital plus a rate of return. This rate of return is equal to or greater than the rate of return that is available in the investment marketplace for similar investments of equal risk. This concept is commonly referred to as the investor's required rate of return.

The weighted average cost of capital (WACC) represents the required rate of return for the business organization as a whole. There are the various ways that a business organization will obtain capital. It is important to consider this fact when calculating the required rate of return for investment projects. This is because business organizations do not generally raise all of their capital from a single source and instead acquire capital from a combination of sources. Furthermore, each method of raising capital has a different cost associated with it, and this must be taken into account.

The WACC incorporates both debt (e.g., bank loans and commercial paper) and equity sources (e.g., common and preferred stock) into calculating a required rate of return. The weight represents the proportion of capital provided by a single source versus all sources of business capital. It is important to note that the WACC calculation can become quite complex given an organization's history of raising of capital over time using various sources at various rates.

The Cost of Capital as a Hurdle Rate

The weighted average cost of capital is typically considered as the minimum required rate of return for any use of the business organization's available capital. When determining the ROI for a given project, it is necessary to consider the WACC as an appropriate hurdle rate for the project when its risk is equal to the risk of the business organization as a whole. If there is added or reduced risk to the business organization from the project, then the required return should be adjusted accordingly.

Generally speaking, the CFO in most organizations has already calculated the organization's WACC. The CFO has also devised a minimum capital project or investment hurdle rate (which in practice is usually higher than a firm's cost of capital) that should be used in the financial analysis portion of your business case. It is beyond the scope of this book to provide a thorough background in developing the WACC or hurdle rates.

THE BUSINESS CASE OR INVESTMENT PROPOSAL DOCUMENT

To understand the steps in preparing the business case or investment proposal document, the best starting point is to review the document's elements or table of contents. The typical business case document will contain the following elements:

- Executive summary
- Background and purpose
- Relevant business issues and opportunities
- Conclusions and recommendations
- Financial impact
- Nonfinancial impact
- Assumptions, risks, and contingencies

These elements are listed in the order where they should appear in the business case. If you have ever read the annual financial report of a publicly held corporation, you may notice some parallels between the structure of a typical annual report and the design I recommend for the business case or investment proposal document. This is not necessarily by accident. The opening portion of the document represents the discussion by management, followed by the numbers (financials), the balanced scorecard (nonfinancial impact), and the fine print or notes that accompany the financial presentation (assumptions, risks, and contingencies).

As previously mentioned, some organizations may already have existing standards for presenting a business case. Before developing your business case around the investment proposal guidelines suggested here, first determine if your organization already has such a format. Then substitute it for the format suggested here. The format your organization uses may contain more or less information. Even if you prefer the format presented here, it may not be worthwhile to adopt this format. You may risk project delay, required reworking, or an outright rejection of the proposal.

The steps in preparing a business case, regardless of its format, revolve largely around filling in the blanks — with the appropriate facts and supporting analyses — for the specific elements needed in the business case. The remaining material in this chapter is largely a discussion of each of the above document elements. Also included is a lengthy review of the contents of the financial impact element.

Executive Summary

The executive summary reduces the entire contents of your proposal to one paragraph. As a result, it is often the last and easiest section to prepare. For example, consider this simple executive summary related to an ERP system proposal:

> *The ABC Manufacturing Corporation should acquire and imple-*
> *ment an enterprise-wide Enterprise Resource Planning (ERP) sys-*
> *tem. After an extensive review of ABC's current business practices,*
> *it has been determined that such a system offers a long list of*
> *both tangible and intangible benefits to this organization through*
> *both process improvements and through heightened levels of busi-*
> *ness operating information being made available to the organi-*
> *zation's management team. **The implementation of such a***
> ***system would require 10 months and could be completed***
> ***by November 1st, 20_, the beginning of ABC's next fiscal***
> ***year. The total cost to ABC for such a system is estimated***
> ***at $1,750,000, while its benefits are projected to be***
> ***$4,250,000 over the proposed system's life of 10 years.***

Some will argue the executive summary should appear at the end of the document, forcing readers to skim through until the end. Others prefer to leave an executive summary out of the document, forcing content review to reveal the proposal's key facts and figures. Both of these tactics are a disservice. I prefer to believe I am dealing with individuals who take their role seriously enough to thoroughly read any investment proposal. They should be able to render an intelligent, fact-based, and carefully thought-out decision, which presumes a cover-to-cover review of the investment proposal.

Background and Purpose

This background and purpose section of the investment proposal sets the stage for the remainder of the proposal. Usually, the reader may have only a limited understanding as to the nature of the investment being requested. The intent is to provide just enough information to place everyone on a level playing field. Just enough information means being concise, and not overwhelming with detail.

The Seed: How It All Began

Every idea begins somehow or somewhere. For instance, perhaps "the 20_ management audit" revealed "opportunities for significant working capital reductions through use of an automated production and inventory control system, such as an ERP system." This statement represents what can be called the seed or moment of life for the business case or investment proposal now being drafted.

Not everyone on the decision-making team may realize the connection between the current proposal and that original seed. Such background information should be briefly stated, perhaps only a few paragraphs at most. This information frames the perspective from which the business improvement or software selection project first sprang and where the process has led (to the investment proposal of course).

What Has Been Done to Date: From Seed to Stalk

The seed statement may have been cause enough to commission or fund a study team or software selection project. It is certainly not sufficient justification to spend the six or seven figures necessary to implement the typical ERP system. More is needed. The business case author must tell the story of from how the current proposal came about — from that original seed — by connecting the dots between past events and the current proposal.

This connection or link, from the past to present, represents the background information leading up to and should be stated in this section of the proposal. Such background information should be presented chronologically, or to use the analogy, from seed to sprout to stalk. This discussion should also link to the sponsor or sponsors of the proposal. For instance, a typical connection between the seed and sprout and to sponsors might read:

> Based upon this 20_ management audit finding, ABC's CFO and senior logistics manager initiated a joint business process improvement project within their business units whose purpose was to review the validity and magnitude of this assertion and to formulate an appropriate course of action if warranted.

The next linkage might then read as follows:

> This team reviewed current business practices in a 6-week study. The team determined that a sizeable amount of plant floor space (approximately 25%) and working capital (approximately $2MM) are today devoted to work in process inventory. In addition, the team found that customer order turnaround times are significant (15 working days) and that customers are increasingly lost to competitors due to slow order turnaround. (Approximately 15% of quotations were rejected due to availability concerns during a 3-week sample.)

The team also found that customer orders were queued in the production process primarily due to inadequate paint shop capacity, where at any given time there was a 2 to 3 day backlog of work. Given this information, the study team concluded and recommended numerous operational and product line innovations, several of which have been implemented and are already providing benefit. (Customer orders now average 12 working days.)

Now, for the final linkage:

The most significant of their findings was to concur with the earlier management audit finding that an automated production and inventory control system would be useful. They concluded that any further business improvements would be realized only through the capabilities that such a system would provide. This lead to the creation of an expanded team involving members of the production and the sales and marketing business units whose mission was to clarify needs, research products, and select an ERP system appropriate to ABC's business model. This effort has culminated into this proposal for the acquisition and implementation of the XYZ system — an ERP software package developed, sold, and supported by 123 Corporation.

This is not a long story, but a summary of significant prior events. The story told invoked sponsorship. It also introduced some of the operational metrics and benchmarks that will be used (later in the investment proposal) to quantify benefits.

Relevant Business Issues and Opportunities

The background and purpose section has likely already planted a few more seeds by referencing some of the business issues and potential opportunities related to the business case presentation that follows. In many cases, they were the driving forces behind any earlier activities leading up to the current proposal. The purpose behind this section of the proposal is to develop a sense of urgency and compelling business reasons to act favorably (by funding) the proposed capital investment.

Presenting Issues

I prefer to use the word issues, not problems, although they are conceptually speaking one in the same. A relevant business issue, first and foremost, serves as *a reason to act*. Like findings in a management audit, some business issues are major concerns, while others are trivial or minor. The relevant business issues must be discussed in detail within the course of the overall business case presentation.

As was the case in preparing the background and purpose section, assume that proposal readers do not have an in-depth understanding of what the business issues are. Also, the proposal must demonstrate business relevance, and more specifically, the correlation between the issues presented and the proposal being made; this cannot be assumed.

Consider a classic cause and effect relationship for a moment. An issue or a problem generally represents the effect. The business case is being made on the premise of what is wrong and here is why. The underlying causes are the drivers of business performance. When searching for drivers, one must first comprehend what the business issues are then work backwards to determine the root causes related to each issue. Consider this example where one issue has been determined to have three causes:

Business Performance Issues Effect	Business Performance Drivers Cause
Inventory value is significantly higher than the competition.	Raw materials: Competitors are using just in time inventory techniques; ABC is not. Work in process: Competitors have adopted a make to order business model, while ABC has remained make to stock. Finished goods: The ABC product line (as measured by stock keeping units) exceeds those of the competition by an average of 25%.

The issues are the easy part of this process. Getting at drivers can be a difficult and time-consuming process. Consider a leaking roof. The problem is obvious — water damage to the facility and perhaps equipment or inventory damage. Where exactly the water is actually seeping through the roof might not be as easy to determine. The question is: How are business performance drivers found? The answer is through rigorous process understanding, such as that suggested earlier in this book.

In the case of the ABC example, assuming that the identified drivers are valid, the solution in this case — implementing a new ERP system — offers ABC the opportunity to resolve some, if not all, of these issues. The example provided here illustrates the issue and its related drivers in a tabular format, although it could be presented in a paragraph format as well. The tabular format tends to force shorter and more precise definitions of the underlying business issues and drivers.

At first glance, the finished goods issue might be considered a marketing or engineering issue. For instance, are all of these stock keeping units actually necessary? Are all of the items turning at an acceptable rate? Are all of the items profitable? Can some of these items be substituted with others? If any one of these questions cannot be readily answered by the organization today (usually because the information simply is not kept or is not available without requiring a significant effort), then an ERP system might help improve the overall management and marketing of finished goods as well. This last assumption will be made for purposes of the next illustration. Now that the business issues and the drivers have been identified and noted, the next step is to quantify the expected benefits.

Presenting Opportunities

I wish I had better news for you, but most, if not all, investments made into new software packages will not directly make any money for the organization. Unfortunately, the direct benefits derived from a software package investment are usually operational in nature. With that said, here is an example of what is a woefully inadequate business case:

New Business Opportunities Effect	Business Operational Drivers Cause
Increased sales	A new customer relationship management system

There are a few special cases in which a software package might be considered as revenue generating:

■ Internet-generated sales through an electronic storefront.
■ Cross-selling opportunities using call center support software. Often such functionality is a part of the customer relationship management (CRM) or services operations management software package could be classified as revenue generating instead of revenue enhancing. These features allow call center representatives an opportunity to also serve as an inside sales force by offering products, such as consumables, or extended service agreements related to the primary product during a customer call event.

Even in these cases, the software only facilitates revenue enhancement through the execution of an overall marketing strategy that includes such activities as a part of the operating plan. The software will not simply make these revenue-generating events happen, no more than will the software perform operational processes.

Consider the CRM system for moment. CRM is similar to Six Sigma in this regard — Six Sigma is not just a quality improvement program, it is about a way of doing business. Now consider CRM in this same context — CRM is not simply a software tool, it is a way of conducting the sales and marketing activities of the firm. It speaks to the intensity and quality of the relationship between the customer and the selling firm. To work, CRM requires not only a good software tool, but a completely different kind of selling culture as well. CRM is not just a software system, it is a way of conducting business with customers. Also, the organization's culture has to accept, embrace, and practice it. Try taking that to the bank!

Take a look at Internet or web marketing. When proposing e-business software packages such acquisitions are frequently tied to loftier goals, such as building a new Internet marketing channel for the core business. Be aware of the risks from channel conflict. Channel conflict occurs when the source of sales shifts from one marketing venue, such as a direct sales force or from retail outlets, to web-initiated sales.

Smaller and middle market manufacturing businesses rely heavily on so-called manufacturers' representatives as a source of business. For instance, a web-initiated sales initiative may infuriate some of these channel partners and cause them to favor a competing product line they represent over your product line. This is an area requiring careful consideration in plotting an e-business strategy. It also has implications for the business case of any purported e-business opportunities and software packages to support them. When considering an e-business strategy, consider also how it will impact revenue from existing channels. If necessary, a downward adjustment to revenues in an existing channel may be necessary to offset e-business revenue increases as customer channel preferences shift.

With this discussion completed, a better formulation or presentation for a business case opportunity and a related driver might read as follows:

New Business Opportunities Effect	Business Operational Driver(s) Cause
Increased sales	The proposed CRM system provides much needed operational support for the sales and marketing team. By staying connected with customers, through regular contact management and promotional campaigns it is felt that *customer retention will increase by 15%*. These are sales that would otherwise be lost to the competition.

The above customer-related metric (in italics) is considered nonfinancial. Generally speaking, an attempt should be made to link any nonfinancial metric with financial metrics. This topic will be discussed later in this chapter.

Internal Stakeholders and Sponsorship

Building a business case for new software requires substantial input and sponsorship from the business units that will actually use the new software. For instance, you will need to understand what unmet business requirements or issues these business units have, how they can be met through software, and how they actually improve business performance. Such metrics must then be recast as monetary measures. Again you have a challenge. Quantifying unmet business requirements is not a simple task. Unfortunately, few new systems actually eliminate costs; they usually escalate them. The business case must be built largely on the basis of indirect benefits to the primary beneficiaries of the new software — the operating business units.

Conclusions and Recommendations

The decision makers in any organization realize that an investment proposal needs funding. In fact, if your business case is marginal or nonexistent, (and some are) the choice may be made to not pursue the project before it reaches the executive team or board of directors. Sometimes we have no choice in the matter. Recall the earlier leaking roof example. With that said, this section of the investment proposal is largely a restatement of the obvious. An example of an ending paragraph from the conclusions and recommendations section might be as follows:

> ABC has made continuous progress in reducing inventories over the past few years. However, without an integrated ERP system that provides real time inventory availability for production and distribution, it will be difficult, if not impossible, to achieve any further inventory investment reductions without such automation. These potential reductions are doable and substantial and have been illustrated previously in this proposal. Given our analysis and efforts of the past weeks, the project team recommends favorable action on this request.

This section should consist of no more than 2 or 3 paragraphs. It should restate significant facts in terms of background, issues, and benefits found within the proposal that give cause for action.

Financial Impact

The financial impact portion of the business case must present both a detailed statement of the costs and benefits or cash flows related to a proposed investment and a financial analysis of those cash flows. The financial analysis itself will contain a series of common return on investment related metrics. The steps to preparing the financial impact portion of the investment proposal include:

■ Identify all tangible costs and benefits.
■ Prepare the statement of project cost and benefit cash flows.
■ Prepare the financial analysis of project cash flows.

I expect that most readers will likely need some assistance or input from the CFO or their staff when completing this portion of the investment proposal document. With that said, detailed discussions of the above steps follow.

Identify and Quantify Costs and Benefits

When preparing the investment proposal all of the costs and all of the tangible or financial benefits expected to materialize during the estimated useful or economic life of the capital investment must be identified and detailed. There are both one-time and recurring costs and benefits associated with most information technology-related investment decisions.

Examples of one-time costs and benefits include:

■ Vendor rebate and incentive payments (benefits)
■ Acquisition and implementation costs
■ Growth and enhancement costs
■ Termination costs
■ Salvage and scrap value recoveries (benefits)

Examples of recurring costs and benefits include:

■ Operating and maintenance costs
■ Change and growth costs
■ Cost reductions and improvements (benefits)
■ Revenue enhancements (benefits)

Generally speaking, project-related costs are much easier to derive than are project-related benefits. In fact, this is often the most difficult and time-consuming aspect in making the business case and building the investment proposal document. This is perhaps the most controversial aspect of the investment proposal as well, because so much of the presentation is based upon assumptions about the future, which are frequently incorrect.

Understanding the Total Cost Picture

It is important to be conservative and thorough in project cost identification. It is the single best way to prevent surprise budget overruns and the accompanying loss of confidence in the project or personnel involved. The list that follows details some of the types of costs your organization will likely incur in a typical technology enablement or software package project:

- The business application software package license. There is wide variation in how software is licensed. Some products are licensed on a per server basis. Other vendors license on a per CPU or server size basis, while other vendors license on a per seat, end user, or workstation basis. Some vendors base license fees on the revenue level of the client. In the case of the financial service industry, software pricing is often based on the asset size of the institution or portfolio. The advantage of these last two pricing schemes is that they will allow the smallest organizations access to what the industry titans would otherwise only be able to buy. There is another twist to consider: Some software vendors sell their application software as a complete product or suite while others sell by functional module (i.e., payroll, job cost) or by application suite (i.e., distribution, financial, manufacturing).
- Add-on modules and core product enhancements. Some software vendors sell their application software as a basic or core product and charge extra for bells and whistles. Some typical add-on and enhancement modules include report writers and development tools.
- Source code. Yes, some vendors do charge extra for this. You will typically need it if you will customize the software in any way.
- Software package maintenance. This is usually an annual subscription-based cost and should cover software patches, help desk calls (sometimes only during normal business hours) and maybe upgrades and enhancements. Premiums may apply for after-hours support.
- Software package upgrades. Usually these are growth-related costs. As your organization grows or expands, you may need to add a

related workstation (i.e., seat or end user licenses). These are frequently sold individually or in so-called client packs. Server licenses may be sold based upon processor or power rating. A hardware upgrade for performance reasons may lead to a forced software upgrade.

- Server hardware. A typical configuration will include application, terminal, database, and web servers.
- Client workstation hardware, including both fat and thin clients.
- Hardware maintenance. For servers you will want an annual contract. For workstations, well anything goes.
- Operating system software, applicable to all servers and fat clients.
- Personnel. Generally, I focus on additions to staff, such as network support personnel. (The incremental nature of costs is what we are considering.)
- Temporary help. Usually this involves the cost of clerical and data entry assistance (e.g., manual data conversions) while permanent staff is being trained.
- Common carrier charges. This includes installation of ISDN or T1 lines and monthly access, service (i.e., bandwidth) and usage (volume) charges.
- Network service provider and other outsourcing costs. These types of costs include charges for ASP, ISP, MSP, and VPN one-time and monthly service (capacity and volume) costs.
- Vendor-provided education and training. This includes any formal classes, computer-based training courseware, and collateral materials, such as training and reference manuals. Vendors generally provide a complete set of document only on CD-ROM. You will need to buy hard copies or print them. My suggestion is to load the software on an Intranet and let end users and trainers print only needed documentation.
- Transportation, meal, and lodging expenses. Covers the costs of employees traveling in conjunction with the project (i.e., vendor training at a remote location, providing end user training or support at a remote location)
- Complementary (third party) software purchased to enhance the functionality of the core software package. Examples include report writing and analysis, external tax calculation tools and output enhancement software.
- Complementary (third party) hardware. This includes bar code printers, bar code scanning wands, RF input devices and document scanners.
- Infrastructure and system management software. This includes middleware tools such as an EAI or ETL software package, network

or performance monitoring software, and the all-important database software. It may also include terminal or web server software for a thin client or browser based system.

- Client workstation software, including both fat and thin client licenses.
- Site preparation charges. These are the costs of developing, conditioning, and powering the server closet or server room and installing any network cabling between servers and workstations.
- Professional services. These are the costs of consultants. They cover such things as software selection, project management, software implementation and setup assistance, training and documentation assistance, and postimplementation support.
- Tradesmen. These costs are related to site preparation. They are usually associated with licensed or union contractors and other professional installers.
- Technical services. These are also consulting related costs. They include the costs of installing networks, installing and tuning the software on servers, customizing or modifying vendor supplied programs, creating custom programs, integrating other software packages, and converting data.
- Chargebacks. Consultants and contractors expect reimbursement for any travel costs, including transportation, meals, and lodging incurred by their personnel to complete any work at your site or at remote sites. These are called chargebacks. Some service providers will charge a handling or billing fee of 5 to 15% of the chargeback amount. Be aware that few consulting teams are ever comprised of strictly local talent.

As extensive as this list is, there are certainly other potential project related costs. Since every organization's situation may be different, expect to have a list that represents a subset or a superset of the costs noted here.

How Much Should I Expect to Spend?

Unfortunately, because every organization and implementation will be quite different, it is hard to be precise. In my experience, I have seen three common measures used to provide a rough estimate of project size or budget. One method is based on a percentage of an organization's annual revenues, another uses total seats, while another uses software value. Some rough guidelines for an enterprise-wide ERP system are as follows:

Estimating Model	Rule of Thumb
Revenue based	Use 1 to 3% of total annual revenues as a total project budget. For example, an organization with annual sales of $100,000,000 might spend up to $3,000,000.
Software value based	Total Project Budget of 3 to 10 times the cost of the software. Assuming a $100,000 software license, the project bill could run $1,000,000.
Per seat (or per end user) based	Total Project Budget equals $25,000 (low) to $50,000 (high) times the number of seats to be licensed. Assuming a 50-user license, the project could equal $2,500,000.

Again, take this information for what it is worth. At best, these metrics provide little more than a rough estimate of value. Consultants, resellers, and software vendors will often quote them. It is perhaps fair to request estimates using these techniques in a nonspecific request for information.

Now That Costs Have Been Considered, What About Benefits?

The first question is: What criteria to consider? In other words, this means what matters most in calculating ROI. As a guide, the following questions should be considered in your selection of the appropriate business case drivers for new technologies:

- How will the proposed capital investment project improve financial assets?
- How will the proposed capital investment project improve nonfinancial assets?
- How will this proposed capital investment project increase revenues?
- How will the proposed capital investment project decrease expenses?
- How will the proposed capital investment project improve cash flow?
- How will the proposed capital investment project reduce or free up working capital?
- How will the proposed capital investment project reduce future capital requirements?

Simply asking these questions is not enough. The second step is the harder task — measurement. A yes answer to any one of the preceding questions will then call for a second round of questions, in particular: By how much and when?

Working with Monetary Metrics

A monetary metric is the simplest to work with in terms of projecting the financial impact when any change occurs in the metric; benefits simply represent a favorable change in the metric. The dollar value change in the metric is the benefit value to the organization that is projected to occur if the business improvement is implemented. Such changes may be immediate or achieved over a period of time. Benefits may occur only once or on an ongoing or recurring basis. Following through on the ABC example, here is a look at the benefits that have been projected. In this case the benefits are monetary:

Benchmark	Current Level	Target Level	Benefit Value
Raw materials	100,000	50,000	50,000
Work in process	200,000	100,000	100,000
Finished goods	700,000	350,000	350,000
Average inventory	$1,000,000	$500,000	$500,000

The narrative related to this presentation might read:

> ABC's business process improvement team has identified and concluded after careful analysis that there are specific methods for reducing ABC's average inventory investment from $1,000,000 to $500,000 — a 50% reduction. These methods are the basis of our recommendation. This action will have a substantial and permanent impact on the working capital requirements of ABC.

The specific methods (your conclusions) for achieving these reductions should appear in the conclusions and recommendations section of the investment proposal document. Monetary metrics are presented in the financial impact portion of the document. Their presentation should precede the statement of costs and benefits and the investment analysis worksheet presentations.

Cost Savings

Sometimes benefits are rooted in cost savings. There are two types of cost savings. The first are readily determinable cost savings. This type of cost savings is more of a direct benefit. For example, they occur when an obsolete mainframe computer is replaced by a client server infrastructure. In this case, the determinable costs would be the monthly hardware maintenance and software license costs, plus any resale or scrap value associated with the mainframe computer that is sold or scrapped.

The second type of cost savings are projections of costs that are expected to decrease. This is usually as a result of a process improvement, such as lower scrap or defect rates, fewer expedited deliveries, and lower delivery costs. These projections are usually derived from a nonfinancial metric that has been monetarized. The next major section in this chapter — nonfinancial impact — will discuss making such projections.

Where Is Your Backup for That?

Although one would like to believe that a numeric presentation is considered objective and leaves little room for challenge, that is simply not the case. There are many assumptions that are made, particularly with respect to the projection of benefits. In many cases, these projections can be highly controversial, if not downright suspect. Expect to be challenged on your numbers. Understand the reasons behind why certain drivers or metrics have been used. The financial impact portion of the business case reduces all of the issues to a few key investment metrics. The next two sections of the investment proposal — nonfinancial impact and assumptions — should contain the financial presentation of costs and benefits.

Costs, Benefits, and Uncertainty

For the estimation or projection of benefits in particular, it may be appropriate to incorporate a risk adjustment into the estimate of a potential benefit. This would typically be done when a high degree of uncertainty about the estimate of benefits exists. This is done by providing a range of possible outcomes — three estimates of benefits to be precise:

- The lowest expected monetary benefit received
- The highest expected monetary benefit received
- The most likely expected monetary benefit received

This is referred to as a probabilistic estimate of benefits. This estimating technique is rooted in statistics. Each estimated benefit value is treated as though it is a random number under a beta probability distribution. The formula to calculate an expected benefit value, based upon a range of estimates is as follows:

$$\text{Expected Benefit Value} =$$
$$(\text{Highest Benefit Value} + 4*(\text{Most Likely Benefit Value}) +$$
$$\text{Lowest Benefit Value})/6$$

Anyone familiar with project management techniques will immediately recognize this formula as the same for calculating task duration under conditions of uncertainty. This is referred to as the program evaluation and review technique (PERT).

Preparing a Statement of Costs and Benefits

There are numerous formats used for making the presentation of the statement of costs and benefits. This book illustrates one format of any number found in practice. In general, this is an accounting-like presentation that details both the costs and the benefits (revenue increases and expense reductions or cost saving benefits) that can be attributed on a causal (cause and effect) basis to the proposed investment. Figure 6.2 illustrates a typical format for the statement of costs and benefits. The statement of costs and benefits is relatively easy to prepare using electronic spreadsheet software, such as Microsoft Excel. I have constructed a standard template that I use. The statement of costs and benefits template is a part of the author's template collection. Consult Appendix A for more information.

Preparing the Investment Analysis Worksheet

Once the statement of costs and benefits has been prepared, the next step is to analyze the cost and benefit information. As a general rule, I present these in the form of an investment analysis worksheet, which provides results for all of these measures, along with a presentation of key assumptions underlying the calculations. There are five commonly used calculations found in use for reviewing capital investment proposals:

- Payback
- Return on investment
- Net present value (NPV)
- Profitability index (PI)
- Internal rate of return (IRR)

Table 6.1 provides detailed information on each of these calculations, including the purpose, interpretation, required data, and the generalized formula used to complete each calculation. This table should provide an invaluable level of assistance in understanding if the business case is strong enough to stand the test of the executive committee or the board of directors.

TradewindsGroup
Tradewinds Group, Incorporated
Consultants to Management
Box 3601
Oak Brook, Illinois 60522

Statement of Project Cost and Benefit Cash Flows
Prepared For: ABC Manufacturing
Project: CRM System

Description	Inception	Year 1	Year 2	Year 3	Year 4	Year 5	Year 6	Disposition
Incremental Cash Benefits								
Benefits Attributed to Working Capital Reductions	0.00	75000.00	75000.00	75000.00	75000.00	75000.00	0.00	0.00
Benefits Attributed to Revenue Enhancements	0.00	75000.00	75000.00	75000.00	75000.00	75000.00	0.00	0.00
Benefits Attributed to Expense Reductions	0.00	25000.00	25000.00	25000.00	25000.00	25000.00	0.00	0.00
Total Incremental Positive Cash Flows	0.00	75000.00	75000.00	75000.00	75000.00	75000.00	0.00	0.00
Incremental Cash Costs								
Computer Software, Unmodified Package	10000.00	0.00	0.00	0.00	0.00	0.00	0.00	0.00
Computer Software, Customized Package	50000.00	0.00	0.00	0.00	0.00	0.00	0.00	0.00
Computer Hardware	25000.00	0.00	0.00	0.00	0.00	0.00	0.00	0.00
Software Operating and Maintenance	0.00	3000.00	3000.00	3000.00	3000.00	3000.00	0.00	0.00
Hardware Operating and Maintenance	0.00	1000.00	1000.00	1000.00	1000.00	1000.00	0.00	0.00
Education	10000.00	0.00	0.00	0.00	0.00	0.00	0.00	0.00
Implementation Consulting	20000.00	0.00	0.00	0.00	0.00	0.00	0.00	0.00
Total Incremental Negative Cash Flows	-115000.00	4000.00	4000.00	4000.00	4000.00	4000.00	0.00	0.00
Change in Pre Tax Operating Income	-115000.00	71000.00	71000.00	71000.00	71000.00	71000.00	0.00	0.00
Amortization Expense for Tax Purposes	0.00	3333.33	6666.67	6666.67	5000.00	3333.33	3333.33	0.00
Depreciation Expense for Tax Purposes	0.00	100.00	200.00	200.00	200.00	200.00	100.00	0.00
Taxable Income	0.00	67566.67	64133.33	64133.33	65800.00	67466.67	-3433.33	0.00
Income Tax Expense	0.00	23648.33	22446.67	22446.67	23030.00	23613.33	-1201.67	0.00
Change in After Tax Operating Income	-115000.00	47351.67	48553.33	48553.33	47970.00	47386.67	1201.67	0.00
Incremental Annual Capital Expenditures Related to Project								
Computer Software, Unmodified Package	0.00	0.00	0.00	0.00	1000.00	0.00	0.00	0.00
Computer Software, Customized Package	0.00	0.00	0.00	0.00	0.00	0.00	0.00	0.00
Computer Hardware	0.00	0.00	0.00	0.00	2000.00	0.00	0.00	0.00
Incremental Free Cash Flows Generated by Project	-115000.00	47351.67	48553.33	48553.33	44970.00	47386.67	1201.67	0.00
Sum of Cash Flows - First Five Years	-115000.00							121815.00

Presentation Assumptions:

Marginal Corporate Income Tax — 35.00%
Section 179 Election Limitation (Allows expensing in lieu of depreciation up to amount of limitation amount) — $ 24,000.00
Tax Depreciation Life for Computer Hardware (straight line, half year convention) — 60 Months
Tax Amortization of Unmodified Computer Software (straight line, half year convention) — 36 Months
Tax Amortization of Custom Computer Software for (straight line, half year convention) — 180 Months
Add 2 Workstations in Year 4

Plunk junk on 6/2/2002

Figure 6.2 The Statements of Costs and Benefits: An Example

Table 6.1 Commonly Used Financial Analysis and Modeling Calculations Related to Capital Budgeting Decisions

Financial Measure	What Is Told	What Data Are Required	How It Is Calculated
Project cash flow statement	Preparing the statement of project cost and benefit cash flows is the initial step in the analysis of a capital investment project. This statement is a detailed listing of the incremental or marginal costs and benefits that can be attributed to the underlying capital investment. This information is developed for all periods of the project's economic life. It is defined as the total number of years or months the asset is expected to remain in service or provide economic value to the business organization. This information is typically presented on an annualized basis, but can be presented on a monthly basis if need be.	Economic life expectancy of project, initial investment costs, periodic cash revenues, periodic cash expenses, tax depreciation expenses, terminating value, marginal tax rate of the business organization	Calculate incremental net free cash flows: *Pretax operating income = Cash revenues − Cash expenses* *After tax operating income = Pretax income − depreciation × (1 − Marginal tax rate)* *Incremental net free cash flow = After tax cash flow − Periodic capital improvements*[b]

Annual presentations are generally acceptable for smaller value projects and when cash flows are relatively stable over time. Periodic presentations are usually preferred when widely varying cash flows exist, in situations of severe inflation or for large value projects.[a]

Return on investment (ROI)	ROI measures the profitability of a proposed capital investment project by the ratio of the project's total benefits to its total costs. ROI is widely used because of its calculation simplicity. ROI is typically calculated and compared to a hurdle rate that an organization uses as a benchmark when accepting or rejecting capital investment projects. The major limitation of the ROI technique is that it does not account for the timing of uneven periodic cash flows or for the time value of money.	Initial Investment, Periodic Cash Revenues, Periodic Cash Expenses, Terminating Value	Calculate ROI (expressed as an average annual percentage): *Total Project Revenues (Benefits)/Total Project Investments (Costs)*[c]

(continued)

Table 6.1 Commonly Used Financial Analysis and Modeling Calculations Related to Capital Budgeting Decisions (continued)

Technique	Description	Data Requirements	Calculation
Payback	Payback represents the period of time needed to recover the initial project cash outlay. Payback is widely used because of its calculation simplicity. Payback measures a project's liquidity more so than its profitability. This major limitation of the payback technique is that it does not account for the timing of uneven periodic cash flows or for the time value of money.	Economic life expectancy of project, initial investment, periodic cash revenues, periodic cash expenses, terminating value	Step 1: Calculate average cash flows: Sum of average annual cash flows/Project life expectancy Step 2: Calculate payback period: Initial project cash outlay/Average annual cash flow generated by the project
Net present value (NPV; also referred to as discounted cash flow (DCF) analysis)	NPV calculates the net present value of a capital investment project by applying a discount rate and a series of future payments (negative values) and income (positive values). The concept of discounting or holds that a dollar receives today is worth more than a dollar received at a future date. This concept is generally referred to as the time value of money. NPV is related to IRR calculation. IRR is the rate at which NPV is equal to zero.	Economic Life Expectancy of Project, initial investment, periodic cash revenues, periodic cash expenses, periodic tax depreciation (noncash) expenses, terminating value, discount rate (the cost of capital)	Step 1: Calculate net free cash flow: Step 2: Calculate NPV: *Periodic Net Cash Flow NPV = Sum (Incremental Net Free Cash Flows)/(1 + Discount Rate) + Terminal Value/(1+ Discount Rate) × Initial Investment[d]*
Profitability index	The profitability index is similar to NPV analysis except that the results are expressed in relative terms instead of in absolute dollar terms.	Present value of total costs, present value of total benefits	*Present Value of Total Benefits/Present Value of Total Costs[e]*

		How to interpret	
		How to interpret the results of the profitability index: If the profitability index is zero, the project is marginal. If the profitability index is positive, the project is accepted. If the profitability index is negative, the project is rejected.	
Internal rate of return (IRR)	IRR is the return received for a capital investment project consisting of a series of periodic net cash flows. IRR is closely related to the NPV calculation. The rate of return calculated by IRR is the interest rate corresponding to a zero net present value.	Economic life expectancy of project, initial investment, periodic cash revenues, periodic cash expenses, periodic tax depreciation (noncash) expenses, terminating value, Guess at what the result of the IRR calculation will be (Many spreadsheets and calculators use this guess to drive an iterative technique in calculating the IRR value [ROI will work].)	Step 1: Calculate Net Free Cash Flow Step 2: Calculate IRR (IRR is the case where NPV = 0): NPV = Periodic Net Cash Flow NPV = Sum (Incremental Net Free Cash Flows)/(1 + Discount Rate) + Terminal Value/(1+ Discount Rate) × Initial Investment[f]

[a] All remaining financial calculations rely on the data prepared for and presented in the project cash flow statement. If the cash flow presentation is made on a monthly basis, then any annualized discount rate must be divided by 12 to arrive at the applicable monthly discount rate.

[b] Figure 6.2 illustrates the statement of project cost and benefit cash flows.

[c] Sometimes this ratio is referred to as the benefit/cost ratio instead of ROI.

[d] Formulas are for illustrative purposes only. Calculation should be performed using an electronic spreadsheet or handheld calculator (i.e., the Microsoft Excel NPV Function).

[e] Formula are for illustrative purposes only. Calculation should be performed using an electronic spreadsheet or handheld calculator.

[f] Formulas for illustrative purposes only. Calculation should be performed using an electronic spreadsheet or handheld calculator (i.e., Microsoft Excel IRR Function).

Payback and ROI are as illustrated by the table. They are easy enough to calculate and can be done so manually. While the underlying calculations for NPV and IRR are straightforward, it is a slow, repetitive process to solve them manually. Previously, when hand calculations were made, it was usually done in conjunction with so-called discount factor tables to simplify at least part of the process. Later using handheld business calculators with built-in facilities, we solved these financial calculations with a minimum of effort. Today, electronic spreadsheet programs like Microsoft Excel, which has built-in functions for these financial equations, have made manual analysis and handheld financial calculators obsolete. Figure 6.3 illustrates a completed investment analysis worksheet using the costs and benefits information presented in Figure 6.2. The investment analysis worksheet template is a part of the author's template collection. Consult Appendix A for more information.

In addition to the results for the calculations or analyses performed, it is necessary to provide decision makers with information to support the presentation. This includes the underlying formulas and any assumptions that were used in completing the analysis. This is especially true for payback and ROI calculations, for in practice there are a number of common variations from the calculation approach as presented here.

On a final note, every organization has varying standards as to which of these measures it desires or will accept in the context of the investment proposal. If desired, one can err on the side of caution and present the results for all of the calculations.

Nonfinancial Impact

As previously discussed, several challenges confront business and technology managers making the business case for business process improvements and software package investments. For most business process improvement and software package investment projects, nonmonetary factors will usually be the key drivers. The first problem is in identifying exactly what business-related metrics are related to these drivers. The second problem is one of translation: recasting, dollarizing, or monetarizing such a nonmonetary metric into a monetary one.

This section of the investment proposal is largely reserved for identifying the driver, the metric, and projecting the benefit. It is intended to provide back-up needed to substantiate the cost and benefit information presented in the financial impact portion of the investment proposal document.

As previously noted, most, if not all, investments made in a new software package will not directly make any money for the organization. The direct benefits derived from the software package investment are usually operational, not monetary. The business application software

Project Financial Analysis
Prepared For: ABC Manufacturing
Project: CRM System

TradewindsGroup
Tradewinds Group, Incorporated
Consultants to Management
Box 3601
Oak Brook, Illinois 60522

Description	Inception	Year 1	Year 2	Year 3	Year 4	Year 5	Year 6	Disposition
Incremental Free Cash Flows Generated by Project	-115000.00	47351.67	48553.33	48553.33	44970.00	47386.67	1201.67	0.00

Calculation of Payback

Estimated Life of Project	60.00 Months
Sum of Cash Flows Over 5 Year Life	236815.00
Average Annual Cash Flow Generated	47363.00
Payback	2.43 Years

Calculation of Return on Investment

ROI = Free Cash Flows/Investment	18.72%

Calculation of Net Present Value

Discount Rate (Weighted Average Cost of Capital)	12.00%
Net Present Value	$56,011.71

Calcuation of Internal Rate of Return

Estimated Rate of Return	6.00%
Internal Rate of Return	30.46%

Calculation of Profitability Index

Present Value of Total Costs	$131,445.63
Present Value of Total Benefits	$171,011.71
Profitability Index	1.30

Recommended Action

Clients Hurdle Rate	15.00%
Recommended Action	Financial Viability Demonstrated, Recommend Acceptance/Approval

Printed on 6/2/2002 — Confidential and Proprietary — Page 1 of 1

Figure 6.3 The Financial Analysis Worksheet: An Example

package simply provides methods or processes for collecting, storing, moving, and analyzing operational information. Recall from the first chapter in this book the concept of return on information — that is what is achieved from software. This does not justify or sell the software package to the executives or board members who decide on the fate of the investment proposal. Return on information must be translated into or recast as a Return on Investment.

When information is used to improve business processes and ultimately to improve business performance, return on information is achieved. Such operational improvements are usually measured through:

- Cost reductions or savings
- Cost avoidance or deferral, primarily through better utilization of existing resources or capacity
- Enhancements to revenue-producing activities, primarily through process improvements or innovations

The first step in representing the nonfinancial benefits is to identify the operational metrics that will be impacted. An operational metric is related to a business process. An operational metric is typically a measure of availability, capacity, defects, yields, throughput, or volume. When a process is benchmarked, it is done so on the basis of an operational metric.

Differences between a desired level of an operational metric — the benchmark to be achieved — and the actual or current performance level are referred to as performance gaps. In the case of ABC, the inventory levels were used as the benchmark. When performance gaps exist, business improvement action plans are formed to address them. Such action plans frequently result in capital investment proposals such as a software package. In the case of ABC, an ERP system is being proposed as a part of its overall business improvement action plan.

Consider External Factors

When making the business case, it is best to consider competitive and other external factors. This is especially true when a new software package is presumably justified on the premise that it will target improvement of an externally affected metric. This is the case in the ABC example. ABC has benchmarked its inventory levels against those it considers its nearest rivals.

Offer Proof to Support Claims Made

In the ABC example, an ERP system is being justified on its ability to help reduce average total inventory investment. If average total inventory can be halved, the benefits that accrue may be more than enough to justify the cost of the system. There is always one big problem with this approach. It is entirely possible that the projected improvement is simply not attainable. There must be some proof offered that such benefits are both reasonable and possible and are not simply conjecture.

Working with Nonmonetary Metrics

Not all operational-type metrics are monetary. In fact, the majority of them will not be. In such cases, any metrics that are not monetary must be dollarized or monetarized. This includes linking them to a monetary metric that relates to the organization's operating performance (the income statement) or to its overall financial structure (the balance sheet). In the ABC example, working capital (and average inventory) is related to the firm's balance sheet. Let's look at another example for ABC:

> ABC's business process improvement team believes that within 6 months of implementation, it will be possible to reduce public (rented) warehouse space by approximately 1,000 square feet (at $10.00 per square foot).

The projection is as follows:

Benchmark	Current Level	Target Level	Benefit Value
Reduce public warehouse (rented) space used by 1,000 feet.	10,000 feet @ $10 square foot	9,000 feet @ $10 square foot	$10,000 (1,000 feet @ $10 square foot)

In this case, the team at ABC has concluded that by permanently reducing inventory investment or physical stock on hand, less space is needed. This is a reasonable conclusion. The ABC team also realizes that the space reduction does not occur immediately — another reasonable conclusion.

Consider the CRM example from earlier in this chapter. Recall that the "bad" version of a benefit was vague. The improved version of the benefit cast the nonfinancial impact as a measurable benefit. Going one step further, once nonfinancial measures or metrics exist, they too can often be stated in terms of their financial impact on the organization. For instance, here is how the CRM nonfinancial metrics can be monetarized:

- Today, 250 customers per year do not make another buy. Assuming we retain 75 (30%) of these customers at an average spend rate of $1000 per year, annual sales will increase by $75,000.
- Customer retention also lowers the cost of developing new business. By focusing on business development through personal contact with existing customers, fewer dollars will be spent on advertising and promotions to noncustomers. A 10% decrease in promotional costs is anticipated. Current promotional costs are $2,500,000 per year. A 10% decrease reduces this figure by $25,000 per year.

Obviously some additional analysis was needed. A much more compelling business case can be made when nonfinancial metrics are shown as quantitative improvements in business performance, or better yet, when they can be dollarized as they were here.

Often times this type of analysis will lead to the conclusion that the monetary benefits produced are modest at best. Being more aggressive in making projections in nonfinancial metrics will certainly have a more pronounced monetary impact. When accepting and illustrating more aggressive nonfinancial metrics, be sure they are realistic. If they are not, then maybe additional benefits must be found or perhaps the software or process change is not realistic for the organization, at least in financial terms.

Assumptions, Risks, and Contingencies

This section of the investment proposal is about making disclosures that are related to the business case that is being made. When any business case is constructed, a number of important assumptions are being made at the same time. The business case presentation should include commentary about these assumptions. Such assumptions are often important, driving forces that will prove to be critical success factors for the project.

In my experience, I have seen internal personnel availability and formal training programs are early assumptions made that somehow are shortchanged throughout the life of a software package implementation. For example, internal personnel availability during implementation has a direct impact on containing consulting costs, while training has a direct impact on post-implementation support costs. Also note that software packages often fail to realize their promised benefits for an organization because of inadequate training initiatives.

A business case calls for making assumptions and arbitrary judgments as well as for developing new data, particularly information to support such assumptions and judgments. This implies a somewhat arbitrary nature to the business case. It means that any two analysts, working independently, could evaluate the same investment differently. There is the potential for two radically different analyses. In both cases, the underlying arithmetic for each would be correct. For example, we often hear about a financial or investment analyst's buy rating for a given stock. These ratings can vary widely between analysts. Each analyst will make different assumptions about the firm's future financial structure and ultimately its financial performance. This results in entirely different opinions about a given stock's future price.

In closing, the assumptions made that are germane to the business case presentation must be presented. For instance, some of the more significant assumptions that will affect the financial impact of a project will include:

- The size of the project team
- The duration of the project
- The percentage of the project team who are employees versus consultants
- The percentage of time each employee devotes to the project exclusively
- The goodness of fit of the software
- The type of rollout (e.g., rolling out all at once — the big bang — versus a planned, staged, or evolutionary rollout of the package into all business units or locations or for all processes)
- The organization's WACC
- The organization's required ROI or hurdle rate

This list is not comprehensive. Each of these assumptions will have a dramatic impact on a project's cash flow or attractiveness as an investment. The longer a project takes, the more it will cost. Starting, stopping, and restarting a project will add to its overall cost. Using hired help (i.e., consultants) will be more expensive than using internal help. This presumes they are available at the commitment levels necessary. Making more or fewer modifications will impact the project's overall cost as well.

BUILDING THE BUSINESS CASE: AN EPILOGUE

A significant aspect of this chapter was the presentation of a framework that would be useful for making a financially driven business case to acquire and implement a business application software package. Some cautions are in order. Although I can offer guidance on how to build a business case, I cannot assure you that your proposal will be accepted. Building a business case is never easy. The arguments for significant business change or a major capital investment must be compelling, persuasive, financially sound, and above all else, doable. Your proposal must ultimately speak to all of these elements.

Rejection of your proposal on either objective or on subjective grounds is still possible. Some examples of why perfectly sound business cases are rejected (or possibly tabled) include:

- The general business or economic climate. (Recessions are bad for business and even more so for new capital investments).
- Political instability (usually a factor for operations in certain countries outside the United States).
- Internal politics. Yes, this happens even at the highest levels.
- A pending, though unannounced business restructuring, merger or acquisition.
- Poor quality, incomplete, or a substance-lacking business case.
- Your personal creditability.

From this list only the last two scenarios are under your direct control. Throughout this chapter I have emphasized ways to strengthen both.

7

UNDERSTANDING SOFTWARE PACKAGE INFRASTRUCTURE

UNDERSTANDING SOFTWARE PACKAGE INFRASTRUCTURE

When I first began outlining the contents for this book I did not anticipate needing a chapter on technological infrastructure. As I reviewed the contents of my original white paper that spurred the development of this book, I discovered that many of the assumptions I made then about the technological underpinnings affecting software packages had changed. I felt that such a chapter would bring added value and new perspectives on this rapidly changing aspect of the packaged software marketplace.

This chapter provides a fundamental understanding of the technical infrastructure behind a typical state-of-the-art or modern, commercial, off-the-shelf business application software package. The technical infrastructure behind a software package represents the collection of standards and software technologies that facilitates the operation of the software package itself.

If your background is from a business or operational perspective, this chapter probably sounds like a real sleeper to you. An understanding of a software package's technological infrastructure is important background information, even for a nontechnical person working on the software package selection and implementation team. Someone with an information systems technology background may only want to glance at this chapter before proceeding to Chapter 8. For other readers, this chapter is considered a prerequisite for Chapter 8. Perhaps most important to all readers of this book is that this chapter provides a list of critical questions related to a software package's technical infrastructure that should be asked of any prospective vendor.

TECHNICAL INFRASTRUCTURE: THE CRITICAL QUESTIONS TO ASK

As previously mentioned, the technical infrastructure behind a typical state-of-the-art, commercial, off-the-shelf software package represents a collection of standards and software technologies that facilitates the operation of the software package. What are the important standards and software technologies that a business application system should embrace today? The best way to address that question is through a series of technology-focused questions asked of prospective vendors regarding their candidate systems. These questions include:

- Is the software package open system based?
- Does the software package embrace the client server architecture model?
- Is the software package event-driven or object based?
- Is the software package component based?
- Does the software package use the relational database model?
- Does the software package provide for integration with legacy systems and other software packages?
- Does the package provide for interoperability with other software packages?
- Does the software package support web deployment?
- Does the package provide for migration of data from existing legacy systems and other software packages?

This chapter will provide lucid explanations of each of these infrastructure characteristics. It will also offer brief explanations as to why these infrastructure characteristics are important to the buyer of a commercial off-the-shelf software package in today's business and technical environment. The next chapter can be best thought of as a strategy discussion and is based upon the topics introduced in this chapter.

THE GOAL: INTEROPERABILITY

Technology buyers are increasingly demanding choices. In short, they want the freedom to choose from a litany of technology products and technology providers that can best satisfy their current and future business requirements. Buyers today want choices in computer architectures, hardware platforms or vendors, operating systems, database infrastructures, and increasingly, business application software packages as well. Buyers are no longer committed to doing business with a single supplier on an exclusive basis. In short, the technology buy is increasingly becoming a commodity buy.

For computer hardware, operating systems, databases, and systems software, this marketplace commoditization is in full swing. The large number of business failures, mergers and acquisitions, the price wars, and fluctuating stock prices are tell-tale signs of such. With regard to business application software packages, these same market forces have not yet had their full impact on this market. All indications are that the business application software package market is now yielding as well. Chapter 8 will discuss some of the changes emerging in the industry that will foster interoperability.

HARDWARE PLATFORMS AND OPEN SYSTEMS

Traditionally, larger computer manufacturing companies, such as IBM, have not been known for openly sharing access to one another's main control program, operating system, or computer architecture. For instance, the IBM AS/400 (now the i series), a popular computer platform among many middle market businesses, uses both a proprietary hardware architecture and operating system called OS/400. The AS/400 also features an integrated relational database architecture referred to as DB/400.

The rules of the game for computer manufacturers have been changing over the past decade. Like its bigger brother, the IBM mainframe computer, the AS/400 midrange computer has been losing momentum in the marketplace. Although microprocessors spawned the personal computer revolution, they initially had little impact on the large computer market. Microprocessors have advanced in speed and microprocessor operating systems have gained multiprocessing and multitasking capabilities. These platforms are now able to process vast amounts of work, especially when they are connected together, either as a massively parallel processor or as a series of networked processors.

As a result of these hardware advances, organizations are increasingly adopting microprocessor-based computers and computer networks instead of selecting midrange or mainframe computers. At the same time, new computer buyers are increasingly demanding so-called open systems.

When Is a Hardware Platform Considered an Open System?

The open system hardware architecture or computer architecture, is an operating platform that generally permits use of one or more commercially available operating systems, such as UNIX, LINUX, or Microsoft Windows NT/2000, instead of proprietary operating systems, such as IBM's OS/400. Open systems are perceived to provide choices — choices that are said to not exist when relying on proprietary or vendor-specific computer architectures.

Over the past decade, computer manufacturers, especially those that cater to the midrange market, have increasingly embraced the UNIX operating system. For instance, midrange computer makers NCR and Hewlett Packard are two companies that have embraced UNIX as their primary commercial operating system. Most recently, IBM itself has made significant statements and investments embracing LINUX — widely considered the most open operating system — as its cross-platform operating system. For now IBM has chosen to retain its existing mainframe and midrange architectures while adding processors that are capable of running the UNIX operating system. It still offers microprocessor-based servers that can run the Microsoft Windows NT-based operating system.

It is also not surprising that many previously successful computer manufacturers that hung on to proprietary architectures have either gone out of business or merged with stronger, open architecture rivals over the past decade. Two examples include Digital Equipment Corporation, which merged with Compaq Computer Corporation, and Wang Laboratories, which left the computer manufacturing business all together. It should also be noted that both Compaq Computer Corporation and NCR Corporation are but two computer manufacturing companies that have in recent years abandoned some or all of their proprietary computer architectures in favor of an Intel or compatible microprocessor architecture.

Even more recently, Compaq has abandoned the Alpha platform, a key asset it acquired from its acquisition of Digital Equipment Corporation a few years back. In addition, Hewlett Packard will retire its long-standing HP-3000 processor architecture over the next several years. A good working definition for a truly open system is that it is largely platform and operating system independent. It is best to pick a computer architecture that is widely embraced. For instance, the leading hardware technology platforms in the server market today include Sun Microsystems, IBM (proprietary and Intel-based processor architectures), Compaq (proprietary and Intel-based processor architectures), and Hewlett Packard (proprietary and Intel-based processor architectures).

The industry trend is away from proprietary processor architectures. Outside of Sun or the IBM AS/400 (known as the i-series nowadays), I recommend avoiding proprietary processor architectures, especially given the Compaq–Hewlett Packard merger or the possible ramifications if this merger fails to materialize. Needless to say, the integration of these two companies causes many concerns. With that said, I also need to make my own personal bias clear for using the IBM AS/400 or i-series products as an application and database server. This platform exhibits high levels of industrial grade performance and reliability. In my experience, it is generally superior to the results achieved on other platforms.

WHEN IS A SOFTWARE PACKAGE CONSIDERED AN OPEN SYSTEM?

For any commercial off-the-shelf software package to be considered an open system, it should be capable of minimally operating under both the Windows NT and UNIX operating systems in today's market. More and more, businesses are demanding that any commercial off-the-shelf software package they buy operate under multiple operating systems. In most cases, you must license a specific variant of the software package for your chosen operating system. If that is the case, it is important to understand what the installed base of users is for that operating system. If the vendor does not have a dominant installed base on the hardware platform, operating system, or database one prefers, then proceed with caution, if at all.

Consider this sad, but true story: PeopleSoft, in an attempt to penetrate the middle market, introduced an AS/400 version of their flagship enterprise resource planning (ERP) software product several years ago. The AS/400 version of PeopleSoft failed to catch on, largely because PeopleSoft did not have strong manufacturing functionality, while the manufacturing sector has been traditionally a strong market for the AS/400 architecture. In a relatively short period of time, PeopleSoft stopped selling and supporting the AS/400 version of its software.

The moral of this story: Understand what remedies, if any, you have under your software warranty, license, or software maintenance agreement should the vendor abandon the platform you have initially purchased the software for. In an ideal world, you will be allowed to cross over to another platform without incurring the full cost (if any) of a new license. If not, consider negotiating this into your purchase contract with the vendor.

Software Follows Hardware toward the Open Systems Model

Generally speaking, computer hardware technological change has occurred at a much faster pace than our ability to leverage these changes through improved computer software. Not surprisingly, as I mentioned earlier, software vendors are as a rule almost always a generation or so behind with their product innovations. As a result, the movement toward open systems has proceeded at a relatively slow rate. As elegant and simple a concept as the open systems model is, it involves adding layers of complexity behind the scenes and therein is the paradox of the open system model — greater complexity, in fact significantly greater complexity. In addition, lack of agreement on standards adds to this complexity. However, software package vendors are beginning to embrace open system standards, including the use of extensible markup language- (XML) based, plug-and-play software components — concepts that will be introduced later in this chapter.

Why Are Software Vendors behind in Meeting Marketplace Demands?

Let us consider ERP software, which is easily the oldest generation software package category discussed in this book. Generally speaking, the ERP software package market has existed for roughly 25 years. During this run, the typical ERP software vendors have seen their product mature in both features and in underlying complexity. This expansion of features and complexity has been largely mandated by a combination of market forces and regulatory changes. Vendors have to continually improve their product to meet the expectations of their current clients and prospects. As a result, most ERP systems are large, complex systems comprised of hundreds, if not thousands, of computer programs that represent millions of lines of computer program instructions or code. Given this underlying complexity, most ERP software package vendors have been slow in reengineering or retrofitting their systems around new infrastructures or technologies, such as the open systems model.

Consider several examples. First, consider J.D. Edwards, one of the leading vendors of ERP software for middle market businesses. J.D. Edwards used to be a one-product company. It was not so long ago, that their World software product would run only on an IBM AS/400 midrange computer system. Over the past 6 years, J.D. Edwards has successfully reengineered its underlying software functionality to operate on many computer architectures and not simply on an AS/400 computer. This was a significant and painful exercise for J.D. Edwards. Their open systems product, referred to as OneWorld, was released prematurely. Early adopters of OneWorld encountered quality and performance problems. Also, some features, available previously in their AS/400 software, were not ready until much later. J.D. Edwards was able to get a handle on these problems, and today OneWorld is a highly regarded package throughout the industry.

In the early 1990s, German software vendor SAP revolutionized two markets. First, SAP successfully ported their complex mainframe-based ERP system, referred to as R/2, into the client server world. SAP R/3 became the first serious or industrial strength business application software available for the relatively new client server platform. Reengineering hundreds or thousands of programs and the accompanying millions of lines of program code is a daunting feat. Many credit SAP as being the first software vendor for being able to successfully do this.

On a final note, prior to the introduction of SAP R/3, client server technology was not taken seriously as an operating platform for major business application processing systems at middle market and larger organizations. SAP R/3 downsized to a more affordable platform. This allowed SAP to become a formidable new competitor, even if only by way of comparison, for old line middle market ERP vendors and packages, including System Software Associates (BPCS), J.D. Edwards (World) and MAPICS (IBM). In short, SAP raised the bar of functionality for ERP software, regardless of platform or price point.

WHY CHOOSE UNIX AS AN OPERATING SYSTEM?

UNIX is generally regarded as the first open system operating system. UNIX wins this honor by being the first commercial operating system that was embraced by and incorporated into the products of multiple business computer vendors. UNIX was an operating system that was first created by Bell Labs and was originally intended to manage the complex operations of computers that served as telephone network switches. It has typically received high marks in efficiency and performance as an operating system. Unlike proprietary operating systems, the UNIX operating system is considered an open system, meaning the operating system's basic command structure has been standardized. The source code, or raw computer instructions, for UNIX and its commands are readily published and in theory can be modified or extended as needed. The UNIX operating system is itself written in the C programming language.

What about LINUX?

It should also be noted that increasingly, business computer users are adopting LINUX, a popular UNIX operating system derivative that is sometimes referred to as the poor man's UNIX. Unfortunately, few software packages have rushed to support the LINUX operating system. That could start to change. IBM has recently decided to parlay a move toward the LINUX operating system across its product line. This could be the nucleus for a new push by software vendors to make their packages operate in LINUX environments.

How Does LINUX Differ from UNIX?

LINUX is a variation of UNIX. Prior to LINUX, if you wanted the UNIX operating system, your choice was to license the UNIX operating system for a specific computer, usually from the hardware vendor. Unlike the

Microsoft Windows NT operating system or IBM's OS/400 operating system, which are both tightly controlled, proprietary operating systems, every vendor that adopts either UNIX or LINUX has likely made extensions to the basic operating system. This makes it compatible with their hardware and not so compatible with others. A modern software package relies to a great deal on infrastructure software, including the operating system, the database, and middleware, All of these software pieces must be compatible with LINUX before a software package can lay claim to full LINUX compatibility.

WHY CHOOSE WINDOWS NT AS AN OPERATING SYSTEM?

The Microsoft Windows NT operating system has become a pervasive force in corporate computing environments. When first introduced, Windows NT was not considered stable or robust enough for business-critical processes. Now the product has matured into a full-featured, industrial strength operating system. The hallmark of Windows NT is that it will operate on virtually all Intel processor based computers. Recently, Microsoft has made claims of 99.999% uptime for Windows 2000 Server, the current version of Microsoft's server-based Windows NT operating system. My personal experiences with other Microsoft operating systems causes me to doubt this availability claim.

While Windows NT has become a serious alternative to UNIX over the last few years, Windows NT is not a truly open system, as Microsoft does not make the Windows NT source code available. A fairer comparison would be between Microsoft Windows NT and the PICK operating system. The PICK operating system is generally considered the original multiple-platform, proprietary commercial operating system. For many years, it was the operating system of choice among midrange computer makers who were competing against the IBM AS/400 or its predecessors.

There is one final note regarding the use of Intel-based platforms using Windows NT or the so-called Wintel platform. This powerful combination has helped bring the power of feature-rich, commercial off-the-shelf software package systems to an entirely new market segment — the lower end of the middle market. Previously, smaller and middle market companies ignored higher-end software products because they generally operated on more expensive, midrange computing platforms, such as the AS/400. The so-called Wintel client server platform has helped to change the rules. It has effectively allowed tier 1 and tier 2 software vendors to down-market their products, which in many cases is exactly what they have done.

WHAT PROGRAMMING LANGUAGE DOES THE VENDOR USE?

Another dimension of openness is the programming language chosen by the software vendor. For many years, three computer-programming languages dominated the business application software market: COBOL, RPG (Report Program Generator), and BASIC. All of these languages originated in the 1960s when mainframe computers, batch processing, flat files, keypunch cards, and flowcharting were popular. In the 1970s, keypunches gave way to CRT terminals and mainframes to midrange and minicomputers. In the 1980s, flat files gave way to relational databases, while batch processing was increasingly replaced by interactive processing. All of these changes were handled primarily by making extensions or revisions to these programming languages.

Three companies have had a profound impact on how computers are programmed and how business application software is expected to operate in today's marketplace. First was Xerox. However, Xerox never fully capitalized on the use of the graphical user interface (GUI) and mouse pointing devices credited to their Palo Alto Research Center (PARC). Apple Computer introduced these devices in the mid-1980s with their Lisa and Macintosh computers. Although technologically sleek, unfortunately for Apple, its proprietary architecture held back widespread adoption of their technology into the business world. It really was not until the introduction of Microsoft and its Windows 95 operating system that business began taking GUIs seriously.

As the use of GUIs in business application software began to take hold, a different breed of computer programming language has emerged and these new languages now dominate. The new generation of computer programming language is object oriented. The object orientation makes it easier to use for event driven programming associated with the GUI. C, C++, and Java are the three dominant object-oriented programming languages along with an object-oriented version of BASIC, a Microsoft product referred to as Visual BASIC.

Software Packages and Java

The world is increasingly moving toward adoption of the Java language. Java is widely considered the programming language of the Internet. Java was originally created by Sun Microsystems and is considered a portable language. Interest in Java is taking on new meaning as the paradigm shifts to thin clients and browser-based presentation. Even SAP AG, which has long used a proprietary language called ABAP/4, has recently embraced Java for use with its ERP software system, R/3.

Why does a browser-based model have such wide appeal for large commercial systems? In one short phrase, it is all about total cost of operations. A browser-based model can operate in a thin-client environment, the benefits of which will be discussed later in this chapter. Although many thought the network computer (NC) was dead, it is just now catching on in the business community.

What Makes Java Special?

Java is considered machine-independent, which the business world likes, and it a form of openness. Java obtains machine-independence through a middleware software component referred to as the JAVA virtual machine. This JAVA virtual machine is written specifically for each computer hardware platform. Any JAVA program will run universally on any implementation of the JAVA virtual machine, affording maximum portability across platforms.

The JAVA virtual machine is by no means a new idea. A similar concept existed with the PASCAL language "P" code compilers that were popular in the early and mid-1980s. Unlike the "P" code compilers, the JAVA virtual machine has enjoyed much greater industry support and gains acceptance in the marketplace on an almost daily basis. The move toward Java is largely fueled by the growing influence of the Internet on basic business models, including business computing, where the trend is toward browser-based delivery of business software applications.

OBJECTS: WHAT THEY ARE AND WHY THEY ARE IMPORTANT

Arguably, object-oriented software development is one of the most radical changes to the design, development, and deployment of business application software since the introduction of high-level computer programming languages in the early 1960s. Over the past decade, the importance, acceptance, and availability of object-oriented software has grown dramatically.

Since I suspect that many of my readers will have an engineering or technical background, I have chosen an appropriate analogy to introduce objects. As a look back in life, my first love in life was drafting, and it was not so many years ago that I had trained as a draftsman. At the time we used T-squares mounted on drafting boards to make parallel lines with mechanical pencils. If you were lucky, you had a drafting machine, which was really nothing more than a deluxe T-square allowing for infinite angles, that was mounted on an arm attached to the drafting board. Foul smelling copies of the completed drawing — a blueprint — could be made with a blueprint-making machine. In just a few years technology has completely altered the process. Needless to say, my drafting skills are now considered obsolete.

Computer aided drawing (CAD) has fundamentally changed the way that a draftsman, engineer, or architect prepares a technical drawing. Technical drawings are now made on a computer screen using a mouse or similar input device and are subsequently printed on a plotter or printer. The end result — a completed drawing — is the same in form and content, but the technique for completing that drawing was fundamentally altered by new technology. In addition, the productivity of a draftsman, engineer, or architect has been greatly enhanced as CAD has matured. Now portions of drawings, usually a standardized symbol such as a valve, motor, door, or window, can be stored and reused repeatedly in related or in completely new, unrelated drawings.

The reason for my short trip down memory lane is simply this: Object-oriented software development is having a similar, revolutionary impact on the software development community. It is impacting systems analysts, programmers, and software engineers in much the same way as CAD had on draftsmen, engineers, and architects several decades earlier. The end result remains a completed computer program that completes a specific business process or procedure, but the technique for creating that program has been fundamentally altered.

Of particular note is that the objects of the software development world are akin to the standardized symbols in the CAD example. Similar to dragging and dropping drawing symbols from a standard symbol palette onto a drawing image, software developers can achieve substantial pro-ductivity breakthroughs by reusing software objects. Unfortunately, reusing software objects has not quite developed to the state where it is a simple and straightforward drag and drop process. Object-oriented software development has fundamentally altered how software packages are being designed and built today.

Almost any discussion of object-oriented software development can quickly become far too technical than is necessary. I have purposefully kept the following discussion at a conceptually high level. There is certainly more to objects than what will be discussed in this book. For the purpose of understanding the impact of objects on the packaged software marketplace, the information provided here should be more than adequate.

Prior to the advent of object-oriented software development, some would likely argue that software was not really engineered. In reality, this is not a completely true statement. If most large-scale, complex software systems had not been previously engineered — at least in some manner — it is unlikely that computers in general would have ever reached their current stature in today's business world. It is my contention that object-oriented software development represents a shift in thinking about how software is engineered rather than a shift to engineered software. In fact, there are a number of earlier contributions that led up to object-oriented programming or software development. These developments include:

- Modular and structured programming techniques that emerged during the 1970s
- The emergence of program or code generators in the early 1980s
- The emergence of computer aided software engineering (CASE) tools during the late 1980s and early 1990s

These developments represent significant milestones within the software industry's evolution toward building engineered software centered around reusable components or objects.

Objects Promote Software by Assembly

Drawing parallels to manufacturing, it can be said that object-oriented software development represents software by assembly. Think of object-oriented software development as a way to construct computer programs out of prefabricated parts, or components, as they are known in manufacturing terms. These components are simply referred to as objects in software development. Software objects are not quite as interchangeable as manufactured component parts are — at least not yet. The greatest impact that object-oriented software development has had to date has been in the area of offering software developers substantial increases in their productivity. This has resulted in shorter times to market for software packages.

Taking the notion of software by assembly one step further, much of the software development literature today frequently speaks of component-based development (CBD), which is closely related to object-oriented software development. A more precise definition of CBD and an assessment of the impact that CBD is having on software packages in general will be discussed in the next section of this chapter.

What Is the Importance of Objects?

Standardized parts or components in manufacturing have been heralded as one of the great innovations of the industrial revolution. Such components allowed for efficient, standardized production on an assembly line basis, providing previously impossible levels of speed, quantity, and interchangeability.

By using objects, software development is making similar strides toward an assembly line process of building software. When computer programs are constructed from preexisting objects or components, they can be created faster, cheaper, and with more predictable results.

Object-oriented software development can provide tremendous benefits. This is even more so the case for software package developers. The opportunity or demand for reuse of large portions of the underlying software code in a complex, feature-rich, integrated software package is great.

How Object-Oriented Software Differs from Traditional Software

The primary and most important difference is that object-oriented programs are event driven. In a traditional procedural language-based program, the programmer had preprogrammed the computer program to operate in a fairly rigid and specific sequence. By contrast, in an event-driven program, the user of the program controls what happens next. The events themselves are implemented through objects and methods, which will be discussed in the next section. The fully navigable GUI is based upon the event-driven program model.

Behind the scenes, programs that use a GUI operate much differently than their forerunners. Prior to being GUI-based, computer programs were largely procedural or sequence driven. As a matter of fact, all of the pre-GUI programming languages are now simply frequently referred to as procedural languages. In a procedural language, the computer program is simply a list of computer program instructions that are executed sequentially, on a step-by-step basis. It can be said that activities carried out by the computer program flowed according to procedure.

In a GUI-based computer program, the program flow becomes event driven, with those events being discretionary and more fully controlled by the computer user. For instance in a GUI-based program, the cursor can be at any position on the screen — from the user's perspective the program is idling. By clicking on a mouse button, the program comes alive. The program action is completely random and must anticipate that a user can request from any number of tasks or events to be performed. Hence we have a definition for the event-driven program model.

Before continuing, it is important to note that just because a software system has a GUI or is browser based does not necessarily mean that the underlying core application programs are object oriented. This just means that the program that a software user communicates or interacts with is object oriented. A good question to ask any prospective software vendor is: Is the entire system — not just the portions of the software — used to access the functions available from the system (referred to as "client side software" in the client/server world) object oriented?

Screen Scraping: Cheat to Win

As mentioned previously, a software package need not be event driven or object oriented just because it has a GUI. In recent years, many software packages have been retrofitted to provide GUI support largely through what is known as a screen scraper. Screen scrapers are programs that extract information out of transactions intended for user interaction on a green screen terminal. That terminal will present this information to an end user through a local workstation program that provides the desired GUI look and feel. Typically, end users manipulate any data presented using this graphical user interface program, then click a submit or send button, within the GUI program. The final click then invokes the reformatting of the information and its subsequent reformatting into a green screen format in order to update the software package's database using the underlying green screen based transaction logic.

Screen scraping is an admittedly sneaky, yet effective way to remediate old software code in order to conform to present day user interaction standards. It should be noted that many software vendors used this approach as a bridge or interim solution while they rewrote their green screen applications into event driven, GUI-based solutions. A few vendors have stopped short of a complete rewrite of their legacy products. Early screen scrapers had both performance and presentation issues. Most of these problems no longer exist in screen scraper based applications.

Objects, Methods, Classes and Inheritance: The Building Blocks of Object-Oriented Software

Objects

In an object-oriented software system, people, places, and things — including business processes, events, and documents — are represented as objects. The manner in which this occurs is to specify the characteristics that uniquely describe any given object used by the system during the software design process.

Methods

There is another important difference between traditional, procedural language programming and object-oriented computer programming. Procedural language programming clearly distinguishes and separates procedures — the line-by-line instructions to the computer that executes a business procedure or process for the user — from the underlying business data. By contrast, in the object-oriented world, the methods or line-by-line instructions to the computer can be combined or encapsulated with the underlying business data into a single entity — referred to as an object.

Classes and Inheritance

Other characteristics distinguish object-based software from procedural-based software as well. The first characteristic is the concept of classes and inheritance. This concept of class can also be related directly to a manufacturing assembly line. The class is akin to an assembly line where similar items, such as automobiles, are produced. A class produces objects of a particular form, or instances of a class, as they are called in object-oriented software development. For example, instances might be automobiles of the same model, but vary by color or body style. The underlying automobiles might be based upon the same chassis, use the same drive train (engine and transmission) components, but use different body panels and interior components.

We use a bill of materials to list all of the components in a manufactured component or final product. If we were to construct such a bill of materials — essentially a list of the underlying classes — for a modern, object-oriented computer program, there would be an important and obvious difference. There only needs to be one physical instance or occurrence of a class in the software bill of materials. This is regardless of how many times the computer program itself might directly or indirectly make use of that class. Unlike a manufactured product that requires a physical unit for every reference or use of that underlying component, manufactured software is a logical assembly, more so than a physical assembly of underlying components.

Reusability and Composition

An important aspect of assembling computer programs using objects is the creation of a series of reusable classes or system building blocks. These reusable classes are then used as the foundation from which an entire system is constructed. When a class is created, it is created only once and reused as often as it is needed. In addition, any changes made to a class are immediate and impact all other instances that make use of that underlying class. The more classes that already exist, the less time will be spent on defining and assembling new classes.

Another important characteristic of object-oriented software is that classes can be defined as special cases of each other. When this occurs, a new class is created. At the same time, the new class inherits all of the properties of the underlying classes that are also referred to as subclasses. This leads to another way to think of reuse. I will again use a manufacturing analogy: the object-oriented software program represents the ultimate indented or multilevel bill of materials.

When objects are built from or contain other objects they are said to be composite objects. Composite objects have an important link to the business world. In particular, they link how we perceive, think about, and expect to manipulate information about real world objects, such as people, places, things, and documents. The composite object forces the underlying computer software to form these same kind of natural, real world links or associations between objects as a person would. When you are using an object-oriented program, a simple click on most fields will yield access to another program where values for a given field can be found, if not added or maintained as well.

The Impact of Object-Oriented Software on the Information Technology Department

Object-oriented programming requires not only a different skill set, but a different mindset as well. It is a process that is considerably different from traditional procedural language programming. The differences are analogous to the earlier drafting versus CAD example I used. To an organization considering the jump to client server, object-oriented software, this will be nothing less than a revolutionary change. It will mean that any procedure language programmers in your ranks will need to learn and embrace the new ways of the object oriented world.

Transitioning your technical staff will require education and patience. Initially, they will not be operating at the same level of productivity until they build up their confidence and experience levels with object-oriented programming tools and techniques. This can be a very difficult transition. In the object-oriented world, less emphasis is placed on coding or writing the line-by-line instructions of a program. More emphasis is placed on the overall design of the software and ultimately on the assembly of programs from predefined objects or components. In many cases, this is being done using visual-oriented tools that are akin to the CAD/CAM tools of the object-oriented world. In fact, these tools have a special name: CASE.

Several popular examples of CASE tools used by software engineers and programmers today include Rational Rose from Rational Software and TogetherJ from TogetherSoft. Many software vendors have built proprietary CASE tools for use in building object-oriented software.

COMPONENT-BASED SOFTWARE DEVELOPMENT

CBD is largely an extension of object-oriented software development. It is a method for architecting an entire system, while object-oriented software development applies to how the underlying computer programs are actually written. CBD permits maximum reuse of the underlying software's functionality. The key advantage of selecting a software package that incorporates and exploits component-based software architecture is built-in interoperability. — Through the software architecture, interoperability with other systems is both anticipated and provided for.

What Is a Software Component?

A component is defined as a unit of software that performs a given process or function. The hallmark of component-based software is the use of interfaces. The component provides specific, predefined interfaces for dealing with the outside world — usually other programs. The use of an interface in effect wraps or masks the internal workings of a given software process or function. The only way to access the functionality or process provided by the software component is through the use of this interface. Another way to perceive of a software component is as a black box, delivering its core functionality to other software and ultimately to software users on demand or an event-driven basis. Component-based software development represents a so-called services-oriented approach to providing software functionality.

Why Do Software Components Matter?

The objective of component-based software development is simple enough — to construct plug-and-play software. For business application software users, this has several ramifications, including agility and interoperability. The relevance of software components to business application software packages is that through software architecture design, entire business processes can be decoupled and unitized into small slices of business functionality. These small slices of unitized business functionality can then be reconnected as desired or needed, providing maximum flexibility in designing and redesigning business processes. Of course, it is still necessary to exercise common sense — referred to as business logic or business rules — when reconnecting the software functionality. Component-based software has strong relevance to the way an organization must function in today's business world — component-based software provides agility — the ability of the business application software package to be reconfigured or adapted quickly to changes in business processes in order to meet new marketplace challenges.

In *Realizing e-Business with Components*, Paul Allen said it best: "The most successful business components are those that can be 'rewired' in many configurations in effective response to business change." Using component-based software architecture promotes and provides for interoperability through interfaces. The use of component-based software architecture by itself does not fulfill the challenge of interoperability. Later in this chapter, some additional challenges to interoperability will be discussed.

CLIENT SERVER COMPUTING

This section provides a high-level introduction to the client server architecture. There are several models or flavors of client server architecture. Often times, the availability or support for a given client server architecture model is an important part of the appeal of a specific software package to an organization.

What is Client Server Computing?

In its most simplistic form, client server computing is a computer architecture that involves clients requesting services from a server. Unfortunately, client server computing is not quite as simple as this definition might lead you to believe.

Although many in the information technology industry are quick to associate the personal computer and the UNIX operating system as the defining enablers of client server computing, this is simply untrue. Actually, there are several simple, but far more important, software engineering techniques that are the true underpinnings of client server computing. These important software-engineering techniques include:

- Modularity
- Standardization
- Messaging

A brief description of each of these software-engineering techniques follows.

Modularity

Traditionally, computer programs were written on the premise that one program could do everything. As business application systems became more sophisticated, the programs grew larger, ran slower, and were increasingly difficult to maintain. Software engineers developed modular programming techniques to solve this one program problem. In the modular program scenario, a main or master program would call or rely on any number of smaller, usually single-purpose programs or modules to perform a given programming operation. Component-based software is a logical extension of this modularity concept.

Messaging

For modular programming to work, another important technique was needed; the modules needed a way to communicate with one another.

Initially, this idea of computer programs passing communicating with one another was referred to as parameter passing. Today, the term messaging is used to describe the program to program communication process.

Standardization

It stands to reason that if messages are being sent back and forth between programs, some formats or standards were needed to ensure the usability of the information within any given message. Unfortunately, this is an area within the software industry that remains a work in process. Standards, including electronic data interchange (EDI), extensible markup language (XML), and structured query language (SQL), all discussed within this chapter, are examples of some of the established or emerging standards found in the computer industry.

Applying These Concepts to Networks of Computers

Once software engineers found and perfected these techniques for breaking apart programs, it stood to reason that these separated parts of the once single-business application program no longer needed to run on the same computer as did the other, now separated parts, of the original business application program. Relying once again on these same techniques, this is truly the entry point to the client server model.

In the client server scenario, it is possible to have client processes or programs and server processes or programs scattered through a network of physically interconnected computers. It can be said that the programs are running on the most appropriate hardware or software platforms as it relates to their role or function in the overall computing process.

For example, database management server software could be operated on a computer processor that is specially designed, configured, and tuned to perform database queries. A more detailed look at what the roles and responsibilities are for both the client and server in the client server architecture follows.

What the Client Does

The client represents the front-end or user-interface portion of the client server application. The client has responsibility for the GUI. Normally a part of the client operating system, the GUI manager detects user actions, manages the display of the form or window on the display, and the display of any data in that window or form. Application programs rely on the GUI manager.

The client validates data entered by the user and sends service requests to the server. In some instances, the client can actually execute application programs that contain business logic processes as well. The client is also responsible for some lower-level processes, including managing the local resources that a user interacts with. Typically, these resources will include the desktop computer and its display monitor, keyboard, and any peripherals (e.g., printer).

What the Server Does

The server is best viewed as a forum or platform for sharing of common resources and executing common processes, tasks, or procedures. The server fulfills client requests by performing the task requested. Typically, the server will receive requests for its services from client programs. Server-based processing can take on many dimensions. The server process performs the back-end tasks that are common among business application systems. Examples of what server programs are responsible for include executing operations, such as database retrievals and updates; managing data integrity; and dispatching responses to these client-initiated requests for services. Sometimes a server program will also execute a common processing or complex business processes, such as financial statement preparation or manufacturing planning.

Server-based processes may run across multiple, physical computers that are attached, or networked together. Server-based processes may also simply be a series of programs that are running on a sole, physical computer processor. For instance, in a networked setting, one physical server computer could be dedicated to providing application-related business processing services, while another physical server computer performs database management related services.

Basic Characteristics of Client Server Architectures

Client server architectures should exhibit the following basic characteristics:

- The client server environment should fully embrace the open system model. A typical client server architecture will be both diverse and multivendor.
- Client and server processes should communicate through a well-defined set of standard application program interfaces (APIs). Industry-wide standards have emerged for the messaging necessary to make client server architectures work.
- Another important characteristic of a client server system is scalability. The client server architecture can be scaled both

horizontally and vertically. Horizontal scaling means adding or removing client workstations with only a slight performance impact. Vertical scaling means migrating to larger and faster server machines or sharing of the computing workload among multiple server machines.

Most software packages support the above client server architecture characteristics to varying degrees.

Client Server Architectures

Several architectural models have emerged for client server computing. These architectures include two-tier, three-tier, and "N"-tier models. A brief explanation of each of these client server architectures follows.

The Two-Tier Architecture

A two-tier architecture is a very simple client server model. In a two-tier architecture, a client communicates directly to a server. Typically, the server handles all database management, while the client provides for all other processing. Two-tier architectures have been found not to scale well. This means that as transaction volume increases, the two-tier architecture is quickly saturated and overall system performance is depredated. To properly scale a client server system to users, a three-tier architecture is generally required. Figure 7.1 illustrates the two-tier client server architecture.

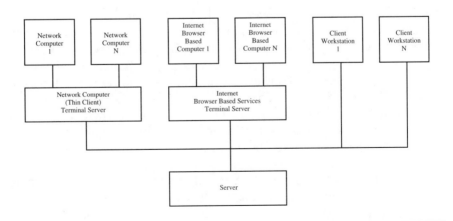

Figure 7.1 The Two-Tier Client Server Architecture

The Three-Tier Architecture

A three-tier architecture introduces another server, referred to as an agent, between the client and the server. The agent has several roles to fulfill in the three-tier architecture; the most important role is permitting the redistribution of workload. Typically, the client performs all presentation, or end-user interaction processes, while an application server handles business logic processing and a database server handles database management services.

The specific services the agent will typically provide in a three-tier client server model include:

■ Network traffic metering services, which monitor transactions and limit the number of simultaneous service requests, made to a given server.
■ Load balancing services that can distribute server requests, such as a batch process request for a report, to another, less utilized server for processing.
■ Intelligent mapping services that will map a single service request to a number of different servers, for instance, to an application server and to a database server, collate the results, and return a single response to the client.

Both three and "N"-tier client server based software packages must provide for these agent services. Figure 7.2 illustrates the three-tier client server architecture.

The "N"- Tier Architecture

The two-tier and three-tier models are the most common variations I have found to occur in practice. A third and somewhat more challenging architecture is the "N"-tier architecture. In an "N"-tier architecture, another level of complexity is added onto the three-tier client server architecture model. The "N"-tier architecture allows for the adding of more servers, referred to as workgroup servers that are typically remotely located servers. This design pushes data and processing out to the physical location where it is needed in order to improve overall system performance.

In an "N"-tier architecture, the agent performs an additional service. In the "N"-tier environment, the agent must also provide services for the replication and synchronization of data and executable programs across the client server network. These agent services are necessary to ensure that both the data and programs that are distributed across multiple clients and servers are kept synchronized. This preserves the overall integrity of the business applications that rely on the "N"-tier client server model.

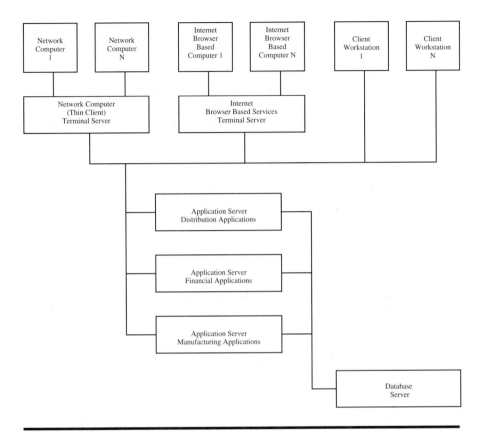

Figure 7.2 The Three-Tier Client Server Architecture

Fat Clients and Thin Clients

Thin clients, sometimes referred to as network computers (NCs), are gaining in popularity among industry advocates. If you have been involved in the computer industry for some time now, you have heard about network computers before. This time, the thin client or network computer is not considered to be a solution without a problem. In most of the sites where I have seen a three-tier client server architecture deployed, it is usually that way because of terminal servers rather than multiple application or database servers.

Many organizations are beginning to grow weary of the seemingly never-ending cycle of buying or upgrading large numbers of installed desktop workstations. In some cases, it is as frequent as every 2 years. The use of a fat client actually compounds the problem — it is entirely possible that upgrades or swap-outs of the desktop workstations used as fat clients might be needed with every application software upgrade.

The attraction of the thin client or network computer is that you replace powerful desktop workstations with bare bones, stripped-down computers. These thin clients handle a relatively small number of operations — the operation of the keyboard, mouse, display, and possibly a local printer and the display of information, is handled by the thin client, but everything else is handled by at least one terminal server. On the terminal server, a client session actually communicates with the network's server resources.

What Is Thin Client Computing?

Thin client server computing pushes all application, business logic processing, and program execution onto the server. The only work remaining for the thin client is to perform GUI manager activities and local desktop management and network connectivity tasks. The thin client plays a limited role, displaying information to the computer user from a server, retrieving user input, and forwarding user input to the server. The thin client is the client server equivalent of the dumb terminal.

Why Use Thin Client Computing?

There are three major advantages to thin client computing. First is the cost of ownership. Thin clients or so-called network computers are cheaper to acquire. Thin clients average about half the cost of a typical personal computer workstation. Second, network administration and management is centralized. Individual personal computer workstations generally require a significant amount of administration. A thin client does not require the same degree of hands-on administration over its service life. This lowered administration requirement may also favorably impact costs in environments with larger networks of clients.

What Is Bad about Thin Clients?

To be fair, thin client computing does have several drawbacks:

- The reliance on additional middleware is a consideration. This middleware adds overhead to the transaction, complexity to the network, and complicates the overall troubleshooting of any network-related problems.
- Typically, one or more additional servers will be needed to service thin clients. These servers are typically referred to as terminal servers. These additional servers will in turn add to the complexity of the network.

- The additional workload may saturate server capacity more quickly — something that a network of fat clients may not do. Fat clients actually off-load some of the processing demands from the application server to the local fat client. A key factor when selecting a thin client solution is how well the thin client middleware will perform load balancing among available terminal server resources.

Despite the challenges of a thin client architecture, momentum for its use is clearly growing.

Browser-Based Computing

There is a second trend at work that is further shifting the balance of opinion toward thin clients and network computers — the Internet. With the Internet, all that is really needed is a device that is capable of running the browser software. This is indeed something that most of the thin clients and network computers are capable of doing.

Increasingly, software buyers are demanding that software vendors provide a ready-made way to allow access to a software package's functionality using Internet-based technologies. Many software vendors have been scrambling in the post-Y2K era to modernize their software around Internet-based technologies in order to remain competitive.

In a web-enabled software package, the end user of the business application software package will typically rely on a personal computer or a network computer that is capable of running a web browser program (e.g., Microsoft Internet Explorer or Netscape Navigator). The end user's workstation must be networked through an organization's Intranet or through the Internet in order to access the organization's server computer where the software package resides. Figure 7.3 illustrates how the browser layer is added onto the software package in either a two- or three-tier architecture.

Client Server Communications

Connectivity is of paramount importance to both the open system model and the client server architecture. Connectivity allows one program, process, or device the ability to communicate with another program, process, or device. For instance, messaging and standardization, which were discussed earlier, provide for connectivity. Another important dimension of connectivity is transparency or the ability to communicate with another program, process, or device. This is regardless of where it is physically located or exactly what it is, as long as it communicates using the correct protocols.

A key enabling element of connectivity for client server communications is the computer or network operating system. The operating system provides services such as routing, distribution, messaging, file, print, and network management services. UNIX, OS/400, and Windows NT are representative of the operating systems that support client server communications.

The operating system relies on communication protocols to provide specific services related to connectivity. These communication protocols are divided into three groups: media, transport, and client server protocols. The operating system and other network service-related programs that run underneath the operating system provide both media and transport layer support needed by the software package.

Media protocols determine the type of physical connections used on a network. Some examples of media protocols include Ethernet, Token Ring, and Twisted-Pair. These standards apply to how devices are physically or electrically connected in a computer network. Typically, networks consist of wires and transmission equipment, establishing a link from the client to the server. Increasingly, Twisted-Pair is the media of choice.

The transport protocol provides the mechanism for moving packets of data from the client to the server. Although there are multiple transport protocols used in the industry, most software packages rely on the transmission control protocol/internet protocol (TCP/IP) as its transport protocol.

Middleware

Other layers of protocols are also involved in a client server architecture. These are typically called middleware layers. Remember one of my earlier comments in this chapter — openness breeds complexity. The required use of middleware is an excellent example of this trade-off. To make multiplatform openness a reality requires some very low-level and not very open, behind-the-scenes programming in order to glue everything together.

Communications Middleware

In the previous discussion of client server architecture we addressed clients requesting services of a given server through an agent. Actually, a special name has been given to these agents in the client server world — these agents are an example of a middleware component. Once a physical connection has been established and packets of data can be moved over the physical network, a final piece is needed — the client-server protocol. The client-server protocol establishes the rule that clients will use when

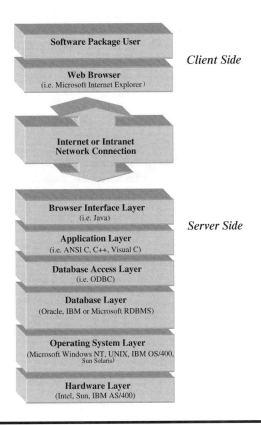

Figure 7.3 How Browsers Layer over the Client Server Based Software Package

requesting information and services from a server. It also establishes rules of how the server will reply to client requests.

A software package requires a middleware component or layer for message handling purposes between its clients and servers. Figure 7.3 is a good illustration of the layers of components or middleware, between the user or source of data and the database management system — the destination of data in a software package.

Database Middleware

Another important piece of middleware is also needed — the database middleware layer. The database middleware layer is the component that provides for software package database independence. For instance, the middleware layer provides a bridge to an open database connectivity-(ODBC) compliant database system. In addition to the ODBC software, which allows for SQL request processing, the software package vendor must also provide a middleware layer or driver for connection to a specific relational database. Without a driver present, the software package will simply not work with any ODBC-compliant relational database. The next section discusses the relational database model ODBC and SQL.

THE RELATIONAL DATABASE MANAGEMENT SYSTEM

Perhaps the most important characteristic underlying the vast majority, if not all, of today's commercial, off-the-shelf software packages is that behind the scenes, a relational database management system is employed. The relational database is a workhorse. It serves as the transaction processor, handling all aspects of organizing and storing all of the data essential to the operation of the software package.

The relational database model was first developed about three decades ago by C.J. Date at IBM Corporation. The relational database model gained widespread acceptance throughout the business community and in the software industry during the 1980s. Today three players dominate the relational database market:

- IBM Corporation with its DB/2, DB/400 and UDB products
- Microsoft Corporation with its Access and SQL Server database products
- Oracle Corporation with its ORACLE database product (currently known as version 9i)

It is important to note that at least in the case of these database systems and in almost all other cases with lesser-known, competing products, the database software is a completely separate software package. It must be licensed and purchased separate and apart from the business application software package.

In some cases, a software vendor distributes or bundles a run-time only license for the database software along with the vendor's software package. As a general rule, this is a practice common with low-end software packages. When using a run-time only version of a database, no changes to the underlying database are possible. It is my experience that in such cases where a run-time only database license is provided, the software package is both a proprietary and closed system. This means that in such cases, the vendor is unlikely to provide the source code to the underlying programs of the software package to the software buyer. This means that any nonvendor modification to or maintenance of the programs in the software package is next to impossible. Even large software vendors have been known to bundle a run-time only databases with their products to widen their appeal to cost-conscious buyers by billing it as an entry-level version of their system.

On a final note, the availability or lack of support for a given database architecture will have both cost and performance considerations that affect the organization's evaluation of any given software package. The remainder of this section provides a general overview on the relational databases model, its importance to software packages, and why an intimate understanding of the software package's data model is sometimes necessary.

The Spreadsheet Analogy

While most readers of this book are likely already familiar with the concept of the spreadsheet, they may not be familiar with relational database. The familiar spreadsheet format also lies at the core of relational database design. Underlying the relational database model are database tables which are, for all practical purposes, spreadsheets. Fox example, assuming you are familiar with the format of a Lotus 123 or Microsoft Excel spreadsheet, you will already have a good idea of how any relational database organizes or stores information. It is stored as a two-dimensional table consisting of rows and columns. Each row in a database table represents a single record in the database table or one instance of an entity or object such as a customer or supplier. Each row or record of data is made up of one or more columns or data fields. At the intersection of any row and column is a data value. Figure 7.4 illustrates this concept.

Contained or stored within these database tables are things of interest to an organization — such as detailed information about business partners and an organization's business dealings or transactions with these partners. These things of interest are referred to as entities or objects in database terminology. Each separate spreadsheet or database table contains a different group of related objects. One of the best examples of such things of interest are the names and addresses of an organization's business partners or its customers and suppliers. The entities or objects in one database table within a given relational database are related to entities or objects in other database tables through key fields or keys. This relatedness of data, from one table to another table using keys, is the essence of the relational database model. Figure 7.5 illustrates this concept.

There are some noteworthy semantic differences between spreadsheet and database terminology:

- A spreadsheet column represents one data field in the database table.
- A spreadsheet row represents one data record in a database table. A database record (row) consists of one or more data fields (columns).
- The intersection point of a row and a column is referred to as a cell in the spreadsheet and as a data field value in a database table.

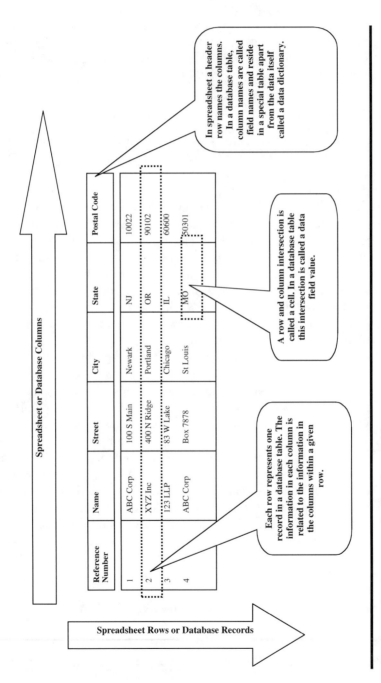

Figure 7.4 The Anatomy of a Database Table

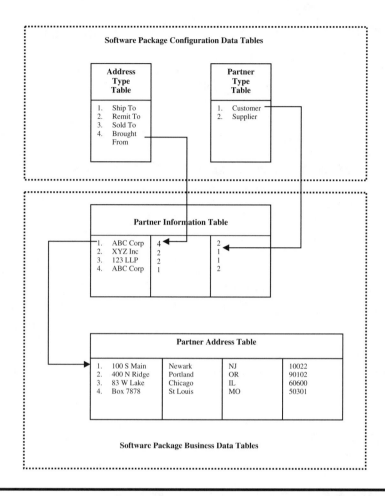

Figure 7.5 The Relational Data Model: A Software Package Based Example

- A worksheet or spreadsheet is really a database table.
- A database table is often referred to as a file.
- A database is a collection of related tables or files.

Although spreadsheets are conceptually similar to a relational database table, there are several important differences between spreadsheets and databases. First, different types of data can be contained in a single column of a spreadsheet, while all of the data in the column of a database table must have a similar underlying format and purpose. Second, a single row in a database should be unique; there is no such constraint on the rows in a spreadsheet. Third, a cell in a spreadsheet can contain a formula, while a database cell must contain a data value.

The Relational Database and the Software Package: The Perfect Marriage

A software package that relies on the relational database model has numerous benefits for both the software package designer and the software package user. Among the benefits are:

■ It provides for a natural integration between objects using relationships.
■ It provides the ability to include data integrity rules.
■ It provides the ability to establish and maintain control over data access and security.
■ It allows for multiple users.
■ It eliminates redundant or duplicate data through a database design concept called normalization. This means that only one common field is needed to form a relationship between any two database tables. Normalization is best described as a set of rules that specify how database tables are designed and how data should be related.

In general, business application software and, specifically, business application software packages, have become far more powerful since the introduction of the relational database as the underlying means for organizing and storing business information.

The typical software package takes the concept of things of interest to another dimension. In the typical configurable software package, the configuration settings are also stored as a series of tables within the relational database.

The Data Model: A Roadmap to the InterWorkings of the Software Package

There are many varied things of interest — entities and objects — in a typical software package. The designers of a software package use a data model to represent these things of interest. The data model is conceptually important to an in-depth understanding of the underlying architecture of the software package. This knowledge is also necessary when determining how to integrate other software with the software package or in order to migrate data into the software package from an existing system.

A data model is usually constructed as a visual model using entity relationship (ER) diagrams. These are drawings that show how the data of one table relate to the data in another table. The data model is then used as the basis for describing the data fields and their characteristics as well as all of the database tables to the relational database software.

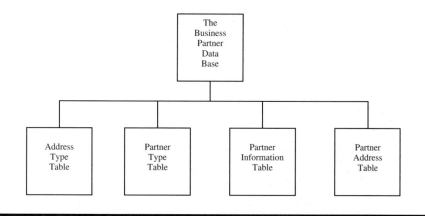

Figure 7.6 The Relational Data Model: A Software Package Based Example

Figure 7.6 depicts a simple entity relationship diagram. Although omitted in this example, these diagrams usually include special symbols at the end of each line connecting or relating one table to another table. Those symbols are an important part of the rules that govern database design. Most software engineers will understand this symbol set or notation and the rules governing database design. They will rely on this knowledge and the appropriate entity relationship diagrams when planning any software package related customization, data migration, or integration project. Some software vendors publish their data model as a separate technical document, while others allow creation of any entity relationship diagram using a function within the software package. In other cases, the software engineer will need to be creative in producing the diagram based upon the database definitions.

The data fields are described to the database through a data dictionary. The data dictionary is usually another table in the database that lists all of the data fields contained in the data model. The data dictionary provides other important information about each data field, such as the type of data or whether the field can contain character or text data versus numeric data. The importance of the data dictionary is that the contents of the database tables rely on the fields described or defined in terms of the underlying data dictionary.

Each software vendor usually has predefined standards governing the naming of both data fields and data tables within the software packages database. It is important to observe all of the software package vendor's predefined standards when integrating with database tables. It is also important to observe these standards if developing custom applications that extend or customize the software package's basic or core functionality in any way. Most organizations will require some degree of expertise in database administration. Usually, such expertise is provided by a database administrator (DBA), a specially trained software engineer who will understand the rules governing how to set up or deploy and tune the database software. The DBA will also assist in setting up the interface between any given database and operating system or database and software package.

Open Database Connectivity

The use of ODBC technology is another important dimension of software package openness and is closely related to the use of a relational database. ODBC is the standard API that is used to allow access to data contained in a commercially available database system, such as Microsoft SQL Server, IBM DB/2, (or UDB as it is called nowadays) or the Oracle database. A special vendor-provided software component, referred to as database middleware or driver software, is needed. It provides the connection between the software package itself and a database system supported by any given software package.

Structured Query Language

Working hand in hand with the ODBC-compliant database is a software package's use of the standardized database programming language, SQL, to interact with the database. Software package constructs database queries using the industry standard form of SQL.

In general, SQL makes programming complex transaction-based systems much simpler. It allows the software package to use standardized SQL requests that will access the database without having to know anything about how to interface with a specific database system. This is accomplished by pushing the complexities and concerns about exchanging information with any supported database into a so-called middleware layer. Figure 7.7 illustrates how ODBC and SQL combine to allow for open database connectivity in a typical software package. For software buyers, ODBC and SQL are particularly important. Many reporting and query tools rely on ODBC and SQL technology to access software package data.

The Universal Data Model Problem

Software vendors have been relatively responsive to adopting open architecture models that allow their software packages to run on a number of database, hardware, or operating system platforms. There is at least one area in which software vendors have been heretofore decidedly stingy about opening up. That area has been in allowing their proprietary business processing models to be activated externally of the software package— this is known as the notion of interoperability. In response to

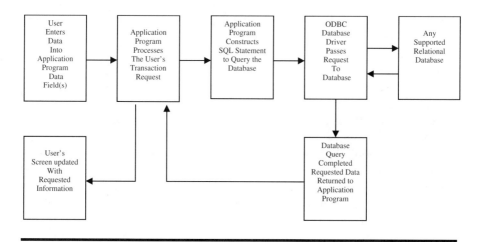

Figure 7.7 Open Database Connectivity: An Illustration

widespread adoption of collaborative, business-to-business electronic commerce, this is starting to change.

Before discussing this newfound trend toward software package interoperability, there is another challenge to interoperability that must be considered. It is the use of proprietary data models. Every software package has a data model — the rules that describe and standardize the way business data must be used in the context of the software package. The standard is local or proprietary to the software package itself. One of the greatest obstacles to interoperability between software packages is the lack of a universal data model to represent business data.

If such a universal data model existed and was readily adopted or embraced by software vendors, business data could be easily used across industries and organizations. Data could also be used between software packages, regardless of which vendor developed the underlying software. Although some leading information engineering and data-modeling proponents have advanced, well-conceived universal data models, they have unfortunately not met with wide acceptance.

On a positive note, the tides may finally be changing. I refer to Hasso Plattner's remarks at the Spring 2002, JavaOne Conference. Plattner commented about what he referred to as "semantics integration." Plattner noted that with regard to software interoperability "the biggest problem is semantics integration." Plattner defined semantics integration in his remarks as "the kinds of information that software applications have to understand about the underlying companies or employees and how they should be related and classified."

This problem raised by Plattner is one that I would largely attribute to the lack of a universal data model within the business application software industry. Will Plattner's remarks change the course of the software industry? Perhaps not, but they do suggest that more standards regarding interoperability — at all levels — are urgently needed throughout the software industry. This will help to address the rapidly expanding needs of the industry's business application software users, particularly for use in collaborative commerce.

The entire software community — software package vendors included — has grown up around the concept of creating largely proprietary data models when building business application software. Consider the common business concept of a vendor — an entity from whom needed business supplies or services are procured. Software vendor may refer to vendors as vendors, suppliers, business partners, or trading partners. These variations are not limited to just the naming conventions of the business data. Often times, the underlying characteristics or attributes of the data will also vary widely. For instance, the most common difference I have encountered between vendor proprietary data models is the number of allowable characters in naming vendors.

XML, INTEROPERABILITY, AND APPLICATION INTEGRATION

Although we have a dictionary for our common, spoken language, a similar dictionary does not exist for business data. For several decades, the only way to readily exchange business data between both organizations and systems has been through the use of several standardized formats for representing information electronically, or more appropriately, digitally. One such standard is the EDI format.

EDI is a widely used format for exchanging information representing commercial transactions, such as purchase orders, shipping notices, and invoices. Another such standard is the Automated Clearing House (ACH) format. The ACH format is used to exchange payment and deposit information, primarily between financial institutions, but it is also used by business organizations to communicate with financial institutions. Most of us are at least indirectly familiar with the ACH format; ACH transactions facilitate everyday financial activities, such as payroll direct deposits and automatic payments of utility bills, insurance premiums, and loan payments.

Both the ACH and EDI formats were established in the early years of business automation. This was when transaction processing occurred not in real time, but through batch processes. Today, collaborative business processes require spontaneous or real-time information exchanges to occur. A new approach to exchanging business information is needed to facilitate such real-time information exchanges. The emerging standard throughout the software community for formatting messages that will ultimately provide the basis for real-time software interoperability is XML.

One of the primary goals for XML is to enable the integration of information across a multitude of business applications.

What is XML?

XML is best thought of as a message organizing framework that, when used, will allow business organizations the ability to exchange business information on an electronic basis, including on a real-time basis. Using XML, business data are exchanged from entity to entity as a document. The XML document is prepared using a preestablished format that includes both the underlying business data and data about the data itself — this is referred to as metadata. XML relies on metadata to facilitate spontaneous information exchange. Metadata is a formal way to describe the contents or format of the business information contained within the XML document.

Why Use XML over EDI?

Presently, EDI still has the upper hand in terms of business-to-business (frequently abbreviated as B2B) information exchange. That is beginning to change as the use of XML is growing fast. So why is XML a better choice for business information exchange? XML allows for a much broader array of business information exchange. Under EDI, the standardized message formats are event driven. Examples of EDI transactions include a purchase order, a shipping notice, an invoice, or a remittance advice.

XML also allows for nontransactional information to be readily exchanged as well. Product specification sheets and material safety data sheets are two such examples of the types of non-transactional information that can be readily exchanged using an XML document. Although it is a misnomer to say that XML processes unstructured data, it is appropriate to conclude that XML handles variable-length data using structured formats. This is a decided advantage over rigid and fixed format EDI transactions.

In the XML world, a document type definition (DTD) represents a standard used to describe the allowable structure of an XML document for a given purpose. These are similar to the standard EDI transaction sets or transaction numbers as prescribed by The American National Standards Institute. Presently, EDI has two advantages over XML. First, EDI includes more defined or standard transaction sets. Second, EDI transactions are more compact, whereas XML transactions are more verbose, because they contain both the business data and the XML-related metadata. EDI was originally created in an age when data transmission speeds were a fraction of the available bandwidth used throughout businesses today. Terse transactions were certainly important considerations then, but are much less so today.

XML has several other advantages over EDI. First, an XML message can be sent in real time as a self-contained service request to another business software application. An XML message can also be nothing more than structured business knowledge. There are no rules saying an XML document must be strictly transaction-related or event-driven information. Second, XML has some additional language components, specifically stylesheets and stylesheet processors that can effectively provide for the transformation of a DTD in one format to another. Third, XML also provides links to other documents. When taken together, these XML characteristics can simultaneously provide a framework for electronic commerce and business application software integration and interoperability.

How XML Provides Integration and Interoperability

In collaborative commerce and electronic commerce scenarios, XML offers a flexible and real-time oriented messaging framework. XML promises to provide for open system support by allowing best-of-breed business application architectures. This may include a strategy of using multiple software packages — and not simply packages provided by the same software vendor. This may also include strategies that combine software package solutions and proprietary systems developed by or specifically for a given organization. Perhaps more important, the fast growing needs in the area of collaborative commerce, where external customers and suppliers in an organization's extended supply chain require real time, system-to-system messaging are better supported. Figure 7.8 illustrates the basic XML-based interoperability framework that is emerging at this time.

For now, the software community is far away from achieving such lofty goals. Integration and interoperability are still big issues for information technology managers. While an ERP package integrates the back office, what about the customer relationship management (CRM) system for the front office? Should one customer master exist for both packages? Should a quote in the CRM system easily — and electronically — convert into a sales order document in the ERP system? The likely answer to both of these questions is yes. Although many ERP vendors are scrambling to add CRM capabilities into already existing ERP products, this might not be enough in many cases.

Presently, the XML community is not quite as established with respect to DTDs as it is to the extent that EDI transaction sets have been defined and standardized. One organization may adopt a given DTD format for handling sales order documents. If a selling organization wants a supplier to direct ship products to its customers based upon a sales order it has taken, the supplier may not be able to understand the sales order document because it uses a different DTD to handle sales orders.

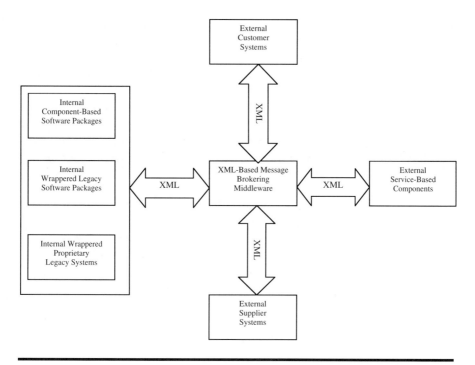

Figure 7.8 The Basix XML-Based Interoperability Framework: An Illustration

There are a number of XML standards-setting initiatives now underway. Some of these initiatives are much further along, while others remain in their infancy. For example, one of the largest and most successful XML standards-setting initiatives to date is RosettaNet. RosettaNet was established in 1998. It is a consortium of business organizations primarily comprised of manufacturing and supplying organizations that participate in the electronics and computer industry. The RosettaNet consortium has undertaken the task of creating XML document standards for business information exchanges relevant to their industry. Subscribing organizations use these standards to then format and communicate their business information to other subscribing organizations within the industry. This enables the entire supply chain to communicate electronically.

While XML does not provide a solution to the universal data model problem discussed earlier, it at least provides some means of reconciliation between different business data models. XML uses a concept referred to as namespaces to reconcile business data naming conventions. Namespaces are used to overcome the prospects of collisions when two business data fields are similarly named, yet have different meanings or uses.

Without an established set of standards, it is not surprising to find differing DTDs in XML for essentially the same information. In the case of software packages, the contents of transactions can vary widely from software package to software package or even between modules within the same software package. However, the XML also provides assistance in reconciling these types of differences as well. XML can reconcile differing document types through the definition of translating or reference documents. These definitional or translating documents are referred to as stylesheets. Stylesheets are created in XML using the extensible stylesheet language (XSL). A subset of XSL referred to as XSL transformations is specifically used for translating or transforming one data type definition into another.

XML and the Software Community

As the need for system integration and interoperability grows, along with the maturity of XML as a framework for system integration and interoperability, an entirely new category of software package has grown throughout the software development community. This category of software packages is known as enterprise application integration (EAI) software. EAI software packages are really technical tools aimed for use by a technical audience — business and system analysts, programmers, and software engineers. These software packages provide the software development community with the tools to integrate business applications systems. This can be one software package with another software package or a software package with a legacy system, typically using XML to do so.

How Existing Software Is Made XML-Compliant

Now for the bad news: The majority of business application software packages that an organization might acquire at the present time will not likely provide any support for XML, much less native XML support. What does native XML support mean? If a software package supports XML natively, then the software components that make up the software package are already using XML; it is the basis for internal software component to software component communications.

In all likelihood, an organization's existing legacy system will not provide any support for XML either. So how do previous generation software packages or any legacy system provide for XML support? The answer is, of course, a software developer's dream come true — more programming. In this case, a special kind of software is prepared — referred to as a wrapper.

A wrapper is essentially a software component that provides for access to a business process or function that is implemented by or embedded in legacy software. Wrapping encapsulates the legacy code inside a software component without the need to rewrite the underlying legacy code using component-based software or object-oriented software development practices. It is safe to assume that many software vendors will use wrappers to implement XML capabilities into their existing software architectures. Software vendors have enormous prior investments in their legacy software and many will be unlikely to rewrite their legacy software. This is because after many vendors have already undertook large-scale remediation efforts in an effort to ensure their existing software code was both Y2K compliant and could support implementation of the Euro — the new European currency.

Figure 7.8 also illustrates how a wrapped legacy system or older generation software package application can be integrated into an XML-based interoperability framework.

What Should a Best-of-Breed Software Package Provide?

If your last major software package acquisition preceded the Y2K rollover, a lifetime has passed in terms of the software community since then. The impact on software packages by the pressures for both electronic and collaborative commerce facilities has been nothing short of revolutionary. Software vendors that, just a few years ago, held out that their proprietary products were above the industry are now being humbled. Software vendors who thought they could ignore the electronic and collaborative commerce revolution will be left behind their competition. This means a best-of-breed software package should provide built-in interoperability through XML.

SOFTWARE PACKAGE INFRASTRUCTURE: AN EPILOGUE

This chapter has discussed the technology or infrastructure behind the configurable, integrated software packages that provide multiple system support. While software packages are increasingly open, they remain behind in the adoption of key architectural features. This is particularly evident in the area of interoperability. Interoperability is an essential software feature if an organization must extend operations beyond its own four walls. It must extend into the systems of customers and suppliers to achieve the vision of collaborative commerce and a truly integrated supply chain.

8

SOFTWARE PACKAGES: GETTING WHAT YOU WANT IS NOT ALWAYS EASY

For everything that a software package represents, there are still certain things that will not be possible within the context of the software. Those that are possible often do not come as easily as one would hope. This chapter is about leveling your expectations for what the software package is and is not. With that said, this chapter discusses a number of important issues, including:

- Migrating existing business data to a software package
- Filling functionality gaps in software packages using workarounds
- Filling functionality gaps in software packages using custom programs
- Complementary technology integration with software packages
- Third party add-ons for software packages
- Interoperability and software packages
- Integrating legacy systems and software packages

One of the most significant challenges the adopter of any software package will face is integration or interoperability. The Swiss army knife equivalent of a software package does not exist. A single software package is unlikely to fulfill all your business objectives.

Even if one package satisfies all of your internal business application processing requirements, sooner or later you will be challenged with extending your business application processes and business data into the offices or systems of your customers and suppliers, given the trend for collaborative commerce and complete supply chain visibility. This chapter provides an overview of both the challenges and promises with regard to software package customization integration and interoperability.

Perhaps most important, is the need for all of these tasks: configuration, customization, integration and interoperability enablement, migrations, and upgrades. Throughout much of the software package life cycle (SPLC), they are essential in meeting an organization's initial and changing business requirements.

WHY SOFTWARE CHANGE IS A CONSTANT PROCESS

Software buyers want the freedom to be different. They want to distinguish their organization and stand out among their competitors. Selecting business application software packages — or perhaps more appropriately called business application software components or services in the future — that represent industry best practices places an organization on a level playing field with its competitors. Moreover, configurable, feature-rich software packages also have the ability to improve an organization's agility or ability to respond to general marketplace changes. It also means the organization can reinvent or reorganize itself or its supply chain to achieve cost or other marketplace advantages.

Software buyers want the ability to add on or complement an existing software package with other software packages that extend their core or back-office business system, which is typically an enterprise resource planning (ERP) system. The speed advantage provided by configurable software packages is derived from the idea that processing changes can be quickly implemented without making wholesale changes to the underlying software. In addition, highly configurable software also allows for a customized buying experience for each customer. This is not just for product configuration, but also for the entire process of buying a product that can be customized to accommodate specific customer preferences.

Supply chain management (SCM) and customer relationship management (CRM) are two significant, external-facing processes that organizations are using in order to improve the customer experience or to stand out among their competitors. Frequently, extensions are needed to the traditional back-office software — an ERP system — in order to automate either of these processes. The ability to integrate with third-party solutions, now or in the future, is both desirable and necessary.

SELECTING BEST OF BREED VERSUS SINGLE-VENDOR SOLUTIONS

There are two opposing schools of thought about software package strategy. The first approach suggests selecting packages that are best in class or best-of-breed in terms of meeting an organization's business requirements. The assumption is that such software packages can be bolted together, or integrated in the back room, and will achieve greater results rather than selecting and implementing a single, integrated solution. In certain situations, (this author feels they are limited) the best-of-breed strategy may have merit. In the majority of circumstances, this is usually the wrong strategy to follow. This is especially true for the smaller and middle market organizations. In these organizations, funds are often more constrained, as there is a cost premium associated with the best-of-breed approach.

When practical, the software buyer should strive for a single-vendor solution. The reasons are simple enough. They include a single point of contact for continuing support, only one annual maintenance fee, a single implementation project (as no two products are ever likely to configure in an identical manner), and technically speaking, seamless integration between applications. The advice I offer to my clients is to make every attempt to satisfy as many, if not all, of their current and anticipated business requirements through a single, integrated business system, more often than not, through an ERP system. A few short years ago this was a tougher prospect, but recent extensions to ERP software packages have made the business case for doing so much more compelling.

There are situations when a single-vendor solution is either an inappropriate strategy or is simply an impossible feat. In such cases, a so-called best-of-breed implementation usually occurs. This implementation involves multiple software packages or a combination of software packages and custom programming being used to fulfill business requirements in the best possible way. When adopting a best-of-breed approach as the business systems strategy, new risks for the organization emerge that should not be taken lightly. I advocate avoiding the use of multiple software packages when an integrated system is available and satisfies the vast majority (usually 80% or more) of an organization's business requirements.

The reason for my recommendation to avoid the best-of-breed approach is quite simple. Usually the lack of software interoperability makes integration so costly and difficult, it simply is not worth serious consideration. To be clear on one point, the best-of-breed approach to selecting software will become more of a reality over the next few years. Throughout this chapter I will discuss exactly why I believe that to be the case. Until then, ease of integration and interoperability between software packages largely remains fiction, not fact.

Integration and interoperability concerns may become less of a headache for software buyers in the years ahead. There will still be some cost duplication that occurs under the best-of-breed scenario, particularly the costs of software maintenance. In most cases, these fees can equal or exceed 20% of the initial software license fees that were paid to acquire the software, and they recur on an annual basis.

I should also point out that, in years past, an integrated system was sometimes not always the best course of action. Unfortunately, the alternative — a best-of-breed of strategy — is not much better for reasons I have made clear. While software packages, such as enterprise-wide ERP systems, have their deficiencies and idiosyncrasies, they are usually more cost effective and easier to manage than a best-of-breed approach.

As I mentioned earlier, systems in general are increasing in scope. This is particularly true for ERP software packages. What this means is that a majority of these systems are offering similar functionality to what only a collection of best-of-breed software packages offered just a few years ago. For instance, almost all of the major ERP vendors now offer a CRM module or provide out-of-the-box integration to a third-party CRM package. On the other hand, electronic commerce or e-business integration and ERP remains a mixed bag. Many ERP vendors offer storefront and customer self-service solutions, but often times these are simply inadequate and unusable solutions.

The point of this discussion is quite simple. When a single-vendor solution is not practical for an organization, it will want to acquire packages that behave well and integrate with other software packages as easily and as seamlessly as possible. This means the underlying software has an architecture that readily supports communication and integration with other software, regardless of who that other vendor is.

Complementary Technologies Integration

While it is all well and good for me to suggest a single, enterprise-wide system over a best-of-breed collection of diverse software packages, this recommendation only solves one part of the business technology puzzle. Even when adopting a single, enterprise-wide system, some integration, usually of other technologies, such as bar code readers and printers, document scanners, or point-of-sale terminals, will likely be required. When these so-called complementary input/output technologies are an integral part of the overall business improvement strategy, I advocate that such criteria be incorporated into the request for proposal (RFP) process for the software package itself.

My reason for advocating that complementing technologies belong in the software package RFP is based on a simple premise: Vendors of software packages today know that most organizations will want or need these technologies in order to complete their business improvement goals of business process simplification and automation. Software vendors have formed strategic business alliances with the makers of products that complement or extend the value proposition for their own software.

Increasingly, software package vendors and complementary product vendors are working together to provide integrated solutions. For example, an industry-wide standards group, the Manufacturing Execution Systems Association, was formed about a decade ago to deal with integration of software packages and complementary technologies.

Perhaps more important, the software package vendor has usually already taken steps to integrate their software package with these complementary technologies. In other cases, they may at least be able to provide client references that have had similar technology requirements. Speaking to such references about their past integration efforts may provide some insights and ideas to your organization before embarking on the same path.

TAKING ON THE TOUGH JOB OF SYSTEM INTEGRATION AND DATA MIGRATION

If you are inclined to believe in or want a best-of-breed approach or strategy of software usage, ease of system integration or interoperability with other software packages should be an extremely important goal in your software selection process.

Unfortunately, I wish I had some better news on the integration front. Outside of perhaps a handful of most requested application program interfaces (APIs), a few conversion or interface programs for specific kinds of data, and usually support for again only a handful of most requested electronic data interchange transactions, most software packages fall woefully short on integration options. Their ease of integration or interoperability with other software packages falls short as well.

Most software package vendors have only recently started to provide support for third-party enterprise application integration (EAI) software packages. These packages can serve as bridges between two or more software packages and represent an out-of-the-box technique for integrating disparate software packages. These EAI software packages have ready-made adapters that expose particularly the application program interfaces that a software vendor provides as entry or exit points into their application processes or underlying database. It is possible that an EAI package will be able to provide the exact linkage desired between several best-of-breed packages that your organization is considering in a relatively straightforward manner.

If your needs are data migration, the one-time conversion of information from an old system to a new system, instead of ongoing integration between two or more software packages, your organization should make use of any standard or optional facilities within the software package to populate the data files in that package. While an EAI software package may be able to ease the data migration problem for your organization, the added software to do so may be cost prohibitive.

With regard to data migration, let me say that in the past many technical personnel have disagreed with me on this point, arguing that it is just data. While it is true that it is just data, most software packages have extremely complex data structures. This is more so than with any software that I have seen that has been developed in house by the typical information technology (IT) department, for instance. This data structure or data model complexity requires an intimate knowledge of the interworkings of both the data model and the underlying software.

In a number of instances, I have recommended to my clients against the direct or field-to-field conversion of legacy system data into a new software package. In such cases, I usually recommend that clients take an indirect path to data conversion. What this means is that an organization must rebuild its legacy system or source data into an acceptable and usable format for the new software package.

There are several reasons why I recommend not doing a direct data conversion from legacy software into the database of a new software package. First, I find that legacy system data (and in some cases a legacy system will actually be a manual system) is either limited or nonexistent with respect to requirements of the new system. Second, sometimes the data are simply in too radically different a format to effectively convert; this is often the case for part master records and is especially the case for configured materials and bill of material information. Third, the legacy data are often of too poor a quality to merit migration. On this last note, the rebuilding of the organization's legacy data is really an opportunity to clean up many past sins. This includes previously flawed data conversions, removal of duplicate records, data inconsistencies, and the adoption of standards to improve future data quality.

Indirect data conversion means extracting the data from the legacy system and placing it into what I will refer to as a bridging format. The bridge format adds containers for the missing fields onto the legacy system file format. I then help clients fill in the blanks for the missing data — a process also known as scrubbing and editing of the data. The bridge format then serves as the data loaded into the new software package's database. There are a number of ways to manipulate the data prior to loading it into a software package. I have found that in most cases, a Microsoft Excel worksheet will do. Some software packages can load this format directly. In other cases the worksheet may need to be saved in an ASCII text format before loading into the software package.

The rebuilding of legacy system business data should be based upon the data model for the new software package along with any appropriate business data rules or standards set forth by the organization or external entities. Example of such organizations include the United States Post Office or the Internal Revenue Service in the case of name and address data. I have successfully taken this approach when loading both master and transaction type data into new software packages from legacy systems. I have also taken this same route when converting mainframe data for use on other platforms.

On a final note, an entire class of software packages has emerged to assist with data conversions. These software packages are generally referred to as extract, translate, and load (ETL) software packages. These packages were spawned by the need to perform such activities on a repetitive basis in conjunction with the increasing use of data warehouses and data marts as an after-the-fact information integration tool for analysis and reporting purposes. This is especially the case when an organization relies on a best-of-breed business application software strategy.

Since the notion of a universal data model has not been readily adopted by the software industry, integration or interoperability and data migration are usually formidable tasks when working with most software packages. An intimate knowledge of a vendor's data model and transaction processing strategy is necessary in order to write data directly to virtually any software package's database (as many of my in-house IT friends are all too often quick to suggest). The typical software package will open up, read, and potentially write to many files for even the simplest of transactions. Replicating the vendor's transaction logic in the form of populated data files can be a formidable task.

Failure to appreciate the data structure or data model complexity of any given software package will ultimately cause problems for an organization. Simply put, data quality is sacrificed. For example, if one were to populate data files directly by making direct insertions to the software package's database using structured query language (SQL) statements, the risk of corrupting the software package's database is great. The likely result can be widespread transaction failure — the inability of the software package to retrieve and process records, or perhaps worse, data loss.

A typical software package will have many inherent field level and process level validations and even follow-on workflow steps. Consider that if the data from an external source flow through a software vendor's predefined integration, interface, or data migration programs that such field-level and process-level validations will be triggered to ensure inbound data quality, transaction integrity, and the "next workflow step ready" state of the data. One might not otherwise achieve this through an alternative and perhaps less time-consuming method of simply inserting existing or legacy system data into a new software package.

SOFTWARE PACKAGE FUNCTIONALITY GAPS

Gap analysis is the usual and customary term used to describe the process of comparing a software package's available and optional features against a list of required features that the organization has prepared. Gap analysis identifies areas where a software package fails to comply with a business requirement, in whole or part. Such gaps will represent missing or incomplete features that have relevance, albeit of minor or major importance to the organization's business model.

Gap analysis usually occurs as a part of the software package selection process. During this process, it is entirely likely, if not inevitable, that gaps will surface. The goal of software selection is to find a software package that is the best fit for your organization in terms of your stated functional and other requirements. The goal, quantitatively speaking, is to find software packages that would yield a compliance ratio of 80% or higher against the organization's stated business requirements. Some of the required features may be completely unsupported, partially supported, require use of a predefined workaround to implement, or have no known workaround.

For example, for as many features as a typical ERP system supposedly provides, any one of these packages will typically leave a number of unfulfilled business requirements on the table. Software package owners are frequently driven over time to implement additional software packages or to sanction custom-developed software programs that fulfill these additional, unmet requirements.

Some software vendors will tell buyers that their software can do it all. Their software represents a dictionary, encyclopedia, or smorgasbord of business processes. But to what depths have the vendors taken their software in support of every business process?

Usually, most all-encompassing software packages are strong in some areas and weak in others. The software may be immature or unproven in any given dimension of functionality. Take for example, an ERP software package. It will be strong in one dimension of functionality, (e.g., human resources), but weak in another (e.g., manufacturing planning). In such cases, a gap is said to exist in the software package's functionality. Because the other strengths of the package outweigh the gaps, it is still the best fit for the organization.

Software package functionality gaps can have a significant impact on the perceived success of any software package implementation. Software gaps must be identified, prioritized, and remedies or workarounds must be sought. Unfulfilled gaps can lead to nonuse, inaccuracies, and statutory noncompliance in certain industries. The key to successful software package gap management is to identify how an organization's core business processes are affected by the gap. If it is an important process or task to your business, it is likely a gap that cannot be left unfilled or relegated to a manual process or workaround, at least not for very long if there is any volume of activity associated with the unmet requirement.

New Gaps Are Constantly Emerging

Once implemented, most highly integrated software packages usually become legacy or stovepipe systems in their own accord. At the heart of a typical complex information processing infrastructure in a modern organization is usually a so-called back-office system; this is usually an ERP system (or something like it). More important, today's business world changes rapidly. A system configuration defined 6 months or year ago may simply be invalid. As business needs dictate configuration changes, new areas of software gaps will likely emerge. Gap analysis and fulfillment are constant tasks that will be continuously on any organization's agenda.

What to Do about Gaps

Most software package functionality gaps are filled in one of four ways:

- Do nothing. After more careful analysis, the gap is considered noncritical and the gap is subsequently simply left open or unfulfilled.
- A workaround is found, usually involving some creative configuration or reconfiguration of the software to close the gap.
- A third-party or add-on software package is sought that can perform the missing or sub-par function.
- When all other avenues fail, the last resort should be a custom program or an in-line code change made to the software package to close the gap. Generally speaking, custom programs are more desirable than in-line code changes.

I have a bias toward selecting from one of the first three choices on this list as the means to fill in a software functionality gap. I will make my reasons clear in the next section, which provides a more detailed discussion of software package customizing considerations.

RECONFIGURATION AND WORKAROUNDS

Few, if any, software packages simply work out of the box for an organization. A case in point: Not so long ago, I was engaged by a small business to review its accounting system setup. This small business had purchased a simple, shrink-wrapped accounting system and then hurried the software into production in order to solve its Y2K issues. During the briefest of implementation efforts, the configuration wizard provided by the software allowed the firm to select a generic chart of accounts, based upon the firm's type of business and legal structure. This was done and the remaining system configuration was then completed.

After this system had been in use for a number of months, some dissatisfaction surfaced regarding the financial reports that were being generated by this system. The scope of my engagement was to identify the management issues and then review the software's capabilities to determine why such gaps existed and provide appropriate recommendations on how to correct them. The biggest problem I found was that a tremendous amount of energy was spent manually developing a gross margin report.

Unfortunately, what I found was that the software had been set up incorrectly for what the business actually needed. Part of the problem was the chart of accounts. Although the correct model chart of account (as provided by the software vendor) had been selected, it was terribly inadequate to support this firm's business model. The vendor's generic chart of accounts was simply too generic, if not unrealistic, and was a bad fit. I recommended reconfiguring the chart of accounts.

But the firm's problems were far from resolved. The second problem I found was due to the type of transaction under which their sales and purchases were being recorded. This was by far a more significant problem. The firm's entire transaction history was simply a mess. To rectify this problem, I did some additional fine-tuning to the chart of accounts. I then experimented with the different types of transactions available in this system until I found ones that were appropriate to the firm's business needs. Although the firm was using transactions that on the surface seemed to support its business, they did not support management's desire to manage by gross profit margin.

The end result was a reconfigured chart of accounts and the utilization of new transaction types. The cleanup required nothing less than a reimplementation. All prior transactions needed to be rerecorded using the correct transaction types in order to reflect correctly in gross margin numbers. The moral of this story: Do not implement any software package without first testing the as built configuration. The next step involves prototyping your crucial business transactions to ensure that the results, on an integrated basis, are acceptable for use by your organization.

Just about every consultant in the business will likely be able to share a similar story where a software package has fallen short of its desired performance goals. Usually similar reasons are noted — improper configuration and inadequate testing. Reading vendor manuals and attending classes on how to configure and use the software are not sufficient substitutes for demonstrable results that match your expectations of the software package.

Another example: I had been engaged by a client's IT department — the client's previous internal IT resource had left recently to review and complete the setup of the client's new financial system. I knew this system well, but I could not seem to generate some sample financial reports by relying on the standard reports delivered with the system using the client's chart of accounts. I was perplexed, but I finally found the problem.

The problem was that the system required each account to be coded with a level of detail. Unfortunately, all the accounts appearing in the client's chart of accounts had been set to the same level of detail. This rendered the reporting and online inquiry features of the system largely inoperable as previously configured. Custom reports and inquiries could have been used instead, but then what is the purpose of buying a software package that already provided this infrastructure? Fortunately, I had caught this problem before its final implementation occurred and corrected it for the client. The client was disappointed with the advice it had been given from a big 5 accounting firm on how to design its chart of accounts. In case you are wondering, it is not the one you have been reading or hearing so much about of late.

These examples are meant to elevate your awareness of the complex, tedious, and time-consuming job of implementing software packages. As a general rule, software that is more complex or that has a more comprehensive feature set will be more difficult to implement. A proxy for complexity or comprehensiveness is software cost. As a general rule, the more expensive the software is, the more likely that all other costs related to the software package, such as consulting services, training, and annual maintenance costs will be greater.

It should be understood that configuration and testing or prototyping of the software is often the most difficult and time-consuming part of an implementation. Configuration requires the formation of a deep understanding of the software, testing configuration settings, changing settings when undesired results occur and reconfiguring and retesting the affected transactions in the software. Many organizations find this critical process difficult enough. They also find it so time-consuming that consultants are widely used during this phase.

HOW THE TYPICAL SOFTWARE PACKAGE IS CONFIGURED

The most basic form of software package configuration is a series of maintenance screens where parameter switches or flags, usually binary or yes- or no-type software switches, can be set. In addition, there are a number of shared tables that must be established. Payment terms in an ERP system are a typical example. Payables, receivables, procurement, and sales order processing often use the same table. Recall that Figure 7.5 illustrates how common configuration-type tables and business data tables are related within a software package. Arguably, such common or shared information can also be construed as master data. Nonetheless, if any given value is not predefined or configured in a table, the system is without knowledge of it. Although configuration is a prerequisite to using any software package, the manner in which it is configured varies widely. Chapter 12 discusses how to identify and incorporate software configuration steps into the software package implementation plan.

Some vendors provide semiautomated approaches to software configuration. In other cases, implementation partners have created proprietary, semiautomated approaches that they will use to configure the software package during its initial implementation. These semiautomated configuration tools can vary widely in their utility. Implementation is a time-consuming and expensive process. If the results garnered from a formal understanding of your business model, policies, and procedures can be codified and catalogued, it stands to reason this information can be extracted and used to populate, in an automated manner, the configuration tables. On the other hand, some vendors use a so-called industry standard practices template that presets the configuration settings in the software package.

The majority of vendors today provide an unusually broad array of choice and flexibility within their software as it is delivered. However, there will be times when your organization's requirements will exceed the software's capabilities. Assuming that your configuration options have been exhausted and that any available workarounds have been explored and deemed unacceptable, your organization's final answer will be to customize the software package.

WHEN CONFIGURATION ALONE WILL NOT WORK: CUSTOMIZING SOFTWARE PACKAGES

Much like configuration, when the answer becomes customization, there is little similarity from one vendor's approach toward customization to another. Most vendors do provide at least some mechanism or tool to allow for such customizing to occur. A customizing tool will usually make the job easier.

Perhaps the first question is: Will any customization of a soon-to-be selected or already selected software package really be necessary? My short and preferred answer is generally no, but the practicality of the matter is that this is rarely true. My experience tells me that I must advocate strongly against packaged software customization and I do. Please note my justification for this answer. While avoiding customization is my short and preferred answer, from a practical standpoint, it is also tough to avoid doing so. These reasons will be explained in this section.

As good as most software packages are, there will always be some degree of customizing that a software buyer will likely need to do. Do not feel that your organization is alone in being required to customize a brand new software package to meet its business requirements. The change could be as mundane as changing the placement of the address information on an invoice document for window envelopes or on a standardized mailer for expense disbursements.

When customization is necessary, a strong business case rooted in your organization's overall strategy, or due to regulatory necessity, should factor strongly into making any customizations. After all, by selecting packaged software you have outsourced the software development process to the package vendor. Quite frankly, software package buyers do not want a customization nightmare on their hands. If they do end up with one, then it is likely that they have bought the wrong software package. Often, the cost of customizing an inferior or inadequate software package will exceed what a more expensive, but better fitting solution would have been.

The good news is that given all the flexibility provided by most software packages, configuration over customization can frequently prevail. The needs of your organization's business processes or other user preferences can usually be met in this matter, or as a workaround that also avoids the customization route. Do not be fooled by today's deep and feature-rich software packages; they still leave some things on the table. For the majority of software package implementations I have been involved with, there has almost always been some degree of customizing that a client will likely need to do.

Although most software package vendors attempt to provide the widest array of choices and flexibility within the core software products they deliver, there are times when the requirements of your organization will exceed the capabilities of the software you have selected and have, or will implement.

Assuming that your configuration options have been exhausted and that any available workarounds have been explored and deemed unacceptable, your organization's final answer will be to customize the software package.

Some software packages make that process easy and others make it difficult. In some cases, changes to a package are simply not possible. This is especially true of most of the low-end software on the price scale.

Software Package Customization in Perspective

The current approach in the system development community is the use of objects. Object orientation represents a paradigm shift for the software industry. Objects offer many advantages to software designers. Object-oriented programming is now the prevalent software development technique in the client server, Internet, and for the emerging web services computing environments. In short, the demands on the software developer have changed and so has the way software is written. Software that is event driven, object oriented, and includes graphical user interface elements is more difficult to design and develop.

As a result of this paradigm shift, software vendors have been creating proprietary design and development tools to make the process of creating, maintaining, and customizing a software package an easier feat to accomplish. However, when the answer becomes customization, there is little similarity from one vendor's approach toward customization to that of another vendor. So while most vendors do provide at least some mechanism or tool to allow for customizing their software to make the job presumably easier, each of these tools will have its own peculiarities and learning curve to overcome.

Customizing Standards

Most software vendors publish specific guidelines or standards that should be followed when customizing their software package. The standards usually cover object-naming conventions, cover file or table-naming conventions, field-naming conventions, and executable program-naming conventions. Vendors will also publish a document describing any API or remote function call (RFC) exits that are available from within their programs. These exits can invoke external custom programs and third-party software packages. In addition, the vendor will usually provide a standards document describing the data model and other technical anomalies related to their software. Following customizing standards prescribed by the software vendor is the best way to ensure your applications will not conflict with software updates from the vendor.

Use External Custom Programs Whenever Possible

When changes to a software package are necessary, it is best to develop customizations as a follow-on or standalone process (i.e., a standalone executable program). This is better than making any inline or internal code changes to any vendor-delivered application program.

In many cases, vendors will provide an API or RFC inside their program that can invoke an external program. Vendors will usually provide a document describing each of the APIs or RFCs they have defined, how each is activated, and what data are to be passed back and forth. As a general rule, inline code changes to a vendor-supplied program should be limited to code corrections initiated by the vendor.

Make Plans for Upgrades before Beginning Customization

An important practice is to consider how any customization will be impacted by future vendor upgrades to the software package. Some software vendors will provide specific advice or guidelines on how to customize their software so that your customization efforts will be minimally affected by an upgrade. While on this subject, the same holds true for configuration actions as well — they too can be adversely impacted by an upgrade if certain rules are not followed.

Customization without Programming

The developer who is familiar with a visual program development tool, such as Visual Basic or Visual C++, should be comfortable using many of the visual application development tools or workbenches provided as a part of a software package.

In general, most software package development tools are intended to keep changes at a high enough level to prevent the need for custom program development at a source code level. As a result, many packages employ an assembly-line approach to developing custom applications using prebuilt components and a point-and-click style development environment. Many calculations will still need to be performed through a hand-coded function. This is usually in a programming language, such as C, C++, Java, Visual Basic, or Visual Basic for Applications, that is called by the custom program. Some vendors will make use of a proprietary programming language, for example, the vendor SAP uses ABAP/4, its own programming language for customizing its software.

Third-Party Report Writers

Reporting is often considered the weakest part in many software packages. While software packages may do a good job of transaction processing and in integrating business data, software packages often score poorly on reporting. This problem is not simply a vendor problem. Even when vendors provide scores of reports, their reports often still fail to meet an organization's expectations. I have found in practice this is largely because it seems that every organization has its own preferences or desired formats — sometimes unorthodox ones — for the presentment of their business data. As a result of this inability to please, many software vendors have simply thrown in the towel on reporting. They will provide perhaps a few dozen core reports and leave anything beyond the basics up to the customer.

To make it easier for their customers to create customized reports and satisfy such unique reporting requirements, software vendors usually rely on a programmable report writer that is specifically attached to the software package's data model. Generally speaking, the software vendor includes a proprietary report writer that often times any core or delivered reports were produced with. The report writer may allow for customizing the core reports and for creating new ones based on the software package's business data model. The latest trend seems to be that software vendors are using a third-party report writer with their software package to produce even their core, delivered reports. Software vendors will then bundle at least a runtime engine of the report writer with their software.

At the same time, it seems that software vendors are endorsing one or more third-party report writers as customizing tools for customized end user reports based upon the proprietary business data model of the software package. The most popular third-party report writers that are increasingly bundled with software packages include:

- Actuate (by Actuate): A report writer for general reporting purposes
- Crystal Reports (by Crystal): A report writer for general reporting purposes
- FRx (by FRx) is a specialized report writer for financial reporting purposes
- SQR (by Biro) is a general-purpose report writer used with SQL database tables

In many cases, an organization may already have one or more of these report writers in house. They may not necessarily be compatible with the version bundled with or included in the selected software package. Verify the need to relicense any existing report writer with the software package vendor or reseller.

It has been my experience that documents and reports are areas where the greatest customizing requirements usually exist. The good news is that these are among the simplest of customizations to make in terms of most software packages, especially given that so many software vendors have begun taking advantage of third-party report writers. In many instances, an organization already has developers on staff that are trained and ready to go on these products. They only need to learn the business data and transaction models and data idiosyncrasies associated with the software package. Although many vendors will suggest that reports can be easily created by an end user, ask the salesperson (a typical "end user") if he can show you how that is possible. If he cannot, then it is likely your end users will not be able to either.

The key to usable end user reports from software packages rests in both design and performance. Report design requires knowledge of the business data and transaction processing models as well as the user's precise requirements. Report performance requires knowledge of relational database concepts and in how to use the report writing tool. Given these guidelines, one can appreciate why end users struggle producing custom reports without relying on the IT staff. Then again, are you paying these individuals to write reports or manage the business? Three of the report writers mentioned above are profiled in the next few sections.

Structured Query Reporter

The structured query reporter (SQR) is not simply a report writer, but is more so a programming language. In that role it is specifically designed for SQL database reporting and information processing. SQR includes procedural programming constructs, such as conditional processing, and other features to facilitate sophisticated report writing (e.g., paging and formatting documents in both columnar and tabular formats).

SQR runs under a variety of operating system platforms, including both Windows and Unix, and works with a number of different SQL databases, including Oracle, Sybase, DB2, Informix, and SQLBase. Because of its platform versatility, SQR has been a popular selection for business application software vendors, such as PeopleSoft, PSDI (Maximo), and Ross Systems (Renaissance), as the custom report writer bundled with their software products. SQR is currently owned and marketed by Brio Software (formerly Brio Technology) and was formerly marketed by SQRIBE Technologies until being acquired by Brio in August 1999.

Crystal Reports

Crystal Reports is published by Crystal Decisions Corporation, formerly Seagate Incorporated, which is better known for their computer harddrives. Crystal Reports became a leading report writing tool when Microsoft began shipping a version of this report writer with its Visual Basic development tool in 1991, and did so up until the latest versions of Visual Basic shipped. As a result of its past Microsoft affiliation, Crystal Reports became a leading database report writer in terms of its installed base. Crystal Decisions reports that more than three million copies of this product have been shipped. This program is included as the standard report writer in more than 100 software packages. One of the more popular features in Crystal is its preview mode. The preview mode includes a drill down feature that allows the viewer to move from a high-level grouping, to a lower-level grouping, to the underlying data with only a few, simple mouse clicks.

FRx

FRx Financial Reporting is a product of FRx Software Corporation. It is a report writing tool specifically geared toward use in an organization's financial reporting and analysis process. FRx Financial Reporting works with many of the leading accounting systems. The product is able to provide an organization with customized financial information in columnar, tabular, and graphical formats. FRx provides for drill down from summary to transaction level details. It is able to consolidate information from multiple companies, databases, platforms, currencies and servers. Additionally, FRx can report on key information, such as budgets or statistical data from spreadsheets.

FRx Financial Reporting is bundled into a number of popular accounting systems. It allows for the design and maintenance of both simple and complex financial reports through a number of built-in features, including support for complex calculations and conditional processing. From the standpoint of an accountant, FRx can create virtual roll-up structures that do not exist in an organization's chart of accounts, allow reporting on both posted and nonposted activity, and provide for side-by-side comparisons of departmental data.

CONFIGURATION MANAGEMENT: AN OVERVIEW

Many of the software packages provide some form of software version control tool. This tool will allow objects to be developed and tested in one environment or instance and then promoted into another for production use.

Think of an environment or instance as a directory or subdirectory in terms of a personal computer workstation — it represents a named or reserved place to store certain files or types of information. For instance, Microsoft Office applications typically use My Documents and My Pictures as reserved or default locations to store documents and pictures created by the Office product user. Creating and managing changes to the environments for the storage of business data and software components related to the software package is typically the most complex ongoing administrative task your IT staff will face in managing a software package (outside of perhaps end user security). Chapter 12 provides some additional insights about environments in the context of installing the software package and making it available for use.

Change management in the software development world, much like machine maintenance work on the plant floor, usually involves some form of lockout. Generally speaking, when an object is being changed, the developer must lock down the object. Only that developer can make any changes to that object until the lockdown is removed using the software version control tool.

In addition, the path to production and to the end user is typically under the control of the software version control tool. This means that objects may need to pass through various checkpoints within the software version control tool before the object is considered production ready and eligible for promotion into the production environment. Figure 8.1 illustrates a typical software package configuration change management model.

Configuration Change Management

In some cases software packages manage configuration changes to the production environment in a similar, if not identical, manner, to customization changes. In many cases such versioning control over configuration changes can be deactivated during configuration and testing, then activated when production readiness is achieved. Though this may seem overburdening, it is a good feature to activate once a new software package is brought live; it is a bit cumbersome otherwise.

In other cases, the only way to promote configuration settings from one environment to another is by copying configuration tables from one environment to another. The software vendor may or may not provide a tool to do this. The most difficult aspect of this process is identifying what tables must be promoted or copied. All related tables must be promoted or copied at the same time. In these latter cases, it is usually necessary to maintain configuration settings in each environment separately after the environments are initially populated.

System Administration and Change Deployment

In the typical client server environment, some of the processing occurs locally on the client workstation while the remainder of processing is completed on one or more application servers. This means that certain programs or executable objects must be deployed from a central site server to one or more remote client workstations. In most situations, the deployment of objects is a discretionary process that requires a system

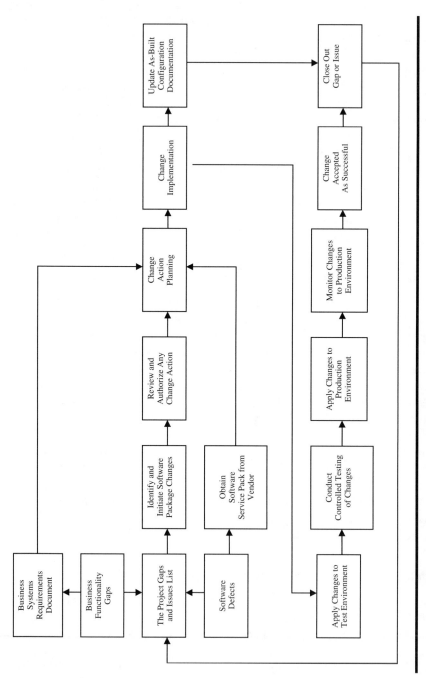

Figure 8.1 The Software Package Change Management Model

administrator. In addition, the objects may cause operational or data integrity issues if they are not deployed properly or completely. For customization, a new object or a changed object must also be deployed to the appropriate system resources.

Change deployment can have an adverse impact on network resources and on other personnel. Changes should be deployed only on an as-necessary basis. An excessive number of change deployments places a strain on your internal support structure. It is generally advisable to deploy changes on a set schedule. A schedule ensures that everyone involved knows when changed objects are due, and when they will be deployed to end users. Perhaps more important, the impact on system resources can be better managed.

THIRD PARTY ADD-ON SOLUTIONS

One method of filling in gaps in otherwise strong software packages, as measured by their ranking along other dimensions of functionality and value, is through a third-party or add-on software package that can perform the missing or subpar function. Sometimes such gaps may be prevalent in an entire class of software packages, not simply for a given vendor's offering. Another situation is when a software gap affects all users in a specific industry segment.

Sometimes a software gap is so widespread that it affects a large number of users of a given software package or class of packages. In this case, a third-party software vendor will view this gap as a business opportunity. The third party provides an add-on or bolt-on software package whose value proposition may be to simply fill in the missing gap. In other cases, there may be a value-added service or benefit provided when using the third party add-on software. There are a number of examples of such add-on and specialty software packages that extend the value proposition of other software packages in this manner. They include external sales tax calculators, demand planning systems, advanced planning and scheduling systems, transportation management systems, and warehouse management systems.

These third-party software package vendors rely on several important tenets. First, the fact that they have the endorsement of the primary software package vendor is usually helpful. This usually takes the form of a formal business alliance between the primary software package vendor and the third-party software package vendor. The existence of such a formal business alliance is certainly better from the perspective of a software buyer. This is primarily the case because the two vendors will usually collaborate on releases of future versions of either software package to insure ongoing compatibility.

When a formal business alliance or relationship does not exist between software package vendors, there can be considerable difficulties in obtaining the necessary levels of support from either vendor. This is especially the case when attempting to integrate the two packages. Second, the third-party software package vendor usually relies on readily available APIs. These APIs are made available by the primary software package vendor to integrate the add-on software with the primary software package. This helps to ensure both smooth integration and operational synchronization.

When evaluating third party add-on software, perhaps the most important issue is error and exception handling. When third-party software fails (and it will) the buyer will need to understand:

- How will its failure affect the operation of the primary software package functions?
- How is the user notified of the failure?
- How does recovery from the failure occur?
- What are the residual effects, if any, on transactions in the primary software package's database and how are they corrected?
- When a transaction usage-related error occurs, how is it handled between the two programs? How is the user notified and how does the user correct it?

Another significant and challenging issue is vendor support. It is complicated enough for any one package, let alone for any two packages, where integration is involved.

When dealing with third party add-ons to the software package, the most important question is generally: "Does the third-party vendor or does the primary software package vendor take ownership regarding any issues or problems that a user has?" I have seen instances of both. Inexperienced personnel at either vendor will often blame the other vendor's software as the cause of a problem. Usually, after escalation of the problem, sometimes with both vendors involved, issues are resolved, so at times problem resolution may seem like eternity. My recommendation to avoid this: Attempt to determine in advance the competency levels (i.e., depth and experience of staff) that each vendor has committed to support their alliance.

When dealing with multiple software packages, it helps to have a written, tested troubleshooting plan in place. Usually, this is a trial-and-error experience that you will have to go through. The key is to document every problem and every solution. They can and usually do occur over and over. Sometimes each vendor will provide documentation that may differ (although hopefully not contradict) slightly. It will usually differ in either level of detail and sometimes about assumptions, namely about your environment. Some vendor documentation will have troubleshooting sections to help with keeping these interfaces working properly as well.

It is important to understand that some of these alliances are quickly broken once the primary software package vendor decides it has a better way of providing the functionality that was previously provided by the third party add-on software. Maybe it is through yet another third party. Or, perhaps the primary vendor has decided to introduce its own proprietary solution. In the latter case, many ERP vendors have been building their CRM solutions by acquiring vendors and their accompanying CRM products, often abandoning any previous CRM software vendor alliances.

WHEN THE VENDOR SAYS: YOU DO NOT NEED IT OR YOU CANNOT HAVE IT (NOW)

Some vendors may imply to your organization that if a given business process or software feature is not available or supported by their software, then it is likely not a commonly accepted best business practice or frequently requested feature and is not worth doing. While this may sound as if it were merely marketing hype, sometimes there is actually some truth in this statement. It could just as easily mean that your organization is an innovator and the unsupported business process represents a competitive or marketplace advantage.

In other cases, the unsupported business practice is specific to your vertical and is not found in practice in other verticals. In this case the vendor may have wider experience within specific verticals (and likely not in your industry if the vendor has no knowledge of its unique requirements). Usually, a vendor's experience is measured by its installed base, or the number of customers who have implemented the software within a given vertical.

Often times, vendors will ultimately provide the needed business process support or software feature as a product enhancement, but it is usually not right away. No matter how hard any given software package vendor tries, generally speaking, it is a generation or more behind in their product design and architectures. Most vendors focus interim or minor product upgrades on problem or performance issues. New software functionality is usually held until a major release or upgrade of the software is provided. More important, your organization may simply not be able to wait out the vendor for an upgrade that provides much needed functionality now. This means that many organizations will turn to the tried and true alternatives They will seek to fill this generation gap by integrating another software package from a third-party vendor that has already responded to this marketplace challenge and fills in the functionality gap today, or will resort to software package customization.

On this last item, software upgrades have several important ramifications for software package buyers. First, software buyers should realize that the versions of software products they are buying and implementing may be obsolete before their implementation is complete. Second, it also means that you, as a buyer of this or any software package for that matter, can expect a near constant upgrade cycle. This will require a new (major) release of the software package to be installed about every 12 to18 months in most cases, with usually at least a few interim (minor) releases in between.

INTEGRATION VERSUS INTEROPERABILITY

I have used the two terms, integration and interoperability, almost inter-changeably thus far. I suspect this is somewhat of a misnomer that I should clear up. Integration is more so a term associated with the coexistence of two software packages that usually have decidedly different business functions. Data, and possibly some transactions, are replicated between two such software packages to support their mutually independent functionality. Both inconsistencies between databases and any manual re-entry of data or transactions are avoided. Interoperability suggests something more, that perhaps instead of different business functions, some overlap of functionality between systems exists. It also suggests that the functionality of one package could be over another with data replication replaced by substitution.

Interoperability: How Close Are We?

Interoperability, or choice, through open systems architecture is very much a reailty for would-be buyers of software packages today. This is the case for most hardware, operating system, and database decisions. It is not uncommon to find that the typical high-end software package will be able to run under a multitude of hardware, operating system, and database platforms. For example, substituting one database for another is relatively straightforward, using something called open database connectivity, which was discussed in the last chapter.

But remember my stipulation on this point — such openness is largely limited to the choice of hardware platform, operating system, and database. I have said nothing about the business application software packages in this respect. This is because, unfortunately, interoperability between soft-ware packages is only beginning to emerge as an industry-accepted practice.

How Much Choice Really Exists?

Here are more practical notes to consider. First, as the software buyer moves down the food chain — into lower-priced software and — when that software buyer has to fill a more complex or specialized business application requirement, the choices can narrow considerably. Second, most software vendors will have specific recommendations that may represent an ideal or optimal configuration for the software package under consideration.

Although you may be free to choose, please exercise some caution. It is not unheard of for a vendor to abandon support for what has been a previously supported hardware platform, operating system, or database. There continues to be tremendous competitive pressures at play as these industry segments consolidate, leaving only a few major vendors in each of these categories. Suppose your organization is considering acquiring software that does not have wide acceptance or substantial market share on a given infrastructure and it is not the vendor's preferred or optimal infrastructure platform for its software. You may want to consider how your organization would be affected if the vendor abandoned support for your infrastructure platform.

Let us examine the interoperability at the process or functional level — the domain of business application software packages. If a business application system can exist in harmony with other systems, sharing information with other business application systems and treating one another as black boxes of secular functionality, then true interoperability has been achieved. Unfortunately, the reality has been that such a lofty goal is steep in theory and admittedly difficult to find in practice.

Previously, most software package vendors have frowned on interoperability. The good news is that the prospects for interoperability have truly improved lately. Recall for instance, Hasso Plattner's comments from Chapter 7. Following SAP's lead, in the months ahead expect that important aspects of application interoperability support will emerge in all of the major software packages.

GETTING WHAT YOU WANT: AN EPILOGUE

This chapter was largely about the reality of software packages meeting business requirements initially and the software package's durability to sustain business precipitated changes over time. Organizations that adopt software packages face five significant issues in order to meet these challenges when dealing with software packages. They include:

- Configuration and reconfiguration
- Customization
- Data and process migration
- System integration and interoperability
- Upgrades and enhancements

These challenges begin early in the SPLC. They often emanate as business requirement gaps during software package selection and continue to challenge the software package user throughout the useful life of the software package.

9

SOFTWARE PACKAGE SELECTION: THE FIRST STEPS

This chapter is the first to deal with the software selection stage of the overall software package life cycle concept discussed earlier in this book. The software selection process is often considered a high-stakes game and is usually regarded as a highly political and subjective process if left unchecked. It is highly desirable to take a planned, deliberate approach that introduces as much objectivity and structure into the selection process as possible.

This chapter is about taking the first steps in a planned, deliberate, and impartial software selection and evaluation process intended to assist any organization in selecting a software package that will provide the sought-after business functionality and business value. More important, it is also intended to help an organization in selecting a software package that can be successfully implemented.

This chapter begins a journey along what I refer to as the software selection roadmap. The software selection roadmap can also be interpreted as a high-level work breakdown structure for the software selection stage. Figure 9.1 illustrates the first steps in the overall software selection process that will be discussed in this chapter and will lead up to the creation of the request for proposal (RFP) document, which is the subject of the next chapter. Note that Figure 10.1 represents the continuation of the software selection roadmap and will pick up in illustrating the software selection process where these first steps leave off.

THE SELECTION TEAM

The logical first step in software selection is to form a selection team. This team is logically the team that might have lead the organization

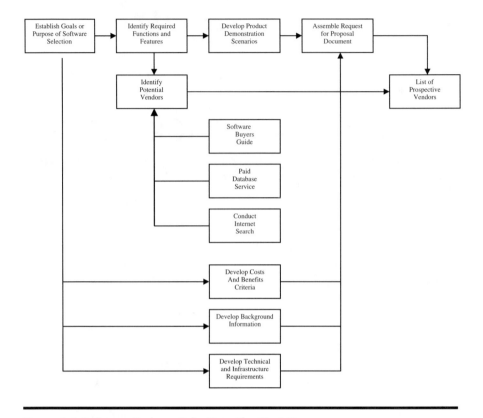

Figure 9.1 Software Package Selection: The First Steps

through the business process improvement initiative. This is because there are many synergies between process modeling, technology-enabled business process reengineering, and software features and functions to be sought. The team will at times rely on other subject matter experts to guide their development, understanding of, and ranking of software features. A consultant may or may not assist in the software selection process. As a general rule, the more inexperienced the team or the organization is with conducting software selection processes, the more value a consultant will provide to the process.

REQUIREMENTS AND SOFTWARE SELECTION

Before determining what software package is appropriate for your organization, it is necessary to fully understand your business requirements. Articulating your business requirements and overall process vision to software vendors is a major part of the software selection and evaluation process. This chapter will introduce the underlying structure for software selection by identifying business requirements. A primary focus of this chapter is to address these primary questions:

- What are you asking or wanting the software package to do?
- What are you expecting from the software package vendor?

These two primary questions are posed to vendors indirectly, through a multitude of secondary and more detailed questions about your specific business requirements. These questions are typically included in an RFP document (explained in the next chapter) that is sent to a software package vendor for its review and timely response in the form of a formal proposal to your organization.

SOFTWARE SELECTION: TAKING A HOLISTIC APPROACH

The successful of software implementation is largely a result of the software selection process. It means that the evaluation and selection process found the best overall software package solution for the organization given the overall criteria in all dimensions. This author recommends a holistic approach to software selection. Such an approach considers that an organization has achieved a totality of requirements within the context of the two primary questions posed earlier:

In the context of a holistic software selection approach, the secondary and more detailed questions about specific business requirements are grouped into four major requirement areas:

- Business application requirements
- Time and cost to value requirements
- Technical and infrastructure requirements
- Vendor relationship requirements

An in-depth review of each of these four evaluation areas follows.

Business Application Requirements

The primary reason an organization will acquire a software package is to satisfy its business application processing requirements. A fundamental portion of the evaluation, perhaps 50% or more, is geared toward assessing the goodness of fit of the software package from a functionality standpoint.

Some of my colleagues in the industry purport that certain types of software packages, especially enterprise resource planning (ERP) systems, customer relationship management systems, and financial application software, have become largely generic or common functionality; they believe that an extensive analysis or comparison between such systems is not necessarily a valuable exercise. My position is that an analysis at the feature level is still necessary. However, perhaps not all of this functionality needs to thoroughly demonstrated as much as the features specifically related to the organization's major business processes. While for competitive reasons the feature sets between any given field of candidate systems may be close, how each vendor implements or performs a given generic or common process can vary widely. Often times the user interface, the number of steps, and the ease of configuration and reconfiguration are all significantly different among a field of candidate software packages.

For certain specialized business applications and industry segments, very few software packages may be available to fulfill a given set of business application requirements or perhaps so for an entire industry. In these cases, only a few software vendors may even qualify as a prospective vendor.

Time and Cost to Value Requirements

Financial considerations can be significant factors during software package selection. It is important to assess carefully not only any one-time charges, but also all recurring charges associated with any given solution. The cost to implement one software package versus another can vary greatly. For instance, one package representing a better fit may cost substantially more, yet a lower cost software package requires more customization, increasing its cost. Understand that the costs of filling software functionality gaps using customization can prove to be costly and will often times lead only to disappointment or delay. Time to value and cost to value criteria must be considered and weighted appropriately as a part of the overall evaluation equation.

Technical and Infrastructure Requirements

Many organizations establish any software package decisions around specific hardware and network and software environments that constitute the preferred architecture or infrastructure in advance. There is much to be said for adopting such a strategy. A deliberate, planned architecture and infrastructure strategy will help the organization leverage resources and control costs. The strategy also promotes discipline in the development of custom business application software or the acquisition of business application software packages.

When an organization has adopted a preferred or mandatory architecture or infrastructure strategy, this should be specifically disclosed in the RFP document. Some vendors may be unable to fulfill all of the architecture or infrastructure guidelines that have been adopted. The good news is today more software packages are supporting multiple platforms, databases, and operating system choices. For specialized software packages, those that are perhaps germane to a specific industry or application, it may be the software that has very specific hardware, operating system software, or database product requirements. They will not be available for use on an organization's desired or preferred platform products. Understand that in some cases overly rigid technical requirements can disqualify all but a few vendors.

Vendor Relationship Requirements

Some vendors are quite professional, highly regarded, and have successfully executed their business strategy over a period of time. They have staying power as measured by their financial strength and the depth of their product. Not all software vendors are in this same position and many are struggling.

There are several reasons for the tough times in the software business, including the economic downturn, the dot.com bust, post-Y2K demand falloff, a renewed interest in measurable return on investment and an increasing interest in products that deliver integration and interoperability out of the box. While the current market represents a seller's worst nightmare, it is also a buyer's dream come true. The information technology industry is downsizing and consolidating. The software industry is not the only one that has been affected. These same market realities are also affecting hardware vendors and the consulting industry as well. Vendors in all of these areas are merging, going out of business, or simply leaving the business.

While it may be true that vendors are hurting and dealing, it also means there are dangers present in the current market. Tough questions must be considered. Will the vendor stay afloat? Will the vendor make the necessary research and development investments necessary to keep its product competitive? In short, it is not simply about the right price and right product; it is also about forming a relationship with the right, long-term supplier.

There are two general categories of relationship evaluation criteria: vendor compatibility and project compatibility. The vendor's suitability on such points as financial stability, depth of staff, compatibility or goodness of fit with the organization, and overall chances of success should be considered. With regard to project compatibility, criteria such as project understanding, methodology, the ability to add value, as well as both the vendor's industry knowledge and related project experience should also be considered.

DEFINING FUNCTIONAL REQUIREMENTS

Business requirements must be the primary driver behind a software acquisition. Until now we have only addressed business requirements at the highest and most strategic levels. Assuming that your business case embodies strategic business requirements, the next level of requirements definition is to understand what operational or tactical requirements your business has for new software. The result of this process is the creation of a list of software package functional requirements. The completion of such a list of functional requirements relies heavily on the work products resulting from a business process modeling initiative. Business process modeling was discussed extensively in Chapter 5.

There are several approaches that can be taken when preparing a list of the functional requirements or features list (a term I prefer to use) that will be used during a software selection. The first approach is to buy a ready-made features list. Such lists are available, but not for all software package categories. In particular, such lists are available for both ERP systems and financial systems. In some cases, these canned lists of requirements may be insufficient. It has been my experience that the depth and quality of these types of lists can vary. Some of the lists will favor one functional area over another.

The second approach is to build the features list from the ground up. This can be a particularly time-consuming process. You will need to inventory your current system capabilities. These capabilities may also be referred to as features and functions. You will also need to determine what outstanding requests exist from within your organization for additional features, which usually must take the form of enhancements to the current system.

A twofold approach can be taken to identify unmet needs. The first part of the approach is to conduct a satisfaction survey with users of the current system. The survey would assess the state of the software. The second part of the approach is to identify additional unmet needs by reviewing the information services department's backlog of enhancement requests related to the current system. An added benefit of conducting satisfaction surveys is that you will begin to involve users at the earliest stages in the search for a new system. If users feel their feedback will guide the process, it stands to reason their overall demeanor will be more favorable when the new system is implemented.

This is a actually a fairly common approach for organizations, especially in organizations not engaging in or coupling a reengineering or business improvement effort with the software selection process. If a business process reengineering initiative is preceding software selection, it is likely that current software user satisfaction surveys will be of little, if any, value.

In such cases, the business process reengineering team will need to architect the software features list. This will be based upon the processes, best practices, and workflows that are being envisioned for the reengineered organization.

Recall from Chapter 5 that radical or clean sheet business process reengineering is done without regard to the current, or even to candidate business system functionality; technology-enabled business process reengineering does consider candidate business system functionality. Ready-made functionality or feature lists generally have wider acceptance for selecting software in conjunction with the technology-enabled business process reengineering initiative.

These two approaches can certainly be combined. An organization can purchase a ready-made list, while adding to or subtracting from it based upon the organization's unique business requirements or situation. For instance, many consulting firms will begin with a ready-made list of functional requirements. This is usually done by business process (i.e., general ledger, payroll, order processing) or vertical industry (i.e., consumer packaged goods, oil and gas, retail, construction).

Building the list of business related requirements requires a significant amount of effort. Do not shortchange the process. If you fail to capture your essential business requirements, you may arrive at a suboptimal decision as to which software is best suited for your needs.

THE FEATURES LIST: DESCRIBE BY FEATURE AND BUY BY FEATURE

Many of an organization's business processes rely on software packages to provide crucial business transaction processing support and analysis capabilities. Business application software packages meet these business needs through specific software features. Earlier chapters have discussed both business needs and techniques of modeling processes and practices that fulfill business needs.

To properly evaluate software packages requires that an organization understand, in advance of any software comparison and ultimately the selection of a specific software package, how it envisions a software package being employed or used in its business model. Consider this the overall purpose of the software package. Chapter 10 provides insights on how to develop a purpose statement for software selection. It may be helpful to read that section in conjunction with this one.

The features list is a detailed presentation of the specific transaction processing support and analysis capabilities required in a business application software package. The term feature is also synonymous with the term function or requirement. A features list is synonymous with the terms functions list or requirements list. This book will use the convention feature and features list. The reasons for doing so will be revealed shortly.

How Detailed Should the Questions Be?

An example of a high-level question is: "Does the package include payroll support?" Such high-level questions have little substance, but they should not be immediately discounted as worthless. The value in this type of question is that it allows for the immediate disqualification of packages that cannot meet your organization's basic functional requirements. There are typically many more payroll-related questions that a software buyer might have. For example, a unionized manufacturing business might have a requirement, such as "Provides for flat rate per hour shift differentials by labor class and grade".

There are several challenges that can occur when constructing a list of business requirements for a software package. First, you need to avoid ambiguous questions. Be clear and concise in stating the requirement. Second, use action-oriented sentences. Third, logically organize the desired features around specific business processes or functions. I have found a particular technique invaluable for developing software-related business requirements. It is called a features list and is the next subject of discussion.

What Is a Software Feature?

My preoccupation and focus on the concept of software features stems not from my software package background, but from some extensive work I did on software development methodologies several years ago. The client in this case was a software package vendor that was just beginning to reengineer their software package for web deployment.

At that time, I came across a concept called feature-driven development (FDD) in *Java Modeling in Color with UML*, by Peter Coad, Eric Lefebvre, and Jeff DeLuca. FDD is an implementation or variant of Barry Beohm's spiral or iterative model for software development. My greatest interest in the work of these three authors was in their approach to describing software features. In the FDD framework, software engineers build software systems effectively one feature at a time. They group and deliver the highest-value software features in the earliest releases of the software system, and lower-valued features are picked up in successive software releases.

Although a complete discussion of feature-driven development is not germane to our discussion here, there are some decided advantages when using FDD. This is especially true for component-based software development and hence for software package vendors. For the purposes of this book, it is the concept of a software feature and how to describe and organize software features that has particular relevance.

Software features exist in systems under development as readily as they exist in commercial, off-the-shelf software packages. Coad, Lefebvre, and DeLuca view a software feature as "a small block of client-valued functionality." I would further submit that a software feature should be thought of as a tangible, demonstrable, and client-valued part of any software system, whether it is a custom developed system or a commercial, off-the-shelf software package. The authors suggest allowing users to describe software features using short statements. I would prefer to go a step further in my definition of a software feature and add that it is an *action-oriented,* short statement describing what a business application system or software package can or must do. A software feature for either a custom developed system or a commercial, off-the-shelf software package can really be described in the same way.

The authors also suggest a framework for organizing features. They suggest organizing features into business-related groupings referred to as feature sets and organizing a series of related feature sets into major feature sets. Although the above definitions seem a bit complicated, an indented bill of materials format of the features hierarchy from the examples below should clear the feature fog.

An Example of a:	In the Context of a Integrated Enterprise Resource Planning System an Example Would Be:
Major feature set	Procure to pay
Feature set	Procurement
Analyzing business results feature subset	Vendor analysis
Feature	Calculate on-time delivery performance level on a per order basis
Feature	Display vendor's overall on-time delivery performance level on an aggregate basis with drill down to specific order on chronological basis

Where Do Software Features Originate?

I must again tip my hat to Peter Coad and his co-author, Mark Mayfield. In their book, *Java Design*, is one of the simplest and best models I have seen for thinking about and describing how business application software should work through software features. The author's approach was written within the context of software development. I have found that with some tweaking, this same approach can be readily applied to seeking out and describing the underlying features needed in a business application software package.

The basic framework or features strategy suggested by the authors is to list the features for setting up and conducting the business and assessing business results. To date, I have found no better or simpler framework for thinking about software in a business context. Although I agree with the three general categories that Coad and Mayfield suggest in their approach to describing the major parts of a business application software system, my model for describing the features needed in a software package does differ slightly. Figure 9.2 represents the business application software model that I have constructed using the author's features strategy that I use in arriving at software package features. A detailed description of this model follows in subsequent paragraphs.

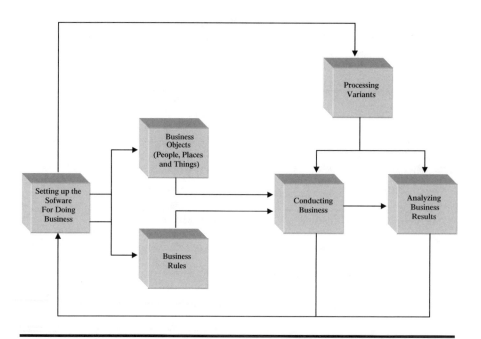

Figure 9.2 Software Package Processing Flow: A Generalized Model

Setting up

When considering software package functionality, there are specific features that your organization will need in order to set up the software package to conduct business using the software package.

The cornerstones of software package generality and flexibility can be found in two concepts: business rules and variants.

What Is a Business Rule?

A business rule is an accepted manner or method for completing a given activity or task. There are many examples of everyday business rules. Many business rules are externally defined by an industry or trade group, through accepted practice, or even by stature. Some well-known examples include:

- Payment terms on an invoice document (e.g., net 30 days)
- Freight payment terms on an order document (e.g., prepay and add)
- Terms of title on an order document (e.g., FOB destination)
- Preparing customer account statements using balance forward method
- Preparing customer account statements using open item method

Any list of software package features should include reference to specific software features that facilitate business rule definition and initiation and application.

What Is a Processing Variant?

Processing variants may also be considered as filters. An example of a processing variant is using the same inquiry or report (e.g., a supplier ledger inquiry) to view three different sets of information: one variant to consider only employees, another to consider only vendors, and a third for taxing authorities. Processing variants affect both the business events found in the Conducting Business section as well as in the software features that provide for Analyzing Business Results.

CRUD: The Basics.

Another common software development acronym applies to software package design — CRUD, which stands for create, retrieve, update, and delete. Implicit in any software package design should be the ability to create, retrieve, update, and delete any meaningful data record — or object — described within a software package's data model. With that said, the software package should provide for creating, retrieving, updating, and deleting the business objects that are needed in the software package's database in order to execute any business event permissible within the software package.

Business Objects: What It Is All about

Business objects include any number of business related entities. Examples include such things as customers and vendors, business units and account numbers, or salable and component parts and assemblies and transaction documents. Many of these business objects are established prior to conducting business in the software package, such as components, customers, and supplier objects. However, at least some of the setting up features in a software package will be used on a routine basis as a part of the normal routine of conducting business using the software package. For instance, the ability to create, retrieve, update, or delete a business document object, such as a purchase order, sales order, or general ledger journal entry represent examples of such transactions.

Conducting Business

At the centerpiece of any software package are the software features that will provide the information support related to the conduct of your business processes. Business transactions are by and large event driven. A business process is best thought of as an event chain. With ERP software, the quote-to-cash processing thread is one example of an event chain. I have also referred to event chains as processing threads and workflows. All of these terms can be used interchangeably.

Consider the following example of a processing chain or processing thread. The quote to cash processing thread is made up of a chain of events. This includes receiving a request for quotation (RFQ) from a prospect or former customer, responding to the RFQ, receiving a firm order from the prospect referencing the RFQ, setting up the prospect as a customer, completing a credit check on the prospect, entering the order, and checking stock or scheduling shipment or production when entering the sales order. When describing software features, the business process event chain, processing thread or workflow is the focal point.

Analyzing Business Results

Once business rules are defined, then business objects can be created. From each of these core system components can spring forth the ongoing analysis of information flowing within the software package.

The basic processing, analysis, and display of results is known as analyzing business results. The nucleus of business planning, control, and management relies on software features described for analyzing business results.

Developing the Features List: Who Should Do This?

The identification of software features relies heavily on an understanding of business processes and the general nature or characteristics of software and software packages. If you do not have such expertise in your organization, such as a business analyst or systems analyst, there are consultants who specialize in software selection work.

These consultants are trained facilitators who have the ability to elicit and describe business application requirements in terms of desired software features. Many will use questionnaires and interviews along with software tools to develop such a list of business requirements. The added advantage in using a software tool is that it can shorten the selection process. Usually these tools work in conjunction with a database of software packages and software package features. This information can be used to develop a list of "prequalified" software packages. In turn, this information can be used for inviting or soliciting specific vendors to bid on the project.

Understand the Business to Determine Features Needed

As previously stated, the identification of software features relies heavily on an understanding of business processes and on the general nature or characteristics of software and software packages. I find the best method for understanding what features are needed in any candidate software package is, first and foremost, to understand the current processes employed by the organization. This is not an endorsement of bad processes. As a matter of fact, it is during this organizational process assessment that process weaknesses or inefficiencies will likely come to light. I generally recommend that business process modeling precede the construction of the features list.

Assuming that business process models are in hand, then any suppliers, inputs, processes, outputs, and customers (SIPOC) process models and the process vision statements prepared during business process modeling can be read for processing actions and specific process criteria. These actions and criteria give rise to specific, process-related software features; hence, it is from these that feature statements can be constructed. Recall that Chapter 5 discussed business process modeling and business process reengineering.

Learning about Software Package Features and Functionality

If you are not aware of software packages or their features, this is one of the areas where a software selection consultant can provide guidance. If you prefer to educate yourself, the most helpful tool available today is the Internet. Search engines such as Alta Vista (www.altavista.com) and Google (www.google.com) are particularly valuable in locating software packages for specific applications. A search at one of these sites will identify vendors and consultants related to specific software packages. From these websites one can gain insights about the various software packages, their features, and the vendors that an organization may want to consider submitting its RFP document to once it is completed.

How Will the Features List Be Used?

The features list is made available to software vendors, usually as a part of an informal request for information or in a formal RFP document. Vendors will be asked to provide a response regarding the availability of each named feature on the features list. Typically, each feature set and each feature within a feature set are ranked as to relative importance to the business. A highly valued feature in a low-value portion of the software may in fact have less weight in the decision than a lowly valued feature in a high-value portion of the software.

Ranking Features

A software feature must satisfy a want for the business unit that is served by the software package or whoever is funding the software package acquisition. In the case of an integrated or enterprise-wide software package, such as an ERP system, development of the features list and the relative ranking or weighting of the features is required.

Once the features list has been established, the tough part is often collaborating on the relative importance of one feature versus another. This can be done in one of several ways. One method is the survey approach. Once features are gathered, the next step is to have the users now rank the importance of each feature. Here is an sample scale for doing such:

- A feature we have now and use frequently
- A feature we have now but would be unlikely to ever use again
- A feature we have now but will not need in the future
- A feature we have now and never use
- A feature we do not have now but would use immediately if available

- A feature we do not have now but would like it available for future application
- A feature we do not have now but would be unlikely to ever use
- A feature we do not have now and will not need in the future

As an alternative, the software selection team can simply rank features given the team's overall knowledge of the requirements. This may be appropriate when business processes are being totally reengineered and users input has little relation to what will be implemented. Ranking the relative importance of desired software features and functionality is often a complex, challenging, highly emotional, and time-consuming process. This process can be conducted at this time, or deferred until the software package evaluation stage, but it must be done.

PRODUCT DEMONSTRATION SCRIPTS

Once the software features list has been completed, the next step is to prepare software demonstration scripts. These scripts will be given to software vendors so they can employ them as a guide in tailoring a software demonstration to your business model. Doing so will ensure the features and functions of the vendor's software package that are germane to your core business processes can be articulated and demonstrated to the software selection team.

As was the case in preparing the features list, the construction of product demonstration scripts assumes that business process modeling has been completed. These scripts rely on the SIPOC models, the process vision statements, the features list, and actual examples of business transactions that are representative of both everyday and unusual aspects of your business model.

Product Demonstration Scripts and the Use Case Format

There are two components of the product demonstration script. The first, is the process component, which I prefer to provide to the vendor in terms of a use case. The primary role of use cases is in software development. Business analysts elicit software development requirements from the system users using use cases. I have also found that use cases are an excellent way to illustrate the logic of a system during a software product demonstration. In fact, many software developers utilize use cases as test cases for new software products.

A use case is best described as a sequence of events or activities undertaken in a system for the purpose of yielding a result of measurable value to the user of the system. Each use case will typically represent a single transaction scenario. When multiple or alternative paths can be taken, a use case is needed to describe each possible flow of events.

The approach I tend to use is to construct a use case for each single business transaction event that should be demonstrated. Examples of such events include adding a new customer, supplier or product; defining a bill of material; entering a sales order; or receiving a shipment. I can also connect a series of use cases together to form a processing chain to demonstrate the entire order-to-cash or the procure-to-pay processing thread within a given system. These connections between use cases are formed through predecessor and successor use cases or activities within the system. A completed use case example is illustrated in Figure 9.3. This use case template is a part of the author's template collection. Consult Appendix A for more information.

In many ways, a use case is similar to the SIPOC process model, but is dialog oriented. This results in a greater level of detail about the system and user relationship in an overall process. A use case should focus on system requirements, but not the system design or implementation. As a result, the use case is written to a relatively high level. This is a very simplistic discussion of use cases and hardly does them complete justice. In fact, entire books have been written in recent years about how to write a use case. Above all else, keep the use case simple.

Preparing Sample Business Data

The second component of the product demonstration script is the sample business data component. If you want the vendor to demonstrate how its software would handle one of your typical business transactions, you must provide sample data. The sample business data can be altered to mask the identity of proprietary content if needed, so long as it can be understood. I prefer to submit sample business data in terms of mock input and output documents or as desired presentations, such as a report or inquiry screen.

Preparing product demonstration scripts is an exacting and time-consuming process. You should start this process well before the scripts will actually be needed in the software selection process. My recommendation is to provide these scripts to vendors as part of the RFP document. If they are not provided in the RFP, then at least a list of the business processes that must ultimately be demonstrated by the vendor should be included within the RFP.

The reason I prefer to provide the scripts is that they can assist the vendor in understanding your organization's business processes in more detail. The features list does not tell much of a story in this regard. Using the use case format I have recommended here does tell a story. The vendor may find this a bit easier to follow and can determine if its software package will meet your requirements.

TradewindsGroup
Tradewinds Group, Incorporated
Consultants to Management
Box 3601
Oak Brook, Illinois 60522

Use Case Scenario for Proposed System

Identifying Information

Client Name	Proposed System	Use Case Reference Number
ABC Manufacturing		

Use Case Information

Use Case Name	Actor	Description of Actor
Enter Customer Order	Internal Order Taker	Any customer service representative or direct sales agent of the organization.

Pre-Conditions

List any pre-conditions for this Use Case	Refer to Use Case Reference Number
1. Product record exists in system.	SOP-080
2. Customer record exists in system.	SOP-090

Use Case Process (List the normal course of events for this Use Case)

List the Actor's Action/Intention	List the Desired/Required System Response
1. Access that portion of the system where a sales order can be entered for any given customer.	1. Opens the order entry form for an "authorized" user.
2. Enters the customer number.	2. Retrieves and displays standard order processing preferences related to this customer.
3. The internal order taker reviews the on-screen information with the customer to insure it is valid for this order. Changes any information as needed.	3. Validates any changes made to on screen information.
4. Enters product number, quantity.	4. Validates product number. Check stock availability. Calculates delivery date. Displays calculated availability on screen.
5. Reviews order with customer to determine if delivery date is acceptable.	5. None

Printed on 08/01/02 — Proprietary and Confidential — Page 1 of 2

Figure 9.3 The Product Demonstration Script: A Use Case-Based Example

TradewindsGroup
Tradewinds Group, Incorporated
Consultants to Management
Box 3601
Oak Brook, Illinois 60522

Use Case Scenario for Proposed System

Use Case Process (List the normal course of events for this Use Case)

List the Actor's Action/Intention	List the Desired/Required System Response
6. Customer authorizes internal order taker to process order. Internal order taker completes on screen acceptance of order.	6. Stores order contents. Reserves inventory. Fax or Print Order Acknowledgement based upon customer preferences.

Post-Conditions

List any post-conditions for this Use Case	Refer to Use Case Reference Number
1. The order must be picked, packed and shipped to the customer.	SOP-110

Assumptions

List any assumptions made for this Use Case
1. Customer places order by part number.
2.
3.
4.
5.

Sample Data (For product demonstration purposes)

Business Data Object	Business Data Value
System (Order Taken) Date	06/10/20XX
Customer	1010
Product Number	1F943-239
Product Description	FASTENER – SS – HEX HEAD – 10/32 x 2.5
Quantity	100
Unit of Measure	Each
Needed By	06/15/20XX

Printed on 08/01/02   - Proprietary and Confidential -   Page 2 of 2

Figure 9.3 The Product Demonstration Script: A Use Case-Based Example

DEFINING BUSINESS REQUIREMENTS: AN ALTERNATE APPROACH

As previously noted, development of the features list and the relative ranking of features can be a complex and time-consuming process. Once completed, the next task is to identify vendors, followed by the development of an RFP; this is all before the actual evaluation even begins. There are proven techniques that your organization, or that a software selection consultant can use to streamline the software selection process. One such technique is available through SoftSelect Systems and is described in the next section.

SoftSelect Systems LLC and the SoftSelect Approach

SoftSelect Systems of Vancouver, WA, provides a series of products and services aimed at providing a more efficient approach for software selection. The SoftSelect process and tools accelerate major portions of selecting software. The application of SoftSelect products and services is not limited to simply software selection. These products and services can be used when conducting effectiveness reviews of existing enterprise software.

The SoftSelect approach is designed for use by a client or an end-user organization. The SoftSelect approach is designed to save time and costs with established methodology and software product research as well as software tools that enable the selection team to collaborate and organize the project. Consultant billings are much higher if the consultant must duplicate the research work that SoftSelect has already done. These are dollars that can then be directed toward actual software implementation or any needed infrastructure improvements. For instance, the SoftSelect approach is ideally suited to an organization that has completed a technology-enabled business processing reengineering initiative and wants to fast track the software selection process.

It is important to note that the SoftSelect Systems products and services discussed here are typically only available through a network of independent consultants. Participating consultants receive training on these products and services from SoftSelect Systems. This training goes well beyond the typical hands-on workshop. The training actually presents strategies that will help consultants maximize the effectiveness of SoftSelect Systems products and services on their client engagements. Consultants can use SoftSelect Systems products and services in software selection engagements and in other business and process improvement engagements as well. The actual SoftSelect products and services are discussed in detail in the next section.

SoftSelect Systems is well known and highly regarded in both the consulting and software package communities. At the National Manufacturers Week convention and tradeshow held this past spring in Chicago, I spoke with a number of software vendors about their products and my work as an author, a consultant, and educator as well. When we spoke about software selections, almost all had heard of and value their product's inclusion in the SoftSelect database.

The SoftSelect Requirements Builder

The starting point for the selection team is to use the SoftSelect Requirements Builder software to collect and organize the software requirements or features needed by your organization. For selected software types (i.e., ERP and supply chain software), this tool provides a predetermined or core set of questions that an organization will answer. These questions address software functional features, technical aspects, and other nonfunctional factors, such as budget considerations, through their innovative "suitability zones."

The SoftSelect Software Selection Report

The organization's answers to these core functionality questions are then finalized and sent to SoftSelect Systems. They are then compared against the database, which contains extensive vendor and independent auditor-verified attributes of software functionality. The resulting report includes candidate software packages along with a series of tools and instructions for subsequent software evaluation.

Even if an organization has already short-listed software packages, perhaps without consulting assistance, but it has not completed the purchase, it may still be want to consider a SoftSelect abbreviated review. This review can quickly and economically confirm the organization's choice of software package.

The SoftSelect Enterprise Software Management Process

Information system obsolescence and information system change are inevitable. Although numerous factors can be involved, being able to compete effectively in a changing, increasingly global, and information-driven world is usually the deciding significant factor. While the typical software application, including the software package, has a life expectancy averaging 7 years, times are changing. Even packages considered state of the art and just a few years old are obsolete if they cannot easily integrate across the supply chain.

A SoftSelect-based enterprise software effectiveness review provides a comparison of the relative position of an organization's current business application system infrastructure and business needs against what the latest software products can offer. The organization's management team can utilize this report to help understand not only if, but also how to provide the business justification for new software technology.

The SoftSelect Software Profiler

The SoftSelect research department uses the SoftSelect Software Profiler, as part of a proven method to collect software product information from software vendors and to keep this information as current as possible. In addition to collecting information from vendors, SoftSelect also relies on other sources to provide an independent, nonvendor confirmation of a vendor's responses to the questions contained in the SoftSelect Software Profiler.

How Does the SoftSelect Approach Change Software Selection?

The SoftSelect approach provides numerous benefits when selecting software. Most important, this approach can vastly improve the selection process. It does this in several ways. First, there is no need to construct a features list; that is an integral part of SoftSelect's tool. Second, there is no need to research or determine the vendors or software packages. The SoftSelect research team has already done this, and this information has been incorporated into its database. Third, once the requirements are identified and analyzed, an evaluation is prepared that matches an organization's requirements against product features to determine which products fit. In addition, nonfeature features are taken into account, saving an organization time and effort in reviewing products. For instance, instead of focusing on building the features list, an organization's efforts can be devoted to constructing business transaction scenarios.

Other Software Selection Tools and Research Sources

There are other tools and services available that can provide standard lists of requirements and current market research. The capabilities of these services and their completeness will vary widely. Two such services include Technology Evaluation (www.technologyevaluation.com) and OnLine Consultant Software (www.olcsoft.com). In addition, a number of larger consulting firms have developed proprietary approaches that are oriented around similar concepts and strategies to those discussed here. The capabilities of these tools will vary. Some of these tools will only build a features list or an RFP template; there is no analysis of data made.

These tools serve to promote efficiency and structure in the overall selection process; they will not make the software decision for you. When reviewing any software selection tool or service, consider these fundamental questions:

- Does the tool select software specific to my industry or business model? Not all of the tools are appropriate for use if selecting a software package for a manufacturing or distribution firm. For instance, some tools are appropriate only for financial software packages. Understand what the bias of the tool or service is.
- How many software packages and/or vendors are represented in the database used by the tool? More is always better. Also, how are the data gathered and validated?
- How many requirements by major business process or function are available in the features or requirements database? Are there ways to filter out requirements that are not applicable or to add requirements missing from the database, but are essential to the selection process? The more questions in each category, the better.
- What nonfunctional parameters about your business are used to discern which software packages are or are not appropriate? For instance, can software package cost and technical factors be taken into account?

These questions can be used to compare and ascertain which selection tools and services will be most appropriate for your organization. Again note that your selection consultant may be biased toward using a particular tool or service.

DO FEATURES REALLY MATTER?

A number of critics have begun to question the value of constructing and using software feature-based lists as the centerpiece of the software package selection process. One such critic is Jack M. Keen, founder and president of The Deciding Factor who refers to this as "feature-mania addiction."

It is a well-known and commonly accepted fact that most organizations use only a small number of features typically available in an acquired software package. Yet, a preoccupation with building lists of software features persists and it is one that this author has also proposed. So if an organization is using only some of the available feature set in a typical software package, why focus on features?

This is a good question and I have a simple, yet persuasive answer to such criticisms. It is rooted in my predisposition toward the FDD model and its particular focus on the notion of client-valued functionality. The process of eliciting from your project sponsors and their users the features they are willing to pay for results in a list of truly needed software package features. What should be left is a listing of the essential software features — *without all the fluff* — your organization must buy to successfully support the information requirements related to your business processes. As stated previously, often times such fluff may relate to software features that are needed today in order to support legacy processes that may be radically changed or even eliminated through the software package acquisition and implementation.

This features-searching process should result in a listing of a few hundred such software features at most to focus on. At the same time, this list of client-valued, core software features is part of the critical factors that must be met if the implementation of the software package is to be a successful one. It represents a sort of postimplementation checklist that can be used to help assure your organization's software investment has achieved, in principle, what it was supposed to do.

So a features list has been built around what the organization values or needs most — around what it is willing to pay for. But this would still not be a valid defense to critics like Jack Keen. How then do you defend yourself to such critics?

Features alone should not be the sole, governing factor in software package selection. To be sure, any software package under serious consideration must score well in meeting the core set of features required to support your business model. The selection and evaluation process must also consider and measure a number of other, nonfeature-related factors; these factors are best characterized as vendor relationship-centric factors. For instance, the Gartner Group refers to this as a software vendor's ability to execute, while others refer to this concept as a vendor's ability to deliver. Call it what you want, but in the end, software package selection must be a holistic decision built on:

- The completeness of a software package's feature set to satisfy your core business information processing requirements.
- A demonstrated ability of the vendor through what are effective case studies of the vendor's past customers to realize success with the software package.
- The vendor's staying power, not measured simply by its installed base, market share, and new license revenue but also through its financial success and service revenue or retention of installed base.
- The vendor's product commitment, as measured through its continuous investment in its software and degree to which its installed base community is involved in the product maturation process.

■ A software package vendor becomes a long-term supplier to your organization. There must be a synergy — an achievable and workable level of trust and respect between your organization and the software vendor — in any software package transaction. Your organization must understand and measure the degree to which the software vendor will be able to help you achieve your desired return on investment.

In the end, the features list is only one part of a much larger evaluation process that includes evaluation criteria that extends beyond software features. Software selection must be a *holistic* process encompassing the product, the vendor, the reseller or implementation consultant, and your organization. The remainder of this chapter focuses on discussing the nonfeature factors that should be an integral part of the holistic software selection process recommended and practiced by this author.

NONFEATURE REQUIREMENTS AND SOFTWARE SELECTION

Thus far, this chapter has focused on business requirements since they usually carry the heaviest weight in the overall evaluation process. The holistic software selection process does have other dimensions. Requirements for those dimensions must be elicited from the organization and documented in the RFP document.

Technical Requirements

Organizations will usually have specific technical or infrastructure objectives. Such goals revolve around acceptable hardware and nonapplication or system software architectures desired by an organization. Usually these technical or infrastructure objectives will more often than not become specific requirements that an organization will have relative to the software packages it will consider. Some specific high-level technical or infrastructure requirements might be:

■ Must operate on an IBM AS/400 (i-series) computer platform
■ Must be completely Internet browser based
■ Must operate on an Oracle database
■ Must include source code

Further discussion of high-level technical or infrastructure objectives and requirements can be found in Chapter 7.

Under ideal circumstances, an organization will have no preferences or bias toward a specific technical requirement, but that is rarely the case. In this section the organization, usually its chief technology officer, spells out exactly what the infrastructure of the organization is and what specific technical or infrastructure requirements must be met by candidate software packages. This information is then used to screen out potential software packages and vendors that will not meet the organization's technical objectives.

Cost and Cost to Value Requirements

Cost is always an important factor when making business decisions. There can be wide variations in software pricing for seemingly identical business application functionality or value provided.

The software package industry competes on features and price. The consulting industry competes on approach, experience, and price. Value added resellers compete on all of these dimensions, but usually have geographic exclusivity for specific software products. All of these factors affect the cost of the software and the cost to value, particularly with respect to features and services received. Chapter 6 provides a comprehensive listing of the cost elements that will affect the software decision.

Chapter 6 also provided some rough budgetary guidelines that vendors, consultants, and resellers may use to determine if a particular client will be able to afford the software package of interest. Some of the buyer guides will provide cost estimates when a vendor has elected to disclose such information. Database services will also qualify vendors on cost criteria, again, when a vendor has chosen to provide this information. In many cases, it will be difficult to ascertain the cost of the software package and the needed requisite services to implement the package before receiving vendor bids.

Vendor Relationship Requirements

Buying a software package is a substantial investment. It is also a long-term decision, given that software packages average a useful life of 5 to 15 years in most organizations. Given the investment and its duration, selecting a vendor that you are comfortable doing business with, both now and in the future, is important. It is also important to understand if a vendor will remain in business for at least as long as the expected life you anticipate for their software package in your organization.

Criteria must be established to guide the evaluation of a vendor in terms of relationship that must be formed and carried out between your two organizations. These criteria are generally formulated along two dimensions: vendor-centric and project-centric. Such vendor relationship requirements or characteristics must be translated into questions posed to the vendor in the request for proposal document. Some examples include:

- Is there a user group for this product? What does membership cost?
- Is there a formal method for the user group to play an active role in the vendor's product enhancement process?
- How many of your clients have implemented this product domestically? Internationally?
- What release level of the proposed software product are most of your clients using?
- What is the average time to implement this software product? If the proposed time line varies from this average, explain why the estimate varies.
- How many clients within our industry group use this software product?
- In what year was this product (earliest version) first introduced?
- How frequently are enhancements made?
- What proportion of your revenues comes from new software licenses? Software maintenance? Training services? Implementation consulting?
- Do you provide implementation assistance through direct employees or using third parties?
- Does software maintenance include an unlimited number of calls to your support center during normal business hours?
- What are the hours of operation of your support center?

This is not an all-encompassing list of vendor relationship issues. The software selection team should consider including the chief technology officer, chief financial officer, and the chief credit officer in any review of vendor relationship questions. The next two chapters provide additional insights on vendor relationship requirements as well. Generally speaking, most of these questions will not factor into short-listing candidate vendors and will apply only to the RFP document and the RFP process.

ROUNDING UP THE USUAL SUSPECTS: FINDING CANDIDATE PACKAGES AND VENDORS

If you are not aware of the available software packages or the features they contain, I previously mentioned using the Internet as a quick way to research this area. If you have done that, you have already found or identified many, if not all of, the vendors that your organization will consider submitting its RFP document to in order to solicit software package proposals for your further evaluation.

In addition to the Internet, many industry and trade related publications publish periodic buyer's guides related to specific types of software packages. Again, the Internet can be used as a source in finding such publications if you are unaware of the ones that may be germane to the type of software being considered. These guides can then be referenced to determine what vendors and products exist that may be able to satisfy your software package requirements. The guides take on all forms. Some list no more than a dozen criteria, while others may contain a hundred or more qualifying features. They can be extremely helpful in paring down a long list of possible software packages and vendors.

Some individuals feel that a buyer's guide will have enough information in it to immediately qualify or disqualify a particular product or vendor. A cautionary note is in order. The information in these lists can be inaccurate or out of date. In particular, product availability on specific platforms or the availability of specific business functions or features may have changed substantially since a list was first published. Do not feel your work is complete until you have verified with the vendor, preferably anonymously through its website, if the product should be added to the short list.

If the SoftSelect software research or a similar approach was employed, this may be an unnecessary task for you. That process may have produced a ready-made short list of prospective software vendors. Whether you are using a ready-made short list or have employed grunt work to arrive at this list, it is your ticket into the RFP process. In the RFP process, the next step will be to determine if the vendors on your short list have a specific interest in bidding on your requirements. Sometimes they may choose not to bid your project, usually because they feel their software will be a poor fit, or your organization will not be able to afford the solution. With that said, this concludes the first steps in software selection.

INITIATING SOFTWARE SELECTION: AN EPILOGUE

This chapter discussed moving from both current or proposed business process models and the organization's process vision toward a list of software package attributes, known as features, that are to be sought out in a software package. Software selection should not be limited to considering only business requirements. Technical and vendor relationship requirements as well as the realities of cost must be considered in the holistic software selection process. Software selection is a well-developed science; specific tools, techniques, and services can be used to streamline the process when desirable. The next step in the software selection process is the construction of an RFP document and the initiation of the proposal process with prospective vendors.

10

SOFTWARE PACKAGE SELECTION: THE RFP PROCESS

The previous chapter discussed how to prepare two important elements necessary for effective software package evaluation: the features list and product demonstration scenarios. It also included tips on how to identify prospective software package vendors. This chapter focuses on two important and related topics in software selection that will ultimately lead to software package evaluation and selection.

The first topic is the process of conducting the competitive bidding process. In this process, vendors respond to the request for proposal (RFP) document with a formal proposal document. This chapter provides an overview of the competitive bidding process and makes some recommendations for conducting a fair, smooth, and successful competitive bidding process.

The second topic is the construction of the RFP document, the formal specification that details your software package requirements to vendors. In fact, the major thrust of this chapter focuses on how to develop the actual RFP document related to the software package acquisition. This document will include both the features list and product demonstration scenarios.

COMMUNICATING REQUIREMENTS TO SOFTWARE VENDORS: THE COMPETITIVE BIDDING PROCESS

The best, most comprehensive and fairest method of communicating with software vendors is through a formal RFP process. This is also frequently referred to as competitive bidding. It has been my experience that buying a software package is a complicated enough purchase decision that most software package acquisitions are worthy candidates for a formal competitive bidding process. Many organizations already require a formal bidding process, so this will not be a new concept to them. This is particularly true of large organizations, especially of regulated businesses; local, municipal, and state government entities; and federal agencies.

A fair number of organizations will prefer a more informal selection process. I would advise against this. An informal selection process can leave many questions unanswered. Unfortunately the consequences do not surface until long after one or more product demonstrations are viewed, a few discussions occur, and a contract is signed, and particularly during software implementation or the attempt to implement the software.

It is sometimes surprising to me when I find that some of my clients are not familiar with a structured software selection process built around an RFP. That is understandable for a relatively new information technology (IT) manager or director, who has perhaps not been a decision maker when making such a major capital expenditure. Most experienced chief financial officers, chief information officers, and purchasing managers will know and appreciate the value of a more structured buying experience, such as a software selection process based on an RFP document.

Perhaps your organization is either uncomfortable with taking on the software selection process alone or does not have available resources to do so. You may want to consider using a consultant to assist and guide the process along. Simply put, it is too important a decision for your organization to make in a haphazard manner.

Figure 10.1 illustrates the continuation of the software selection roadmap, first introduced in Figure 9.1. The competitive bidding process illustrated in this chapter is a part of the overall software selection roadmap illustrated by these two diagrams. The competitive bidding process outlined in this chapter is a compilation of the best practices that I have employed in practice throughout my professional career. Certain steps in the process can be deemed as optional. When they are, I will specifically say so.

The Request for Proposal

The formal bidding process will usually revolve around the preparation of a formal RFP document and its presentation to qualified vendors. Vendors are then asked to prepare a formal reply to the RFP, which is usually referred to as the vendor's proposal or bid document. Subsequently, the organization soliciting such proposals must have a process in place to objectively evaluate any replies to an RFP that a vendor submits for consideration.

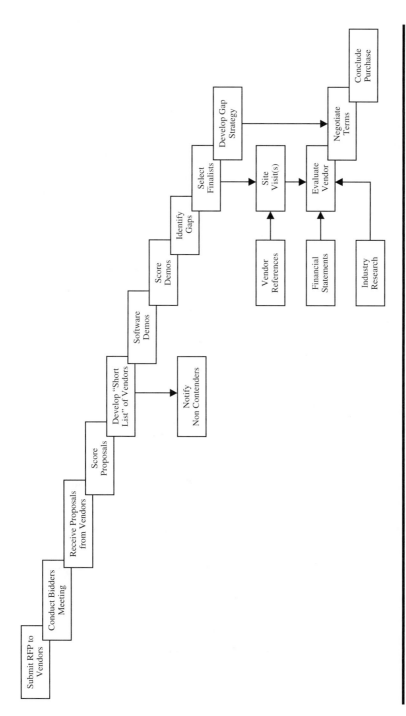

Figure 10.1 Software Selection: Constructing the RFP and Evaluating Proposals

I consider the RFP document a key deliverable in the overall software selection effort. The purpose behind an RFP document is to solicit information from potential software vendors that will help your organization make the best purchase decision possible. The creation of the actual RFP document may rest within the IT department, the purchasing department, or with an external consultant.

All business units considered, stakeholders in the software decision making process should participate in preparing the RFP. Generally, this participation will require them to identify the specific functions or features they may need from the software package that will support their business interests, such as in automating the business processes supported by their business unit. Likewise, these stakeholders should also participate in scoring responses, selecting semifinalist vendors, and observing demonstrations of software features and functions.

An RFP will typically save the selection team some time. The RFP process delegates some of the mundane work of comparing software features, functionality, and cost into the hands of the vendors. A well-written RFP will allow you to gather information that applies specifically to your organization's needs. The well-organized RFP process will allow you to evaluate the various vendor proposals quickly. Later portions of this chapter will discuss how to assemble the RFP document that is used as the basis for the competitive bidding process.

The Bidders' Meeting

The bidders' meeting is a brief meeting, usually a half day or less in duration, and is intended to address specific questions that potential bidders (vendors) may have. The session usually begins with a brief introduction to the proposal objectives and the selection process. The session may then review briefly the major sections of the RFP and address specific issues about its parts. The concluding portion of this meeting is an open forum where vendors may ask specific questions. It is recommended that the entire selection team attend in order to hear the questions asked and answer them. If any questions cannot be answered immediately, answer them afterwards and publish that answer for the benefit of all vendors, not just the one that made the request. If there are specific document formatting requirements in which the reply is to be made, it is also appropriate to review them.

Note that all potential bidders are invited, though not all may choose to attend this meeting. In addition, even though a given bidder requests an RFP and attends the bidders' meeting, that bidder may still choose not to respond with a formal proposal or bid. On a final note, the bidders' meeting is one of the steps in the software selection process that can be viewed as optional.

The Expression of Interest

Less common than a bidders' meeting is using a preannouncement letter or a public announcement in a newspaper or trade publication. Agencies and organizations in the public sector must usually make public announcements of their intentions to buy products or services and will publicly seek bidders to an RFP. This is usually done through tombstone ads in the legal notices section of a local newspaper. The private sector usually operates under no such requirements. Regulated companies and other large organizations will sometimes publish announcements of their intentions to buy as well. The major problem here is that unless the vendors are reading the same publications you have published an announcement in, you may not hear from them at all.

To alleviate this problem, many organizations maintain preferred vendor lists, then send a preannouncement letter to preferred vendors seeking their interest in or intention to bid. It is best if these letters require an explicit reply. The letter should indicate the scope of the upcoming RFP, the date the RFP will be issued, the time and place of the bidders' meeting, and the due date of any RFP reply. This is also an optional step.

Protecting Confidentiality During the RFP Process

The expression of interest may also require attachment of an executed confidentiality statement. In this case, an organization will require that a vendor execute a confidentiality statement prior to receiving the RFP document. The confidentiality agreement is not something every organization requires, so again this may be an optional step. Invariably, during the course of any complex software selection, it is likely that an organization will be compelled to reveal details about the nature of its business or transaction information to a vendor that will have some proprietary content or nature to it. Careful attention must be paid to the task of constructing any sample data that will be provided to vendors for use in any product demonstrations.

ASSEMBLING THE REQUEST FOR PROPOSAL DOCUMENT

An integral part of the software selection roadmap illustrated by Figures 9.1 and 10.1 portrays the use of an RFP document. The preparation of the RFP document is a time-consuming process. Recall that the first steps of the software selection process were illustrated by Figure 9.1. The remainder of this chapter is devoted to assembling the actual RFP document for software package selection purposes.

The Request for Proposal: Some Document Preparation Guidelines

Many organizations use boilerplate templates for constructing an RFP. Likewise, many vendors use boilerplate templates when constructing a reply to an RFP document. In fact, you can buy software that will help you prepare the RFP document. Organizations that build RFP documents on a regular basis, such as a government agency or regulated industry, may already have RFP builder software. There are sometimes canned RFP documents already available for the type of software package you wish to buy. Do not assume you will be able to use any boilerplate RFP template without making some changes to it. A boilerplate request for proposal document is a part of the author's template collection. Consult Appendix A for more information.

Document Preparation

I typically use Microsoft Word and Excel as my RFP writing tools and Microsoft PowerPoint to prepare the presentation for the bidders' meeting. I use only Microsoft Office 97 formats for all documents. I find that most everyone is at least using Office 97 or later versions of Microsoft products. As for the more recent versions of Microsoft Office products, it is a mixed bag.

Although I mentioned there are software packages available to prepare RFP documents, I have generally elected to prepare RFP documents using traditional preparation techniques and software tools — namely Microsoft Word and Microsoft Excel. I have seen some examples where traditional worksheets are replaced using a Microsoft Access database, but Excel worksheets work just as well in most instances.

One early word of caution about preparing an RFP document: Adding too much detail or placing too many conditions on the process will overburden both your organization and the vendors. Make sure that the RFP document is a well-organized, concise, readable, and workable document. The RFP is not a legal agreement and does not need to read like a contract, though I admit some of the elements of the RFP document will.

I favor simpler, fill-in-the-blank formats whenever possible, although some portions of an RFP will not lend themselves to that. The more one can utilize fill-in-the-blank worksheets for the core responses, such as features and costs, the easier it will be to compare responses.

Electronic Responses

I am a strong advocate of delivering RFP documents electronically and receiving vendor replies electronically as well. There are times when a vendor cannot practically reply to all portions of an RFP without submitting at least some hard copies. With that said, my strong preference is for the vendor to enter its core responses to RFP questions into an Excel worksheet. Assuming that responding vendors do not change the worksheet format, one is then able to combine all inbound replies into a single, consolidated worksheet. This worksheet yields a feature-by-feature comparison and facilitates easy scoring of vendor replies.

The Model RFP Table of Contents

The best method to explain what elements should be contained in the well-crafted RFP document is to take a close look at a model table of contents for such a document. The model RFP table of contents recommended for software package selection is as follows:

- Purpose and nature of request
- Proposal requirements and guidelines
- Background and demographics
- Functional business objectives
- Technical and infrastructure objectives
- Product demonstration scenarios
- Pricing and support options
- Software infrastructure requirements
- Vendor background information
- Vendor references and potential site visit locations
- Detailed product information
- Case studies, cost benefit analyses, and calculators
- Model contract documents
- Implementation methodology and time line

The remainder of this chapter discusses the formation of an RFP document following the above content areas.

Purpose and Nature of Request

The purpose statement is the opening for the request for proposal document. This opening statement should identify the purpose of the software package and what *tangible business results* are expected from the software package. An example purpose system for a financial management system desired by a nonprofit organization appears below:

> The ABC Foundation wants to obtain through the competitive bidding process a single, integrated financial management and

accounting system that provides support for the following general business activities, including:

- General ledger processing that supports fund accounting
- Accounts payable processing and purchase order processing that supports encumbrance accounting
- Accounts receivable processing
- Cash receipts processing
- Fixed assets processing
- Payroll processing
- Human resources administration
- Project accounting
- Budgeting
- Cash and investment management

This purpose statement is clear and concise. The purpose statement should not exceed one or two short paragraphs. It may not be necessary to list the specific business functions to be automated through such a system, but it presents a clearer picture to the reader of exactly what is required from the very start. In practice, I like to extract the purpose statement and use it as a project mission statement when at all possible. The project mission statement is discussed in Chapter 12.

Proposal Requirements and Guidelines

This portion of the RFP document outlines the proposal submission requirements and provides information on the desired format of the vendor's proposal to your organization. This portion of the RFP document should provide specific instructions on how to respond to the proposals. Although I said an RFP is not a contract, one might not think so when reading this section of a typical RFP. It is necessary to provide some rules governing the process and this section should provide them. Note that each subsequent RFP section will also present its own set of rules or instructions that vendors should follow. The rules here generally represent overall submission guidelines. The proposal requirements and guidelines section of the RFP document should minimally indicate:

- The proposal due date and the street address (not a post office box) where the proposal should be delivered. The reason for the street address is a simple one. Most vendors will submit their proposal to you via an overnight courier service or will hand deliver it to your location.

- The person to contact regarding any questions about the RFP, along with phone and fax numbers and an e-mail address.
- Any specific submission instructions, such as the desired number of copies to be submitted or the desired method of response. For instance, while you may require an electronic response, is that response going to be an e-mail, diskette, or CD-ROM in a binder with hard copies attached?
- A request that a vendor not change the format of any worksheets provided. Instead, request vendors to provide attachments that reference a given proposal section and subsection or line item.

This list represents a minimal set of submission requirements and guidelines. The next section discusses other provisions that may need to be included.

Depending on your organization's specific circumstances, there are a number of additional guidelines you may want to consider including in the proposal requirements and guidelines section. Here are just a few examples of other inclusions that might be included:

- A statement allowing your organization the right to amend or modify the RFP document at any time prior to the due date. Exercise of this privilege should be avoided. If you amend the RFP document, expect to receive requests to extend the due date depending on the extensiveness of any changes made.
- A statement allowing your organization the right to cancel or rescind the RFP document or to postpone a decision on any proposal submitted. Again, be careful in exercising this one. Vendors do not appreciate the customer who cries wolf too many times.
- A statement allowing your organization the right to obtain clarification of any point in a vendor's proposal or to obtain additional information deemed necessary to properly evaluate a particular proposal. The statement will also disqualify the vendor if such clarifications are not provided within a reasonable, although typically short, period of time.
- A statement allowing your organization the right to expect responsiveness and integrity of reply. A typical general instruction is to require bidders to respond in an honest and forthright manner to all requirements in this RFP to the maximum extent possible. Bidders are also required to clearly identify any limitations or exceptions to the requirements inherent in the proposed system.
- A statement requiring the submitted proposal to include the requested information only in the formats indicated in the RFP document, or the proposal submitted will be subject to disqualification or rejection. Allow and encourage the vendor to include

any other material. This usually means they will attach their standard sales literature, adding to the persuasiveness or clarity of their recommended approach. Indicate to vendors that these items should be organized as an appendix to the proposal response they provide.

There are a few, more creative inclusions that might be considered necessary depending on the circumstances. One can also argue these guidelines might be placed in other sections of the RFP document, particularly the pricing and support section. Since the nature of these statements may drive the construction of the vendor's response as a whole, it is best to place them under the proposal requirements and guidelines section. You may optionally choose to briefly restate them under the pricing and support section as well. Here again is a list of some typical items:

- Your organization's desire for a turnkey proposal (if that is the case). This usually means that one vendor will provide everything — the hardware, software, infrastructure, implementation assistance, and training — that your organization will need to get the software into production. Value-added resellers (VARs) and integrated solution providers are examples of firms that will provide a turnkey proposal. Most software vendors will not provide a turnkey proposal. They may choose to provide a joint proposal designating one of their qualified alliance or business partners to address those elements of your requirements they cannot fulfill.

- Your organization's expectation or desire that the responding vendor serves as the primary and responsible contractor if the use of subcontractors will be necessary to fulfill any portion of the proposal. This condition is tandem to the concept of the vendor providing a turnkey proposal.

- A statement indicating how the vendor should label or present multiple proposals. Usually a vendor should designate one of its alternate proposals as its primary proposal. For example, a VAR who is a respondent to the RFP represents competing software packages and wants to propose each package to your organization. Another example: A vendor provides a hosted solution as an alternative to buying the software package and wishes to propose it as well.

- A statement allowing your organization the right to line item purchase any specific item or items listed on the proposal from other vendors. When expecting a turnkey solution, this is a frequent inclusion.

Line item purchasing is an important consideration in many cases and especially with turnkey proposals. Oftentimes, a given vendor will have a particularly strong price advantage over another for one or two items on a proposal, but not for the proposal value in total. Although you may have a strong desire for a turnkey solution, your organization may decide to break its own rule and forgo it, instead opting for a multiple-vendor solution. This may be especially true when there are significant line item variations. The only problem is that a vendor may be unwilling to provide the same line item pricing to your organization when the solution is unbundled. This type of clause is intended to overcome that type of problem.

Again, with regard to the line item purchasing clause, when it is included in an RFP, I also recommend adding the following additional clause to the RFP document:

Vendor must be willing to cooperate with other vendor(s) by supplying interface information such as details on application program interfaces [APIs], file layouts, and any additional information as may be needed to support the integration of one software vendor's product with that of another in order to fulfill our complete business requirements.

If you invoke the line item purchasing clause, your organization will want some assurances that a vendor will help carry such a line item acquisition strategy, particularly with respect to integrating competing and third-party solutions. It has been my experience that most vendors will welcome the opportunity to work out the details of an interface with another software vendor, especially when the two products complement one another. While this stipulation sounds like and should be language also contained in any contract negotiated with the vendor, it arguably has a place in the RFP should the vendor decide any such integration is undesirable. This decision is usually for competitive reasons related to a future and unannounced product enhancement that would duplicate or overlap features and functions provided by the third-party product.

Background and Demographics

This section provides an overview for the vendor of your organization and the business problem you have and want to solve. First, do not assume a vendor will know much about your organization, especially if your organization is privately held. A brief history of your organization and business philosophy or corporate mission should be provided. More important, discuss your industry, products or services, provided and relevant details of your business model. You should indicate the size of your organization in terms of both revenues and total employees.

Second, describe your organization's vision for the software. This description should represent the prevailing view within the organization about how the software package will be used, what its value proposition will be, and what specific areas are being targeted for improvement. Perhaps the mission and objectives of the software selection team will provide the nucleus for this discussion.

Third, discuss current and future demographics as it pertains to the software package. This should include an overview of your current software systems, current and projected number of users who will simultaneously use the software at any given time, current and projected transaction volumes and master data record counts, and the number of locations where processing is initiated and how it will typically be initiated (e.g., through dial-up, web browser-based workstations).

Finally, each functional area that is a stakeholder should be able to provide other metrics that will be considered useful to the vendor's overall understanding of your business problem. A good practice when considering an enterprise-wide software package, such as an ERP package, is to have each area prepare its own key business process demographics or metrics for inclusion. For instance, human resources and payroll might want to include annual volumes with regard to applicants, interviews, new hires, payroll and personnel record changes, head count by employee, and frequency of and types of payroll classes (i.e., union, nonunion, exempt, nonexempt) runs completed.

Vendors are typically interested in learning about your organization. Part of the reason is to be sure their software is an appropriate fit to your organization, both from the standpoint of software features offered and affordability. Consider the following list of questions that a vendor might typically want answered in terms of your RFP:

■ Products and Services:
  What is your end product or service? If you have a complicated business model, consider listing each standard industry classification code and the percentage of sales in each.
  What is the total annual revenue size of your organization? What is the growth rate in revenues for your organization over the past 5 or 10 years? What are the gross and net profit margins?
  What market place position and market share does your organization have within its dominant markets or segments?
  What is your manufacturing environment (i.e., make to order, make to stock, assemble to order, process)?

- Locations:
  How many sites does the organization have where products are produced or services are provided?
  How many employees are located at each site?
  Where applicable, how many sites does the organization have where products are stocked (not produced) for distribution to customers?
  How many employees are at all sites?
  Is this organization a subsidiary of a larger organization?
  What is the name of the parent organization (if applicable)?
  Where is the corporate headquarters located?
  Is this software evaluation being conducted for the entire organization or strictly for the subsidiary?
- Future Business Environment:
  Would you like your customers to check their order status online?
  Would you like your customers to place or update orders and release schedules online?
  Would you like your suppliers to check their requirements online?
  Would you like your suppliers to receive or update orders and delivery schedules online?
  Are there specific critical business issues that the software must address?
- Current Infrastructure Environment:
  What software are you currently running to support your manufacturing, financials, order entry, inventory control, and procurement activities?
  If known, how many users would likely use, at any one time, the business application software being considered for acquisition?
  How long have you been using this software?
  When was your last upgrade?
  What is the hardware platform you currently run software on?
  When do you plan to make any changes to your operating system?
  Does your system run on a LAN? Is your server on site?
  Do you currently have a website. If so, is it for marketing or transactions purposes?
  How many transactions are processed daily? Provide count by type of transaction.
  How many days, months, or years of transaction history retained online? Provide count by type of transaction.
  How many customers, suppliers, employees, and products (counts for each) are managed using the current systems?

This is not an all-inclusive list. Combine this list with the previous comments about what background information your organization should include in the RFP to round out this section's contents.

Functional Business Objectives

The functional business objectives specified in your RFP document will serve as a comprehensive listing of the desired software features and functions needed for conducting business. I have previously recommended the use of a features list for this purpose, described in Chapter 9.

Before discussing features and functions in more detail, this is also the appropriate place to list specific financial and nonfinancial benefits that the software package is expected to accomplish. It is appropriate to request the vendor to note (and attach) any case studies. Also, request that the vendor provide specific client references where one or more of these business objectives using its software package has been successfully accomplished. This information can be useful to further support a business case and develop a list of possible sites that can be visited during the evaluation process.

As for the software features, their evaluation is largely a mechanical process. To expedite their preparation and review, I recommend providing the features list as a separate worksheet document, which I will refer to as the vendor response table. Vendors should be instructed to provide their answers on the worksheet. The worksheet document or response table can then be combined with the response tables received from other vendors to form a master worksheet. This worksheet will then serve as a comparative features analysis.

The response table or worksheet should be kept as simple as possible. The recommended format of a vendor response table or worksheet related to functional requirements appears in Figure 10.2. This table is available as a template in the author's template collection. Consult Appendix A for more information about these templates.

The most important aspect of the vendor response table is the response. A standardized coding scheme or response scale should be adopted. Vendors should be instructed to provide a response to every line item, otherwise it will be coded as not available/not possible. Table 10.1 provides a recommended vendor response scale.

At this point it is appropriate to discuss exactly what information to include in the general instructions for this section of the RFP document. First, include a statement similar to this one:

> *Vendors must provide a response for each desired software feature on the vendor response worksheet. Any line item for which a response is incorrect or blank, we will assume the answer to be not available/not possible.*

Vendor Response to Request for Proposal
Proposal on behalf of: ABC Manufacturing
Proposal For: ERP System

TradewindsGroup
Tradewinds Group, Incorporated
Consultants to Management
Box 3601
Oak Brook, Illinois 60522

| Vendor Name: | ERP Vendor Name Here |
| System: | ERP System Name Here |

Feature Number	Major Feature Set	Feature Set	Feature Sub Set	Required Software Feature	Vendor Response (See Instructions Below)	Vendor Commentary
101	Procure to Pay	Procurement	Vendor Analysis	Calculate On Time Delivery Performance Level on a Per Order Basis	STANDARD	
102	Procure to Pay	Procurement	Vendor Analysis	Display Vendor's Overall On Time Delivery Performance Level on an Aggregate Basis with Drill Down to Specific Order on Chronological Basis	OPTIONAL	Requires Business Intelligence Monitor, an optional module.

Vendor Response Instructions

Vendors are asked to limit their response to one of the following statements which best characterizes their availability of any given software feature:

STANDARD   Included in the software package as a standard feature
OPTIONAL   Feature is available through an optional software package component
CUSTOM   Feature is not available, but is possible through customizing tool(s)
NOT AVAILABLE Feature is not available; no known workaround or customizing option

Printed on 6/2/2002   - Confidential and Proprietary -   Page 1 of 1

Figure 10.2 The Vendor Response Worksheet

TABLE 10.1 RECOMMENDED VENDOR RESPONSES TO FUNCTIONAL REQUIREMENT STATEMENTS

Check in This Column...	When the...
Fully supported standard feature	Software fully supports this line item as a standard feature of the software and is operational out of the box, requiring no customization.
Partially supported standard feature	Software partially supports this line item as a standard feature of the software and is operational out of the box, requiring no customization. Note that for any partially supported feature, direct vendors are to specifically state what is not supported in the comments/explanation column of the response table.
Optional, fully supported, vendor provided feature	Software provides full support of this feature as an optional, added cost feature and is operational out of the box, requiring no customization. Note that for any optional supported feature, direct vendors are to specifically state the cost of the optional feature in their detailed presentation of costs.
Optional, third-party provided feature	Software provides full support of this feature only through an optional, third-party provided solution that is operational out of the box, requiring no customization.
Workaround	Although not a specific feature of the software, one or more clients have successfully facilitated this functionality using a workaround scenario.
Nonstandard feature available through standard customization tools	The software must be modified to perform the required function. This modification can be completed using the basic customization tools provided with the software.

TABLE **10.1** (CONTINUED) RECOMMENDED VENDOR RESPONSES TO FUNCTIONAL REQUIREMENT
STATEMENTS

Check in This Column...	*When the...*
Nonstandard feature available through optional customization tools	The software must be modified to perform the required function. This modification can be completed using the optional customization tools available for the software. Note that for any optional customization tools, direct vendors are to specifically state the cost of the optional customizing tools in their detailed presentation of costs.
Nonstandard feature available through optional vendor customization	The software must be modified to perform the required function. The vendor, at an additional cost, must perform the customization. Note that for any optional customization, direct vendors are to specifically state the cost of the optional customization in their detailed presentation of costs. Customization tools are included with the applications.
Not available/not possible	This line item is a feature that is not available and is not considered possible within the software.

Second, include a statement similar to this one:

Vendors are expected to predicate their responses as to the availability of each feature noted in terms of the version of their software that is readily available for implementation today and is already in use at multiple client sites.

Third, instruct vendors to:

When a feature is not fully supported, or supported through a workaround, provide a brief explanation in the column labeled "Comments/Explanation."

Finally, instruct vendors to:

Provide the cost of any optional features, third party provided features, customization tools, or vendor performed customization as separate line items referenced by feature number.

Can the Responses Be Further Simplified?

One can make a case for even further simplification of the standard response nomenclature proposed in Table 10.1. The problem is that few packages will fully support every feature or functional requirement your organization may have. Unless you specifically ask about how to provide for the gaps — the 5, 10, 15, or 20% of your requirements left on the table by any one software package — you will have gathered incomplete information about cost, viability, or the overall goodness of fit of that vendor's software package to meet your requirements.

Vaporware and Software Selection

Now that I have spoken about vendor responses, I need to point out that I have intentionally omitted what I call the vaporware choice. Although I have seen many RFP examples include it, I feel it does not have a place in an objective evaluation process. The best intentions of vendors — those being to provide a feature or function in a future, or even the next release of their software — simply have no place in a firm proposal. If it cannot be delivered today, then it should not be proposed. Unless that future software version is now in beta testing and will be available for general release and use by clients by the time a contract is signed, such information will be of little value.

I would not suggest allowing the vendor to reply to an RFP under that premise. This is because all too often early releases of new versions of a software package are riddled with bugs and as a general rule, are to be avoided. In addition, testing may yield so many such issues that a vendor will defer the general release date of a new version, while such problems are analyzed and hopefully resolved. I am sure a few vendors will not appreciate my candor after having read this section. I am sure their lack of appreciation was because the section conjured up some of their own bad memories and not what I have said here.

Technical and Infrastructure Objectives

There are times when your organization will expect a software package to support one or more particular technical requirements. Bar coding and wireless communications are examples of broad, technical requirements. Of course, it could be a more pointed or direct response, such as asking about compatibility with a specific handheld scanning device. Support for thin clients, web browsers, the availability of APIs for certain functions that will be linked with other software packages and legacy systems are all good additional examples that one might ask here.

At the same time, there will be other technical requirements, more or less infrastructure requirements, that your organization might believe it should include here. For example, a requirement could include support for a particular database, operating system, middleware package or a particular programming language. As to whether or not such infrastructure requirements should be included is a judgment call on the part of your organization. It depends largely on how committed it is to its current infrastructure strategy.

As a practical matter, I find many middle market organizations facing this question today as they consider their future on the IBM midrange (known also as the AS/400 or i series) platform versus choosing a UNIX or a Windows NT solution. This is a big decision and has many ramifications. Such a decision can minimally render your current computer hardware and software obsolete. In many instances, the impact may be even more sweeping. It may render your network cabling infrastructure and workstation architecture obsolete as well as the skill sets of your application development and system support staffs.

I am usually reluctant to include too many specific technical requirements like the ones I have mentioned here. My reasoning is that, first and foremost, a software package decision is a business decision. If technical constraints, such as support for a specific platform will drive the decision, you may not select the software package that will provide the best overall fit for your business requirements. Only your organization can decide on what is the right balance between its business strategy and its technology strategy. It is this balance that should influence the questions asked here.

At the same time I suggest balance, I remain steadfast in my opinion of the IBM midrange platform (and so are many of the client organizations I work with). It is a solid choice for any middle market organization that wants industrial strength computing performance. At the same time, I know (and my clients know) that such a commitment will potentially limit an organization's software choices.

On a final note, I need to point out that the RFP's infrastructure requirements section has a close relationship with the technical requirements section. Consider working up these sections in tandem for the RFP document.

Given the comments above, some technical and infrastructure questions you will want to consider answering for the vendor as a part of this section include:

- Will you consider changing the hardware platform you currently run software on?
- Will you consider changing the database system or operating system currently used?
- What is the time frame for the evaluation? For implementation?
- Will all locations be implemented simultaneously or in phases?
- Has there a budget been set? If so, can a price range be provided?
- Are you looking into e-commerce packages? If so, will any e-commerce/e-business applications be integrated with the software package being considered?

This is not an all-inclusive list. Combine this list with the previous comments about what technical and infrastructure objectives your organization has and include them in the RFP to round out the contents of this section.

Product Demonstration Scenarios

Product demonstrations are an important part of the software selection process. For maximum benefit, it is a process your organization will want to control as much as possible. The way to control the process is by providing to the vendor carefully crafted business transaction scenarios that can be used as the basis for a software demonstration.

Many vendors welcome and appreciate the opportunity to showcase their product to you through real life examples from your business. It will make their job easier when the product sells itself by decidedly handling a complex or everyday transaction from within your business model with relative ease. Unfortunately, some vendors would prefer that your organization not provide business transaction scenarios. Instead, they prefer to substitute a canned product demonstration. This is because many vendors conclude that it is simply too costly a process to prepare custom demonstrations. Yes, vendors have been known to simply disregard these requests and instead provide their canned demo while talking to your business issues during the demo. Simply put, vendors who disregard your instructions are the ones whom you may not want to further consider. Try to ensure each semifinalist vendor will follow your script. If necessary, meet with the vendor ahead of time to see a preview of what the overall selection team will see.

A business transaction scenario must be thoughtfully prepared. The business transaction scenario is prepared only after reaching a thorough understanding of your business. If you have been closely following the recommendations in this book, here is another example where a great deal of synergy must occur between the steps in the software package life cycle. This is because these business transaction scenarios make use of the business process models developed in the earlier reengineering and process modeling stage. Again, as I recommended earlier, I strongly advocate that business process modeling should be completed prior to commencing the software selection. This prerequisite step of modeling business processes is discussed in Chapter 5.

Product Demonstrations

Ever encountered the vacuum cleaner salesperson at the shopping mall that pours a cup of dirt, sand, and other goodies over a small piece of carpet (usually white) in the middle of the aisle? The salesperson then snaps on a small, flimsy looking vacuum cleaner. In just a few moments time all of that previous mess disappears and, in the process, another vacuum cleaner is sold. In this case, the salesperson knew how valuable a good product demonstration can be in closing a sale. But the salesperson also knew their product. This person demonstrated only what the product was capable of doing and nothing more. For instance, a spilled cup of chocolate milk was likely something this vacuum cleaner could not handle and remained off limits for the demonstration.

Product demonstrations are an important part of the buying process. The problem is that business application software packages are much more difficult to demonstrate than most products. The software package demonstration problem is similar to the challenges in assessing plans for the new office or factory building. In these cases, reliance on drawings and perhaps a scale model is necessary to visualize the end result and to assess its utility or functional value.

There are three possible scenarios for software package demonstrations. The first scenario is the vendor directed or canned demonstration. Most vendors have already gone to the trouble of configuring and entering sample data into a demonstration version of their product. In addition, they have likely scripted and rehearsed (presumably) a demonstration of their product's essential features using this sample data that will be presented to the client. Software vendors obviously like these kinds of demonstrations the best — they represent the software salesperson's vacuum cleaner of sorts. Why do they like these kinds of demonstrations? They require less time to prepare and give the salesperson more control over the presentation. In this case, the software vendor decides what to show. What is shown may have little or no relevance to your organization and features that are important to your organization may not be seen at all.

The second scenario is simply a modified version of the vendor directed or canned demonstration. In this scenario the vendor and the prospective software buyer select from the vendor's canned demonstration what is germane to the evaluation. This is a slightly better approach, but it is still not a perfect situation.

The third scenario is the tailored demonstration. This approach represents the ideal scenario. Under this scenario, the prospective software buyer provides demonstration scripts and sample business data built around its own business transactions. In terms of the software package demonstration, it is best to pick out several representative transactions that reflect the organization's core business processes. It is best to provide meaningful (though disguised) sample data to the vendor along with the step-by-step details of how these processes occur (or are envisioned to occur). Expect that one or more members of the selection team will need to be available to work with the vendor to set these scenarios up on their system. It may be necessary to have a working meeting with the vendor for this purpose. In some cases, it may be necessary to conduct a dry run of the demonstration before showing it to the entire selection team.

The tailored demonstration is sometimes not the easiest feat to accomplish. The vendor does not necessarily want to set up or configure the software simply to demonstrate a few transactions. This is an expensive and time-consuming task. In addition, the complex nature of certain transactions may make it difficult to articulate the information to the vendor without first-hand knowledge of the software, compromising the demonstration.

It is desirable to provide a list of demonstration scenarios and sample data as early as possible to the vendors involved, especially if the evaluation window is short. They can be included in the RFP or withheld until semifinalist vendors are selected and then provided.

Pricing and Support Options

First, it is important to point out that Chapter 6 provides a comprehensive listing of the costs that are related to a typical software package acquisition. Refer to this list when building the vendor's bid response matrix as proposed in this section. In addition, many other points and issues are raised in this chapter regarding pricing and support options that must be considered.

The many pricing models for software licensing and support are varied and often complex. Forcing vendors to adhere to a standardized pricing model is the only way to arrive at a presumably level playing field for the purposes of your evaluation. First of all, a general statement may be in order, if you will accept a partial bid:

> *If you do not have offerings for each of the stated applications, clearly indicate which modules you are proposing. It is not necessary to have offerings for all applications or features; however, proposing a more comprehensive system would be clearly advan-*

tageous. All functions that your proposal encompasses, including any recommended third-party solutions, should be fully integrated.

What is an example of a partial bid? A partial bid may occur when a vendor has all of the modules related to a desired financial system, except the vendor does not offer a fixed asset accounting module. The vendor may recommend this functionality be obtained through a third-party solution. This is usually from another vendor and typically one that will interface or integrate in some way with the vendor's proposed core products. The vendor may not have included pricing for that third-party solution in its proposal because it is not involved in selling the third-party solution.

Another partial bid scenario may also come into play. The vendor or perhaps maybe a good number of the vendors you are evaluating simply do not offer (at least not yet) what you have requested in terms of features or functionality in a software package. The danger when relying on your To Be models to develop the features list is that your organziation is ahead of the market. If you are using a consultant to help you develop both current (As Is) and future business (To Be) process models, that consultant should have a working knowledge of the software you are considering. The consultant should not let you become too frivolous or futuristic with your requirements.

This portion of the RFP should instruct the vendor to provide a sequentially numbered, line item listing detailing all one-time and recurring charges related to buying their software. Further instructions should request that any item or items noted as optional on the features list response worksheet should be priced by reference to that feature.

Time and Materials Billing of Professional Services

Professional service fees are usually a big part of the costs associated with any software package implementation. In fact, these charges will typically at least equal and will often exceed the cost of the software. A few comments about what to expect in the way of professional service fees are in order before moving on.

At least for the moment, assume that all professional services will be provided on a time and materials basis. That means any professional, such as a consultant, technician, software developer, or project manager will be charged on a per hour basis. The vendor will estimate the hours of each individual resource required for completing a given aspect of a project, multiplied by an hourly rate. These rates will vary widely. They are rarely less than $100 per hour (usually a rate for more junior level or lesser skilled individuals) and usually less than $300 per hour (the rate one can expect for senior level individuals). Note these are per person charges.

It is rare that a vendor will support your site with a team comprised entirely of local talent. Some or all of the vendor's project team will need to travel to a given project location, usually on a weekly basis. This will mean a line item estimate of travel, lodging, and meal expenses for each professional resource. Travel costs to larger cities are usually less, but are generally offset by higher local accommodations; the reverse is true for smaller cities and rural locations. Travel time to smaller cities and rural locations are usually much greater. Some vendors will attempt to assess travel time charges. Often, they are a percentage of the hourly rate or a flat number of extra billable hours. There is no need to pay such frivolous extra charges. Simply negotiate them out of the final contract with the vendor. Most vendors will yield on these charges in all, but a few isolated cases.

As mentioned previously, expect to see a line item for travel, lodging, and meal expenses for each professional resource. As a general rule of thumb, expect these charges to average between 15 and 25% of the total hourly charges on a per person basis. Some firms will attempt to assess a service charge of 5 to 15% when passing these expenses, or chargebacks as they are frequently called, along to their clients. Again, as I see it, there is no need to pay such frivolous extra charges. Simply negotiate them out of the final contract with the vendor. Most, if not all, will yield.

Although many of us would like to believe we have good ideas about how to reduce travel, lodging, and meal expenses, most of them are usually impractical, but there are two exceptions. Using shared rental cars is one. The other is using a long-term executive housing facility for long-term project team members instead of using hotels on a weekly basis. Do not count on meal expenses to be reduced however. Most traveling professionals work long hours and simply want to grab a quick meal on the way back to the hotel before calling home, catching up on e-mail or reading, and then call it a night. Life on the road is not as grand as many may believe. Another way to save costs that may work well is if you have substantial volume discount arrangements with travel-related providers. Insist that a vendor's traveling personnel make the arrangements through your travel desk or agent. This way all of your organizations' discounts will be applied. If you allow providers to direct bill your organization, it will also help to lessen any of the vendor's service charges on expenses if the vendor has not relented on them.

The norm in recent years is for traveling professionals to usually work 4 or $4\frac{1}{2}$ days a week, 10 to 12 hours per day during the noncritical stages of a project. During the critical periods of a project, such as during go-live periods, they may work 7 days a week for several weeks. Working 4 days a week does help to reduce both hotel and rental car charges.

Also, if everyone uses the same hotel, special rates can usually be negotiated and are usually $5 to $25 less per day.

Most vendors want their professionals dedicated to and engaged at a single client site for a full 40 hours per week (or even more). In most cases, this will work to the advantage of the client and the vendor. When this happens, vendors are more willing to forego travel time charges. As an added bonus, this too will bring savings in travel related costs, allowing for earlier travel reservations.

Fixed Bids, Fixed Fees, and Fixed Rates

As a buyer, a fixed price contract is always desirable, although there are a few problems with fixed bid contracts. First and almost without exception, a vendor will add an estimating error factor into any fixed bid quoted. It is my experience that a vendor will create a fixed bid in the same method as if the work were going to be done on a time and materials basis. The vendor then escalates the total cost anywhere from 10 to 50% to account for the risk it is taking.

Fixed bids for hardware and system-related software implementations and training programs usually work out fairly well for the vendor. There are generally fewer unknowns and certainly less politics involved in those areas of an implementation. With regard to application software implementation work, it is a mixed bag. Unless a vendor has solid prior experience doing a nearly identical project, it is unlikely the estimate will be exact. Few, if any, implementations are ever really that similar. This is especially true for an enterprise-wide implementation, such as an ERP system implementation.

Unfortunately there are positive and negative dimensions to a fixed bid. First, since it is more of an unknown for the vendor, the fixed bid risk escalator will be higher. This is bad for the client, meaning the project comes in at a higher cost. At the same time, with a fixed bid in hand, the client has bought protection from these same unknowns that played havoc with the vendor in trying to reach the bid amount.

Generally speaking, fixed bids will make for a more controlled (not to be read or construed as more adversarial) relationship between the vendor and the client. The vendor will be adamant about scope control, change control, and project management almost to a fault. That is not a particularly bad thing when the organization is pressed against a tight deadline or budget. Fixed bid contracts are typically more difficult to negotiate.

The biggest problems usually come from determining what is in scope, what is out of scope, and how to define what scope is. If a vendor insists that something must be in scope, ask why. Often, the vendor is not trying to sell you more than you need. It may be that all or a portion of a seemingly unrelated module must be implemented — usually because it provides a core function needed by other modules considered in scope for the implementation.

One-Time Charges

A one-time charge is a fee that is paid to the vendor, presumably only once. When buying or licensing the software outright, one-time charges would apply. For one-time charges, I suggest a worksheet containing the following columns that the vendor would complete:

- A description of the line item, usually a module within the software
- The list or base price of the line item
- Any discount percentage applied to this line item
- The dollar amount of any discount applied to this line item
- The net price of the line item
- Number of simultaneous users or other resource units required for this line item
- Number of resource hours consumed for this line item (applies to services only)
- Total extended net price for this line item
- A final column on the worksheet reserved for vendor notes and explanations

I suggest this worksheet should then be divided into subsections. Some suggestions include these major categories:

- Application software products
- Application software related services
- Infrastructure hardware and software products
- Infrastructure related services

The worksheet can be further divided into subsections. Some suggestions include:

- Application software products — Functional software
- Application software products— Customizing tools
- Application software products — Third-party add-on functions
- Application software products — Third-party customizing tools
- Application software services — Training
- Application software services — Implementation support

- Application software services — Implementation project management and administration
- Infrastructure products — Database system
- Infrastructure products — Operating system
- Infrastructure products — System administration
- Infrastructure products — Messaging, communication, and integration middleware
- Infrastructure products — Server hardware
- Infrastructure products — Workstation hardware
- Infrastructure products — Workstation software
- Infrastructure products — Networking hardware
- Infrastructure products — Networking software
- Infrastructure services — Network cabling
- Infrastructure services — Training
- Infrastructure services — Infrastructure installation and implementation support
- Infrastructure services — Implementation Project Management and Administration

The cost worksheet can get quite lengthy depending on the scope of the project. For instance, if a turnkey proposal is being requested, expect to include all such sections. If the RFP covers only the application software, then fewer sections will be included.

Why Columns for List versus Discounted Prices?

By now, one might wonder why I have included such a complicated pricing scheme in the cost response worksheet when I have stressed simplicity. By using a response presentation that requires the vendor to frame the bid in terms of list and discounted prices, it will preestablish a desire or intent to negotiate a price with the vendor that is less than its list or base selling price. This is a really an advance negotiating tactic. The vendor will typically feel compelled to put its cards on the table early in the game by providing at least some incentive for considering its solution against competitive offerings. The discount columns are optional and can be omitted if you want to take a simpler approach, but still work at not paying list price in your own other ways.

Note that one column is used to indicate the number of simultaneous users or units required for a given line item entry. Typically, an organization will require a far greater number of end user or per seat licenses for functional portions of the software than it will for developer tools. This difference in seat count may or may not impact the organization's final cost. Likewise, for self-service or portal-type applications the organization may need a dramatically larger number of user licenses than it will for specific software functions.

Also note the inclusion of a specific line item for project management and administration costs. In practice, I have found that many organizations mistakenly believe that any project will either manage itself, or that vendors and consultants provide project management services on a pro-bono basis. Unfortunately, none of these statements are true. In fact, expect that these costs will be among the highest on a per hour basis.

Recurring Charges

If you license or buy the software package outright, most recurring charges are going to be for software maintenance provided by the vendor. If you have chosen or desire an application service provider arrangement whereby an application is hosted for you, there are usually monthly maintenance fees, per transaction fees, and storage fees. These fees may increase or decrease as your transaction or storage volume increases or decreases. Sometimes vendors have lower teaser rates that escalate quickly as transaction and storage volumes increase. At other times, vendors may have a set minimum or base service level that is a part of a flat monthly service fee; any transactions or space consumption above the minimum will incur incremental per transaction fees and storage fees.

As a general rule, during contract negotiations, seek to stabilize any recurring charges for an extended period of time and limit any escalations in rates to some form of inflation or cost of living index. Sometimes vendors will provide substantial discounts for prepayments of maintenance costs. These arrangements also allow an organization to lock in services for an extended period at a preferred or lower rate.

Hosted applications have gained an increasing amount of interest because of perceived lower costs. These lower costs are not always what they seem to be. You may still need to license the software separately and will still likely have implementation-related costs. If you operate in a stable industry, your ongoing costs will be more predictable. I should point out that the majority of software acquisitions remain purchase arrangements, not application leasing.

A closing note about recurring costs: The spreadsheet or budget provided by the vendor should ideally contain all start-up and first-year cost projections.

Software Infrastructure Requirements

This should be a fill-in-the-blank section. It can also be a part of the Excel worksheet (perhaps a separate worksheet tab) that a vendor is required to complete. Request information about the vendor platform and minimum sizing requirements, including processor type and speed, core memory required, and disk storage requirements programs. In addition, for each business data environment (i.e., production, test, training) request operating system and version requirements, database and version requirements, and any other middleware components and versions. This section is closely related to the the RFP's technical and infrastructure objectives section.

Vendor Background Information

It is customary to request a copy of the vendor's financial statements for its most recent fiscal year. If the company is publicly held, this is a relatively straightforward request. For a privately held company, it may be more difficult to get this information and it may be not be audited. In addition, request other background information about both the product and vendor's history. Also, request local and national user group information and information and locations of local and national support centers and their hours of operation. Many times vendors will have a corporate profile booklet already prepared that provides much, if not all, of this type of information.

Vendor References and Potential Site Visit Locations

Request the vendor to provide at least five industry references (organization, contact person, and phone number) that currently use the software package. Request a general reference list of at least 25 references in all industries. Request that the vendor identify at least two locations (preferably local) where the software is currently installed and operational. In addition, see if these references would be willing to accommodate a site visit from your selection team's representatives. If you have a large selection team, it is unlikely the entire team will be able to visit the site. A good rule to follow is to limit the site visit team to just three individuals. A larger group can sometimes be accommodated, but remember, your team is the guest of the hosting organization, not the vendor.

Detailed Product Information

This section usually instructs the vendor to provide at least one set (and perhaps multiple copies) of product information that provides detailed information about the features, functions, benefits, and technical requirements related to the proposed software package.

It is also desirable to request sample screen illustrations for each step in the core business processes that will be demonstrated. This affords an offline reference and side-by-side comparisons of these illustrations against other products.

Documentation and Output Samples

Request that the vendor provide a representative sample (but not necessarily a complete set) of detailed user and technical manuals for the application software proposed. A list of standard reports for the different functional areas should be included. If specific reports are of significant interest, request inclusion of a sample copy.

Case Studies, Cost Benefit Analyses, and Calculators

Vendors go to a lot of trouble on their own to make a business case as to why an organization should buy their software package. While every organization will have its set of reasons and metrics to achieve, it is useful to review what the vendor has prepared. Often the vendor will have noted a benefit or return on investment dimension that was not previously considered. This information could apply to your situation to further strengthen the business case presentation for a given type of software package (not necessarily this vendor's software).

Model Contract Documents

Request a copy of the software license agreement, software maintenance agreement, implementation services agreement, and any other relevant document that must be signed to complete the software acquisition transaction if the vendor is selected as the finalist. Oftentimes, these documents may contain unfavorable or undesirable clauses. It is useful to determine if there are any red flag contractual issues that would rule out further consideration of a given vendor before expending a lot of energy evaluating the software. For example, you may not want to proceed with a vendor that will not remove an arbitration clause or will not disclose or provide access to its source code.

Implementation Methodology and Timeline

Every software vendor will have specific recommendations, usually in the form of a formal approach or methodology for implementing its specific software package. This section requests the vendor to provide details of this approach, as recommended for your organization's situation. This section also requests a detailed project plan that illustrates the time line and resource assumptions. These assumptions are for your internal resources and any external vendor or consulting resources that will be needed to achieve the proposed implementation schedule.

Public Sector Considerations

I have found that some vendors have an aversion to replying to an RFP document. Usually they mistakenly associate an RFP as a process used only for government work. That is simply not true, although selling to any government agency will have many unique implications. For this reason, many vendors have special sales staffs for dealing with the public sector. In some cases, certain VARs and consulting firms will be ill equipped for dealing with the public sector and may specifically avoid selling to this market.

Regulated Industry Considerations

If your organization is in a heavily regulated industry and when deemed appropriate, you may want to include a statement in an RFP. The statement should indicate that although your organization is not an agency of government, it is regulated by various local, state, and federal agencies and these regulations will specifically affect your organization's software requirements. In addition, you should specifically point out in the list covering the desired software features and functions any such items that are governmental requirements.

RFIS VERSUS RFPS

A document that is closely related to an RFP is the request for information (RFI). The most obvious difference between an RFI document and the RFP and the RFP process, in general, is that your organization is not considered ready to buy. An RFI implies your organization is only gathering or seeking information at the current time.

The RFI document can be central to the process of establishing a short list of vendors. Your organization might send an RFI to every vendor on a trade publication's list of software packages. The RFI document is a decidedly different and much shorter document.

The major content differences between an RFI document and an RFP document are formality and scope. The RFI document should contain background information about your organization (similar to an RFP's). It should be void of any proprietary information. In other words, it should contain no more than what might be publicly available about your organization. It should provide a broad statement of your objectives and list the functional areas considered within the scope of these objectives (again similar to the RFP's purpose statement).

The RFI document should specifically request product literature, general platform availability, infrastructure requirements, and any vendor case studies related to your vertical market or industry segment. Unlike the RFP, only one or two copies of this information should be requested. In many cases, your consideration of a vendor or product will not go any further than this. Why waste the vendor's time or money on an elaborate preparation or mass mailing to the selection team? Only one point of contact should be listed. In most cases, it will be the project manager, chief information officer, IT manager, or IT director who will serve as the contact.

Does the Vendor Want My Business?

Almost all vendors decide how to pursue your business based upon one of several criteria. The industry you are in is one such determinant and the potential size of your organization's software package budget is the other. The largest prospects are often sold or serviced through a direct sales staff employed by the vendor. If your organization is in a specialty field, such as a federal agency, a state or local government, or a university or other educational institution, the vendor may have a special accounts department to serve such markets. For smaller and middle market prospects, the vendor will refer your interest to a local VAR or to a local sales agent, acting in a similar capacity to a manufacturer's representative.

It is appropriate to request in the RFI a statement from a vendor indicating if the vendor will serve your interest in its product directly or through its agent or reseller. It is also appropriate to ask if multiple resellers will compete for business in your geographic area or if the reseller has an exclusive in your geographic market. If the vendor has multiple, competing resellers in your market, it is also fair to request a listing of those resellers. You may also add a statement to the RFI asking the vendor, if invited, would it want to provide a short (a half day or less) presentation on its firm and a brief overview of its product for your fact-finding team. (Notice I did not say evaluation or selection team.)

PREPARING THE REQUEST FOR PROPOSAL: AN EPILOGUE

Preparing a formal RFP is the first dimension of an effective and structured software selection process. It is a time-consuming process that must identify the financial, functional, technical, and vendor relationship objectives that must be accomplished from the proposal and ultimately through the selected software package.

11

SOFTWARE PACKAGE SELECTION: THE EVALUATION PROCESS

The previous chapter discussed how to prepare a request for proposal (RFP) document related to a software package acquisition. It also briefly touched on both the selection steps and some of the evaluation considerations related to vendor responses — the proposals — that a vendor delivers in reply to an RFP. The focus of this chapter is on proposal evaluation or ultimately, the actual selection of a software package.

Once the RFP document has been prepared and distributed, it is a waiting game until the replies trickle in for review and evaluation before the real work starts. Some of the evaluation work can be done in advance, such as the creation of evaluation spreadsheets and weights on the relative importance for each of the evaluation criterion. Once proposal replies are in hand, the next task is to evaluate the strengths, weaknesses, costs, and the overall goodness of fit represented by each software package and of each vendor considered. This process ultimately leads to a decision about which software package and vendor is right for your organization.

This chapter discusses these major topics:

- The evaluation criteria underlying the holistic software selection
- Scoring the vendor's proposal document
- Scoring the software package demonstration
- Checking references
- Conducting a site visit
- Negotiating the final deal with the selected software vendor

In addition to these topics, several other important issues related to the overall evaluation and negotiation process are also discussed.

HOLISTIC SOFTWARE SELECTION

A holistic approach to software selection focuses not only on eliciting and scoring how well software packages compare on a feature-by-feature basis, but also considers nonfeature comparisons as an integral part of the overall evaluation and ultimate decision. Recall from earlier discussions that the holistic software selection approach suggested by this author relies on four fundamental software evaluation areas, which are as follows:

- Business application requirements
- Time and cost to value requirements
- Technical and infrastructure requirements
- Vendor relationship requirements

The successful software implementation is largely a result of the software selection process. It means that the evaluation and selection process found the best overall software package solution for the organization given the criteria along these dimensions. An in-depth review of each of these four evaluation areas follows.

Business Application Requirements

The primary reason an organization will acquire a software package is to satisfy its business application processing requirements. Therefore, a fundamental portion of the evaluation, perhaps 50% or more of the weight of the evaluation is geared toward assessing the goodness of fit of the software package from a functionality standpoint. The features list, discussed in Chapter 9 is used to identify functional business requirements and to elicit vendor responses about whether or not they meet such requirements.

Some of my colleagues in the industry purport that certain types of software packages, especially ERP systems, CRM systems, and financial application software has become largely generic or common functionality and that an extensive analysis or comparison between such systems is not necessarily a valuable exercise. My position is that an analysis at the feature level is still necessary, though perhaps not all of this functionality needs to be thoroughly demonstrated as much as do the features specifically related to the organization's core or major business processes. While for competitive reasons, the feature sets between any given field of candidate systems may be close, how each vendor implements or performs a given generic or common process can vary widely.

Evaluating software features on paper alone is difficult. Although a vendor may indicate conformance to a requirement, only the product demonstration will speak to the usability or degree of conformance of the feature to your organization's specific requirements. Oftentimes the user interface, the number of steps, the ease of configuration and reconfiguration are all significantly different among a field of candidate software packages. Hence the reasons why product demonstrations are so important and also why this is even more so for the core, high-volume business processes that will be performed by the software package.

When vendors score similarly against an organization's financial requirements, generally speaking, attention turns to the degree that a software package achieves or exceeds the desired functionality objectives the organization has established for the software package evaluation.

Time and Cost to Value Requirements

Financial considerations and time to implement can be significant factors to the overall acceptability of a given software package during the final moments of the software package selection and evaluation process. This is especially true when price or schedule variations are extremely wide between solutions.

Technical and Infrastructure Requirements

Usually, the evaluation of technical and infrastructure requirements is benchmarked to a preferred architecture or infrastructure of choice for the organization. Although this is an important consideration, consider also reliability and throughput criterion in the evaluation process. Such criterion may suggest changes in such strategies. This is especially true for newcomers to the software package arena. The processing and storage demands placed on a system by the typical software package can seem excessive at first blush, but do not undersize or underestimate their importance simply to meet a budget or technical objective. The software package decision must first and foremost be a business-based decision and that means that the package selected must first and foremost satisfy the functional business requirements before technical and infrastructure requirements. This means that technical considerations should have a lower overall weighting in the evaluation to the functional business requirements.

Vendor Relationship Requirements

There are two general categories of relationship evaluation criteria which must be addressed; they are vendor compatibility and project compatibility. The vendor's suitability on such points as financial stability, depth, knowledge and professionalism of staff, compatibility or goodness of fit with the organization and overall chances of success should be considered. With regard to project compatibility, criteria such as project understanding, methodology, and ability to add value, as well as both the vendor's industry knowledge and related project experience should be considered.

Developing the Evaluation Criteria

The merits of proposals received from bidders must be evaluated on a level playing field. Developing objective criteria is an essential step in the evaluation of competing proposals. Proposals should be evaluated against both general and specific criteria. The proposal evaluation approach or methodology, as recommended by this author, centers on the use of tables or worksheets that list the evaluation criteria to be considered.

The evaluation criteria used for the holistic software selection are ideally developed in a group setting by the selection team. If this is not done, then at some point a collaborative meeting will need to occur. During this meeting, a consensus on the criteria to be included and their relative importance (or ranking) is established. This can be a politically charged and heated process for some organizations. A possible alternative is to poll stakeholders. Their responses will be weighted based on the relative importance of each of the four components in the holistic software selection evaluation described here.

UNDERSTANDING RESPONSES TO AN RFP

Some vendors will do a very good job of answering your RFP in the desired format, while others simply make vague references on your document with their boilerplate reply. If the vendor has done a poor job in making their reply, the task of reconciling the RFP response is a more significant one. It is important to write an RFP document in such a way that it is not ambiguous. An ambiguous RFP document will only result in ambiguous responses.

Responses that are improperly prepared by a vendor can be immediately disqualified or they can be returned to the vendor for correction and resubmission. Some will do so, but many others will not. Unfortunately, some vendors do not take RFP documents as seriously as they should. In other cases, your organization may not have allowed enough time for the vendor to craft an appropriate response. Having been on both sides of the RFP process, I can tell you that usually a vendor's reply suffers most when it has assigned or delegated the wrong resources to the task of responding to the RFP document.

Remember that you will want the vendors to put as much thought into making their reply as you did in preparing the RFP document. Although vendors should realistically be able to turn around a reply to any RFP almost as a matter of routine, they will need some time to assemble the right team to make their response.

Why Some Vendors Do Not or Will Not Respond to an RFP Document

There are a number of reasons why a given vendor does not reply to an RFP document, including the vendor's own opinion that it is unqualified to complete all the work. In other cases, a lack of response may simply be an unwillingness to bid a particular type of work. For instance, at my consulting firm, we, as a general rule, do not reply to an RFP indicating that only fixed bids will be considered.

PROPOSAL EVALUATION: THE BASICS

The evaluation of proposals received from numerous vendors is a time-consuming and challenging process. These evaluations must generally focus on:

- The vendor's understanding of the RFP
- The product's fit to your overall business and technical requirements
- The capacity of the vendor to be successful
- The vendor's fit to your organization (i.e., how comfortable will your organization be in dealing with and working with a given vendor)

The use of a carefully planned, organized, and deliberate evaluation process reduces the inherent subjectivity in this undertaking to a minimum. Standardization also promotes maximum efficiency in the reading and evaluation of the typical software package proposal response, an often complex and lengthy document. This section is to be used as a guide in preparing for and evaluating proposal responses from vendors.

As a general rule, the best format for evaluating proposal responses is through the use of an electronic spreadsheet. I use Microsoft Office products, but that is not to say that the Lotus SmartSuite, Corel Office, or Star Office equivalents will not work if those are the standards in your organization. As a general rule, most of these other products can read a Microsoft format file and save to a Microsoft format file. The remainder of my discussions in this area will focus on the use of Microsoft Office products.

I recommend eliciting as much of the vendor's proposal reply in a Microsoft Excel format as is possible. This will save time. If that is not possible, at least have the vendor enter replies electronically into a Microsoft Word document, then cut and paste replies into a spreadsheet for the evaluation process. Preparing the evaluation spreadsheets is largely a mechanical process. This workload can be shared among selection team members to expedite the process.

Understanding Workbooks versus Worksheets

I am accustomed to using Microsoft Office products and understand their terminology, but realize that not everyone does. To set the record straight, a workbook is a file containing multiple worksheets and will be represented by a series of labeled tabs across the bottom of the worksheet area. I use the term electronic spreadsheet generically to mean an Excel workbook file, whether it contains one or multiple worksheet tabs. A Microsoft Word document can contain a formatted table comprised of rows and columns that are similar to a spreadsheet. In fact, the contents of tabular cells from a Word document can be copied and pasted directly into Excel spreadsheet cells.

My preference, in concert with the intent of the holistic software selection process that I have prescribed in this chapter, is to devise four workbooks. These four workbooks are named as follows:

- Business application requirements evaluation workbook
- Time and cost to value requirements evaluation workbook
- Technical and infrastructure requirements evaluation workbook
- Vendor relationship requirements evaluation workbook

The specific questions contained in the RFP are categorized and then added to these four workbooks. This is usually done during the RFP construction process when vendor response worksheets are being prepared. If that step was not previously done, it must be done now.

What the Individual Worksheets Look Like

Within each Microsoft workbook file, I create as many worksheets (or tabs) as I have vendor replies, plus one. The plus one worksheet (or tab) will be used as a summary worksheet. Each vendor reply worksheet will be identical in format. The format usually contains the following columns:

- Proposal question
- Vendor response
- Response value
- Response weight
- Response score
- Vendor comment

A lot of work goes into developing the content and format of the evaluation worksheets and tabulating the responses. This task is easier when the structure of the evaluation is considered early on in the process. Again my recommendation is to formulate the nucleus of the evaluation worksheets or the evaluation criteria while the selection team is constructing the proposal document.

Developing Scores

Scoring vendor responses must be based upon objective criteria. The selection team must develop a table of standard responses (or at least standard units or formats, such as dollars for cost criterion or days for time criterion) and associated standardized values for each proposal question. For requirements that were posed to the vendor in the form of a list, such as a list of required business related features, the standard responses should have been defined at that time. The associated standardized scoring values may or may not have been assigned at that time. Examples of such standardized responses and values appear below:

Proposal Question or Evaluation Criteria	Possible Standardized Vendor Response Values	Assigned Value for the Standardized Vendor Response
Ability to create a check payment document on demand without processing all check payment documents (i.e., truck driver waiting for a cash on delivery payment)	Standard feature Optional feature Requires customizing Not available	Standard feature = 10 points Optional feature = 5 points Requires customizing = 1 point Not available = 0 points

This standardization should be practical for every potential question posed in the RFP. This will require some creativity at times. Assume the question was: What is the project duration (in business days) that will be required to implement this software package based upon your assumptions and assertions in this proposal? Here is a potential way to score this type of question:

Proposal Question or Evaluation Criteria	Possible Standardized Vendor Response Values	Assigned Value for the Standardized Vendor Response
Implementation project time line	Days (any value)	91 or more days = 0 points 90 days or less = 5 points 60 days or less = 10 points

As stressed in the development of business cases, nonfinancial metrics were translated into financial metrics. The goal in proposal evaluation is similar — to frame or translate all proposal evaluation criteria into measurable or valued assertions.

Developing Weights

Generally speaking, replies are weighted based on the importance of the feature in light of overall business requirements. The presumption is that not every requirement is of equal importance. Weights are made on a consensus of opinion basis by the selection team. Once the evaluation criteria have been established they are then weighted according to their importance. This is done by considering the relative importance a specific evaluation criterion should have with respect to the overall importance in the decision-making process. Assign a ranking, in descending order, to each criterion statement. For instance, if there are 20 criterion statements, the highest-ranking criterion is assigned a value of 20, while the lowest ranking criterion is assigned a value of 1.

The alternative method of weighting is to assign a specific weight based upon the business criticality of each business requirement. The typical standardized weighting scale might be as follows:

Business Criticality Rating of the Business Requirement	Assigned Weight for This Business Criticality Rating
An essential requirement	10
A desirable, but non-essential requirement	5
A currently unknown, but perhaps future requirement	1

This alternative method obviously works when the business requirements were given such criticality ratings as they were developed. These business criticality ratings then transfer readily into evaluation criteria.

Each individual requirement or feature reply is scored by multiplying the response value by the response weight. The scores are then tallied at the end of this worksheet column. This is the vendor's cumulative score within a given evaluation area. Figure 11.1 illustrates a portion of a vendor evaluation worksheet.

What the Summary Worksheet Looks Like

The summary worksheet repeats several of the columns from the vendor reply worksheet:

- Proposal question
- Vendor response
- Response weight

In addition to these columns, the summary worksheet contains a column that will contain the corresponding score value from each vendor's worksheet and a column for the arithmetic mean (average) of all vendor scores. Figure 11.2 illustrates a portion of a vendor evaluation summary worksheet.

The completion of these worksheets will be lengthy process. Once these four worksheets are created, the next task is the handling of proposal components left unscored by this process.

Scoring Proposals

It is now time to read the proposals received from vendors. Members of the evaluation team should first read and score the proposal on an individual basis. It is best to read all of the proposals twice. The first time one should read to understand, making notes of observations as needed. Now make a second pass read of the proposals. During this read, the evaluation and scoring of the proposal's merits will be accomplished. With the evaluation criteria worksheet in hand, read and score the proposal accordingly. This step is completed for each proposal.

Tabulation and Evaluation of Results

After the proposals have been scored and tabulated, a collaborative review of the individual proposal evaluations by the selection team should then occur. The results should be reviewed in detail. Make two

Vendor Evaluation Worksheet
Client: ABC Manufacturing
Proposal: ERP System Selection

TradewindsGroup
Tradewinds Group, Incorporated
Consultants to Management
Box 3601
Oak Brook, Illinois 60522

Vendor Name: ERP Vendor Name Here
System: ERP System Name Here

Feature Number	Major Feature Set	Feature Set	Feature Sub Set	Required Software Feature	Vendor Response (From Response Worksheet)	Response Value	Business Criticality	Assigned Weight	Vendor Score
101	Procure to Pay	Procurement	Vendor Analysis	Calculate On Time Delivery Performance Level on a Per Order Basis	STANDARD	10	ESSENTIAL	10	100
102	Procure to Pay	Procurement	Vendor Analysis	Display Vendor's Overall On Time Delivery Performance Level on an Aggregate Basis with Drill Down to Specific Order on Chronological Basis	OPTIONAL	5	DESIRABLE	5	25
		TOTAL FOR VENDOR							125

Possible Scores

STANDARD	10	ESSENTIAL	10
OPTIONAL	5	DESIRABLE	5
CUSTOM	1	FUTURE	1
NOT AVAILABLE	0		

Figure 11.1 Vendor Evaluation Worksheet

Vendor Evaluation Summary
Client: ABC Manufacturing
Proposals For: ERP System Selection

TradewindsGroup
Tradewinds Group, Incorporated
Consultants to Management
Post Office Box 3601
Oak Brook, Illinois 60522

Feature Number	Major Feature Set	Feature Set	Feature Sub Set	Required Software Feature	Vendor: Vendor 1	Vendor: Vendor 2	Vendor: Vendor 3	Vendor: Vendor 4
101	Procure to Pay	Procurement	Vendor Analysis	Calculate On Time Delivery Performance Level on a Per Order Basis	100	50	100	50
102	Procure to Pay	Procurement	Vendor Analysis	Display Vendor's Overall On Time Delivery Performance Level on an Aggregate Basis with Drill Down to Specific Order on Chronological Basis	25	50	25	25
		SUMMARY (TOTAL) SCORES			125	100	125	75

Figure 11.2 Vendor Evaluation Summary Worksheet

lists as you are going along. One will be a list of questions that can be posed to the vendor where clarifications about specific proposal items are necessary. The second list should identify gaps between the software package and the business, cost, or technical requirements. This list will have multiple purposes throughout the remaining evaluation and selection process. It will factor into assessing the overall goodness of fit, guiding the negotiation of a final contract with a vendor and determining the final costs of the proposed solution.

SCORING PRODUCT DEMONSTRATIONS

The first rule of product demonstrations is to avoid the canned presentation. The second rule of product demonstrations is to develop a meaningful set of product-related evaluation criteria to be used during the software demonstration. Of course, the best way to do this is to provide the vendor with a business transaction scenario to guide the features and function demonstrated for a given business process. The business transaction scenario document provides a solution neutral perspective on how the process is completed. The process vision document provides the ideal method of completing the process step. These two documents provide the benchmark for evaluation purposes. Scoring of the product against these benchmarks should be done during the demonstration process. The example below provides the typical criteria that can be applied to each processing step demonstrated:

Question	Target Response	Response Value
The vendor demonstrated this process as per the business transaction scenario.	Yes No	Yes = 10 No = 0
The steps taken to complete this process were clear, logical, and straightforward.	Yes No	Yes = 10 No = 0
The user interface for this software feature is well organized and uncluttered in appearance.	Yes No	Yes = 10 No = 0
The transaction results were as expected.	Yes No	Yes = 10 No = 0

Question	Target Response	Response Value
The process met or exceeded the process vision goals and objectives for this business process.	Yes No	Yes = 10 No = 0
A particular software feature failed to operate properly during the demonstration.	Yes No	Yes = 0 No = 10
The vendor used the sample data provided by our organization to complete this portion of the demonstration.	Yes No	Yes = 10 No = 0

This list is only a suggestion and can be added to or subtracted from as desired. The intent is to measure or evaluate the functionality, usability, and degree of completeness of the demonstrated software features.

Product Demonstrations: When Should They Be Conducted?

As a general rule, software demonstrations using demonstration scenarios should be limited to the semifinalists in your selection process. They are one of the last steps in the overall evaluation process. Do not put a vendor through any extra effort until it has made the final cut. Any software demonstrations received prior to those during the formal RFP process should be limited to the vendor's standard sales presentation and its canned product demonstration.

This is also a good time to point out that I am reluctant to contact and work with software vendors prior to commencing a formal bidding process. There are times when an introductory session with an obscure vendor may be desirable, especially if you are considering the vendor as a semifinalist. This is a touchy area. To be fair, if you allow one vendor this opportunity, you must provide the same for all vendors. I call this short listing prospective vendors.

Postproduct Demonstration Activities

After the product demonstration has occurred, collect the demonstration evaluations completed by each individual team member. Next, score and tabulate these into a consensus score for each criterion. A selection team postdemonstration meeting should then be held. This meeting is a collaborative review of the consensus scores as constructed from the team member demonstration evaluations. Each criterion is then discussed. If a person disagrees with the consensus opinion, this is the time when that person should be heard. Once consensus is established for a given criterion statement, the process is repeated for each remaining criterion statement.

This overall process is obviously repeated for each product demonstration that has been made to the selection team. At the conclusion of this process, you will have reached a consensus opinion on the merits of each proposal. This can be a time-consuming and controversial process, but is an important step in ultimately selecting a software package.

VENDOR REFERENCE CHECKING

An important request made in the RFP document is a call for vendor references. Most vendors (when they can) will dazzle the prospective buyer with a long list of who's who in corporate America and from a litany of industries. It is impressive on the vendor's part. There are a few problems that surface with reference lists, including:

- The reference list is stale. For example, the contact person is no longer at the reference or the reference firm has stopped using the software. It is usually not a performance issue.
- The reference list has no organization on it that approximates the size, industry, or business model of your firm or is not for the version (or platform) of the software package you are considering.
- The reference list has many foreign businesses noted, but few domestic businesses.
- The reference includes only satisfied customers or users of the software package.

The vendor will usually provide additional references to satisfy the first two problems. If the vendor cannot provide new or more specific references, then treat that as a red flag. In the case of the third problem, this could be construed as a yellow flag. It usually means the vendor is not strong in the United States or is a new entrant. In this case, ask the vendor:

- How long has your product been sold in the United States?
- In what areas was your software package changed or enhanced before its introduction into the United States?

- At how many locations has the software been implemented in the United States?
- Given the market is very competitive in the United States for this type of software, what is your firm's commitment level to the long road ahead in obtaining and advancing your own market share?

Checking on foreign references can be difficult due to language barriers. English is widely used in business today and is the predominant language online. In some cases, an e-mail or fax may work better in obtaining answers to your reference related questions.

Finding dissatisfied users is a job that is tougher to address. One way to partially overcome this problem is to ask the vendor several pointed questions. These questions include:

- How many active total installations of the package you have proposed are there?
- How many active total clients do you have in our industry?
- What are the three top reasons why clients have failed in their implementation of your software package?
- When customers select another software package over your product, what are the top reasons cited for doing so?

Depending on the honesty of the vendor or salesperson, you may get a good insight into what some of the challenges are that this particular vendor is experiencing. Another way to overcome this problem is to obtain independent research reports and trade reports about the software package or vendor and investment analyst reports about the vendor. The use of independent research is discussed in a later part of this chapter.

A final way to check on bad experiences is through the user group for the software package. Although the bad apples may not appear on the reference list, they are likely members (usually vocal) of the vendor's user group for the software. Sometimes vendors will invite you to attend an upcoming user's group meeting. If that is doable within the project's time frame, send a few representatives from the selection team and try to network as much as possible with other users while there. It may be money well spent to confirm whatever feelings your organization has about the choice it is about to make.

The first rule of reference checking: Do not call any vendor references until scripting a series of questions related to the product, vendor, and implementation and support experience. As a general rule, the selection team should meet and agree on the contents and format of the reference-checking questionnaire, then divide the list up and make the calls.

306 ■ Maximizing Business Performance through Software Packages

There are a number of questions that can be asked of vendor references. The second rule of reference checking must be applied: The list should be short and manageable, perhaps made up of only 10 to 12 questions. With that said, expect to complete the reference check within a relatively short period of time, perhaps 20 minutes or less. During the call, some folks will tell it all, while others will simply respond with short, curt answers. In some cases, your questions or calls may go unanswered, and in other cases you may get passed around to several individuals before getting to someone who can or will answer your questions. Here is a representative list of exact questions that should be addressed with each reference:

- What were your particular reasons for selecting this particular software package (vendor)?
- Did you get all of the functionality you were promised?
- What features have your users particularly liked (disliked) about the software?
- Can you cite any ways in which your business operations were changed or improved through the use of this software package?
- Have you made upgrades to the software package? Were they difficult or time consuming? If so, why do you feel that way?
- Are there areas of the software where you feel usability or performance can be improved?
- How long have you been working with this particular vendor?
- How would you characterize the ease of doing business with this vendor on an overall basis?
- Was your project completed on time or in advance of the promised startup date?
- Was the project completed on a fixed price contract? If so, were there any problems that arose on in of scope versus out of scope issues under the fixed bid? If not, was an up-front project budget provided by the vendor and how close was the final cost to that budget?
- Did the project start when desired and were resources readily available throughout the project as needed?
- How quickly and professionally has the vendor addressed any issues that have arisen during the life of your relationship?
- What has been your experience in dealing with the vendor's project managers, consultants, and technical support people? Are they knowledgeable and honest? Do they present themselves in a professional and businesslike manner? Do you see or speak to the same individuals over time, or is there always someone new to deal with?
- On an overall basis, how satisfied are you with this vendor?

- What is your single greatest concern about the future of this vendor? For this particular software package?
- Will you upgrade this product in the future? If not, will use of the product be abandoned and why is that the case?

It is not necessary to ask all of these questions. There may also be several questions you will add that are germane to your business or industry. Again, try to limit the overall list to 10 or 12 questions.

Objectively evaluating references is not always easy. Open-ended questions make the task difficult. One possible way is to structure the questions in such a way as to elicit a targeted response. This means it will be necessary to also provide the vendor's reference with specific replies to your questions. Associated with each response is a numeric value.

Targeted responses work well for a fill-in-the-blank style of reference check. That type of reference check will not yield much in the way of additional information or insights. Unfortunately, paper questionnaires either get pushed aside or tossed away too easily. A conversational reference check is more effective and is the recommended method of checking references. The problem with targeted response surveys is they often do not provide any useful commentary besides the reply to the question. It is recommended that some open-ended questions should still be posed to the reference. The reference checker can then make brief notes about respondent's comments. In a verbal interview format it is possible to learn more than simply the answer to the survey questions. If possible, and if the respondent agrees to it, consider placing the person on a speakerphone so several selection team members can participate.

A typical reference check question formulated with a target response and an associate numeric response might appear (or be asked) as follows:

Question	Target Response	Response Value
How would you rate the vendor's project managers, consultants, and technical support people as to their knowledge, integrity, and professionalism?	Exceeded expectations Fulfilled expectations Below expectations	Exceeded expectations = 5 Fulfilled expectations = 3 Below expectations = 1

A qualitative assessment of reference checks works similarly to how functional and technical portions of the proposal response are evaluated.

The selection team can weight each question as to its relative importance to the vendor evaluation. Multiplying the response value by the assigned weight yields the earned point value for the question. The summation of the earned point values for all questions yields a reference check score. Summing and averaging all reference check scores related to a given vendor yields an overage average score for the vendor.

Generally speaking, it is desirable to consider checking with between 5 and 10 vendor references. Certainly call on all of the industry vendors with the balance being randomly chosen from the reference list. The team may not be comfortable with a few of the responses or unable to contact a significant number of the references initially chosen within a reasonable time period. If this is the case, then pick an additional group of references and repeat the process.

Reference Checking: When Should It Be Conducted?

Unlike software demonstrations, reference checking can and should be done for semifinalist and finalist vendors. In some instances, the results of reference checks can help to determine if a vendor should be included as a finalist. Note that some vendors will provide references only when they are notified that they have been selected as a finalist. It is entirely acceptable to request a vendor that is on the cusp of becoming a semifinalist to provide references if not previously submitted and the vendor wants to be a semifinalist.

Postreference Checking Activities

After all the reference checks for a given vendor have occurred, these separate evaluations can be summarized and tabulated into a consensus evaluation. A meeting is then held with the entire selection team to review the results of the reference checking process. The consensus evaluation can then be rolled into the overall vendor relationship evaluation and scoring.

SITE VISITS

Site visits are meant to confirm the findings and conclusions you have already reached about both the vendor and the product's overall suitability toward meeting your organization's business requirements. This was accomplished through the fact-finding and evaluation processes.

Site visits are often done only in conjunction with the finalist vendor. In fact, I make every effort to lead to a conclusion on the finalist vendor without conducting the site visit. Understand that a vendor will not take a prospect to a site that it cannot use as a reference. In many cases the site may be known as a showcase account for the vendor. Often vendors will not provide a local reference. There can be several reasons for this and they may be innocent or deliberate. First, the vendor may be new to the region or to a given industry and may not have an established local presence. These are certainly factors to consider in determining the vendor's suitability, but the solution must still be judged in a holistic manner using other criteria as well. Second, the vendor hopes that by picking a similar, but distant reference, your organization will forgo the site visit altogether.

Site visits require preplanning. The site visit is an opportunity to see or experience the software in action. The well-planned site visit should have preestablished objectives in terms of what your selection team wants to ask or see at the site. As with conducting reference checks, it is not realistic to expect that every team member will be able to visit the reference site. Out of courtesy to the hosting business organization, the size of this group should be limited to just a few team members.

If the site was also a reference that was previously checked, do not repeat the reference check questions (though you might ask about elaborating on some part of a previous response). It is best to visit with several managers or observe several critical business processes in action. Develop and ask a series of probing questions based upon what is observed or said. Coordinate development of the agenda and your expectations for the site visit with the vendor's salesperson.

Scoring site visits is not an overly difficult task. Score the site visit against the predetermined objectives as in the example below:

Question	Target Response	Response Value
The site visit confirmed assertions the vendor has made during the product demonstration or in the proposal.	Yes No	Yes = 10 No = 0
The vendor's client site staff is satisfied with the vendor's postimplementation support.	Yes No	Yes = 10 No = 0
The vendor's client site staff seemed satisfied with the software package's reliability and stability.	Yes No	Yes = 10 No = 0

Question	Target Response	Response Value
The vendor's client site is making use of the same or similar functionality of the software that we would likely use.	Yes No	Yes = 10 No = 0
The vendor's client site staff was able to provide examples of how the software package has improved business processes or business performance metrics.	Yes No	Yes = 10 No = 0

This list of sample objectives also gives rise to the kinds of questions that team members should ask during the site visit. As needs or objectives dictate, this list can be altered.

Postsite Visit Activities

After the site visit is conducted, a trip report should be prepared by those involved that summarizes and tabulates the findings and observations. The trip report is then distributed to the selection team for review. A meeting is then held with the entire selection team to address any specific questions members may have about these findings and observations.

EVALUATING THE VENDOR'S FINANCIAL STRENGTH AND BUSINESS MODEL

When your organization obtains a new customer, the sales department has ideally done some preliminary research about a new customer's business. Oftentimes this will include a preliminary assessment of the prospect's financial resources or the ability to pay. This is usually done with the help of the credit department that will ultimately establish a credit limit for the prospect should the prospect become your customer.

When it comes to vendors, the purchasing department will similarly research new vendors. Although we often assume — and wrongly so — that the purchasing department makes all decisions based upon price, that is not the case. This is especially true for noncommodity type products like software packages. An important criterion that purchasing will be interested in is the ability of the vendor to be a long-term vendor. This means that the vendor is financially stable and has a history of meeting its delivery and product performance obligations. Important sources of information to the purchasing department in evaluating and selecting vendors include:

- References
- Financial statements
- Industry and trade press mentions (especially regarding the vendor's innovations and product evolution experience)
- Investment community research about the vendor (if it is publicly held)

Of course, nothing less applies to software vendor evaluation.

One of the finest, shortest, and most candid accounts I have read about a particular software vendor comes out of India and was written by Arun Jethmalani. Jethmalani is an investment research analyst who wrote the investment research report, "Visesh Infosystems — Yet Another Software IPO." Although I found Jethmalani's grammar a bit less than perfect, the contents of this report (from the viewpoint of the software buyer) represents exactly the kind of information to be gleaned from an investment community research report about a software vendor. This report provides a quick take on the software vendor, its product, and the market in which it is competing. In short, it is a frank assessment about whether the organization being reviewed can be *financially* successful.

Of course, a software package buyer wants its selected software providers to be financially successful, though maybe not entirely at its expense. After all, a major impetus for buying a software package is to outsource its software maintenance and development to the vendor. That means you will want the vendor around at least for as long as you continue using its software package. Beware of vendors who will use your business to springboard their package into a new market or as the launch site for a new product offering. Unless the vendor has a proven record in the marketplace, competing against already established players is difficult and cash consuming.

Consider Microsoft's recent announcement about entering the customer relationship management (CRM) software market or its desire to pursue the middle market or sweet spot for software packages. The company accomplished this by first acquiring Great Plains and then announcing its planned acquisition of Navison, both well-known middle market software package solutions. This is a bold and perhaps good move for Microsoft. However, this is a challenging market to enter, looking at the scores of competitors and ongoing purging of marginal players in a market that is no longer perceived as a growth industry. Even if it is not financially speaking a good bet for Microsoft, the company has strong enough financial reserves and product revenue diversity to tough it out and likely factor in as a long-term player (if it chooses to stay).

This does mean that a relatively new, financially challenged software vendor should be avoided entirely. There may be situations where the vendor has a unique value proposition — an exciting or innovative new product — that is paving a new market. Your organization may be left with few, if any, software package or vendor alternatives. I have also seen a number of smaller niche software players with innovative products or unique value propositions acquired by larger software firms. These firms quickly bundle the acquired product into their own product line. Under a worst case scenario, which happens frequently, this will mean the previous firm's installed base can be immediately orphaned. Yes, it is still buyer beware and in the grueling software marketplace, its relevance is that much more so.

I have repeatedly said that the software package marketplace has changed in the last few years, especially for enterprise resource planning (ERP) vendors. License revenues are down, growth prospects are lower and the market for software packages, in general, is smaller. While this information is good news for the software buyer, it is not particularly good news for software vendors, especially those without strong balance sheets and strong residuals in the form of software maintenance revenue. Strong residuals exist only when the vendor has a large installed base. Those residuals remain strong only when a software vendor is able to minimize defections from its product that is largely driven by the vendor's reputation for customer satisfaction. Customer satisfaction is measured by how well existing products work, how easy it is to do business with the vendor, and the firm's commitment to the future and its customers in the form of their product investment and innovation.

The next section discusses the product and market analyses conducted by information technology (IT) research houses, such as the Gartner Group, and their key analysis work, the Magic Quadrant. This type of research can assist an organization in assessing the position of a vendor and their product in the marketplace. Certainly, when a vendor scores marginally in an industry research report, it does not mean it is going out of business. That low score is simply an educated opinion about the vendor or its product, the market obstacles it faces, and the degree to which it can, or will, overcome such obstacles.

Unless a vendor yields almost single-handed influence over a market, like Microsoft has achieved in Operating System and Office Suite software, a software vendor, like any other business, exists only by maintaining competitive advantage. This is done by offering a unique value proposition to the marketplace or the vendor risks being eliminated. The vendor can maintain this advantage by improving their products, strengthening their reputations, by retaining existing customers, and by obtaining new ones. When the investment community pans a particular software vendor, the vendor may not get the chance to improve upon its lot in life.

For software vendors that are publicly traded, I strongly advise obtaining investment industry research reports that may have been written about the software vendor. Organizations should try to obtain these reports from sources with as much independence as possible. For instance, if an investment bank or brokerage house is a market maker for a given software vendor's stock, there may be some potential bias toward the positive in the report. Also, not as valuable, but worth a look, are the industry outlooks that cover the financial prospects for an entire industry. These reports are usually published by many investment banking and brokerage houses or by a government agency. They are usually available for free or for a small fee.

On a final note, consider by what criteria your organization might judge the credit-worthiness of your customers. The same objective review criterion used for making customer credit decisions also applies to vendor selection decisions. The emphasis, however, is altered slightly, highlighting profitability, revenue growth, reinvestment in the business, and sufficient reserves to weather business downturns.

SCORING THE VENDOR PROPOSALS: SOME POINTS TO CONSIDER

It is far easier to create an RFP document than it is to analyze multiple proposals in disparate formats. Analyzing vendor proposals is the most difficult part in the RFP process. The good news is, software package functions and features have been consistently rising. The bad news is, it is increasingly difficult to differentiate among the various software packages from rival vendors. This situation will not change in the years ahead. In fact, it will only get tougher.

Buying for the Future

The push is on to create plug-and-play, component-based, and largely commoditized software products. As this vision takes shape within the industry, for the first time taking a best-of-breed approach to software selection will finally make sense. Even SAP, the world's largest ERP system vendor, long known for the proprietary nature of its software, has recently indicated at the annual Sun MicroSystems Java Software Developers Forum a movement in this direction.

This concept of future vision may eliminate from contention the products of some vendors who are bound by the realities of tradition or their financial condition. As previously mentioned, even older generation software can be wrapped and componentized, so it is about a willingness to embrace this new market vision and any given vendor's ability to execute it successfully. Vendors that are providing an industry specific solution are in the best position to avoid the new market realities. If they cannot avoid them completely, they can at least avoid them until they are at the threshold of having a completely obsolete solution. Industry specific vendors must be cautious. In many ways, this emerging industry trend truly favors niche roles that some software vendors fulfill over the role of providing general purpose, generic software solutions.

The realities of the future are that it is far more difficult to execute than simply prognosticate. For the time being at least, all that can be done is to future proof software selections to the extent that such is possible. The future has several important ramifications in today's software selection process:

- Does the vendor embrace that future vision?
- Is the vendor moving its products toward that vision?
- Will the vendor be able to deliver on their promises?

The vendor should be able to provide a statement of direction about the future of its product. This may require your organization to sign a confidentiality agreement prior to the vendor making such disclosures. If the vendor is truly moving in the right direction, it may have actually begun delivery of a part of its future vision. In the absence of such, all one has is a vendor's promises. How do you evaluate a vendor on its promises? The vendor's current financial condition and its past product success or track record can only answer this last question.

Some outside objectivity can be introduced into the evaluation phase regarding the semifinalists. It comes in the way of industry and product research provided by third-party research houses. Gartner Group is one such organization. Its magic quadrant approach, in many ways, provides an independent assessment of a vendor's statement of direction. The next section of this chapter discusses these research houses and their value-add to the selection and evaluation process in more detail.

Obtaining and Using Third-Party Information in the Evaluation Process

The package software marketplace is a significant industry. It has attracted the attention of the major players as well as scores of smaller players that provide independent research and opinion services. To a certain degree, these various services serve as the *Consumer's Report* for the IT industry. Often a major research service may offer a favorable opinion in its research for a particular software package or vendor or for the market and business imperative for a particular class of software package (e.g., CRM systems). It is not unusual for software vendors to include this kind of information in their sales pitch to prospective customers.

Most of the research these organizations provide is of a proprietary nature; it is not free, nor is it usually available in the public domain. Selling this type of research to prospective software buyers is a major revenue stream for most of these research houses. Unfortunately, this type of research is not inexpensive. Research of this sort can easily cost several thousand dollars for reports that may only be several dozen pages in length. Given that, the cost to license most software packages can easily run into six figure ranges, it is generally money that is well spent. This is especially the case when the research pertains to finalist vendors in a selection process. This research may have a decidedly higher role in the decision-making process when an organization's evaluation finds two vendors or products pitted in a dead heat.

As a general rule, industry outlook reports help to put an overall perspective on the players within a software package segment. These types of reports will typically cover how the major vendors stack up in a given market. This information is usually cast in terms of technological leadership, market share, financial strength, license growth, current installed base, and numbers of increasing importance to most software buyers — software maintenance revenue trends and research and development outlays.

If your organization is on a tight budget, some of these services provide abstracts of their more complete reports at no charge. In other instances, scan the press releases available on the research houses' websites. These press releases are often peppered with key quotes from their more complete research reports and may provide sufficient industry insights. Finally, vendors will frequently make these reports available to an organization considering its software package, especially when they are positive.

Speaking of software vendors, it is important to understand that software vendors are a major revenue source for the IT research houses as well. Unlike Consumers Union, which is the nonprofit publisher of *Consumer Reports*, the IT industry research houses are for profit entities. In fact, vendors may actually sponsor some of the research, especially market analysis type reports. In other cases, research that reflects positively on a vendor or its product can be purchased and distributed by the vendor in its sales cycle, representing another revenue source for the research house.

Aberdeen Group

Founded in 1988, Aberdeen Group is what I would refer to as more of a marketing research firm. Aberdeen Group is an industry leader in this category and its IT marketing research is often cited in vendor press releases and vendor sales presentations. Aberdeen Group focuses its research content and marketing efforts toward the software vendors that are hoping to establish themselves within a given market segment, rather than toward end users.

Aberdeen Group's influence in the marketplace is not strictly behind the scenes. While the firm provides packaged research on followed areas of interest (research that is primarily of interest to the vendor's), it is often engaged by a software vendor to prepare third-party market or even product reviews. It is important to understand that, while looking authoritative and independent, these third-party reviews are vendor sponsored and are primarily part of a given vendor's arsenal of sales and marketing collateral.

Aberdeen Group characterizes a given vendor or its product in a positive way within the context of the market. Aberdeen Group's research will, as the firm puts it, "amplify a client's positioning message and unique value proposition" so as to "differentiate the vendor in a crowded market." While I do not in any way want to diminish the quality of research work Aberdeen Group provides, it is important to remember that this work is often vendor-sponsored research. While it may be third-party research, it is not truly independent research. With that said, I have found that Aberdeen Group's vendor-sponsored research work is often informative and insightful. For example, your organization may want to cite Aberdeen Group as a third-party observer for a given market analysis or industry trend when building a business case for new software.

Forrester Research

Forrester Research, Inc. is headquartered in Cambridge, MA, and boasts over 400 employees on its staff. Current CEO, George F. Colony, founded Forrester in 1983. Forrester is a leading independent research firm that "analyzes the future of technology change and its impact on businesses, consumers, and society." Forrester suggests that organizations can use its research "as a continual source of insight and strategy to guide their most critical business technology decisions." It is the Forrester view that "technology changes everything".

From the above comments one can sense that Forrester provides a different kind or level of research. In fact, what Forrester provides is information about how your organization might better leverage its technology investments in reaching its strategic objectives. Forrester has something referred to as its WholeView™ research strategy. This research strategy focuses on three areas:

- Technology evaluation
- Technology strategy
- Marketplace understanding

Forrester addresses each of these areas through specific research products.

To address technology evaluation, Forrester provides its TechRankings™ research. TechRankings combines lab-tested evaluations of various software packages conducted by its research partner, Doculabs Inc., with competitive market analysis, user interviews, and Internet-based tools for selecting and implementing software infrastructure and application products.

Forrester's TechStrategy™ research is intended to address technology strategy issues through thoughtful analysis of technological changes. This analysis can help an organization decide how and when to deploy technology for competitive advantage. This is a qualitative research offering. The centerpiece of this research is extensive interviews conducted with approximately 3,500 global companies with revenues exceeding $1 billion dollars. In effect, this is the customer base for the bulk of smaller and middle market manufacturers and distributors in the business-to-business marketplace.

Forrester's Technographics® research is a quantitative research program. This research focuses on how "technology is considered, bought, and used by consumers and businesses." The information looks at issues such as buyer behavior, product adoption, spending, and tolerance for technology risk. Forrester's Technographics quantitative-based research work complements Forrester's TechStrategy qualitative-based research work. It can be used to determine how to incorporate technology into your business strategy in a way that will best satisfy both customers and future prospects.

Forrester provides research in several areas of relevance to the subject of the book. Specifically, its work focuses on enterprise software applications, customer relationship management, supply chain management, manufacturing, and a specialty area on consumer packaged goods. Much like Aberdeen Group, Forrester makes its research available free of charge as a method of promoting its research work to prospective clients. I have found Forester's research work to provide accurate, candid, and objective analyses of its subjects.

Gartner Group

Perhaps the most well known of the IT research houses is the Gartner Group. Gartner Group is based in Stamford, CT. It has been in business since 1979. Gartner Group's body of research covers more than 200 topics including customer relationship management, business-to-business e-commerce, supply chain management and ERP software. In fact, many credit the Gartner Group with coining the widely used phrase "enterprise resource planning".

With respect to the software package marketplace, Gartner Group is perhaps best known for its Magic Quadrant™ market positioning assessment tool. Vendors will often quote their position on the Gartner Group's Magic Quadrant during their presales process. Gartner Group refers to the Magic Quadrant as a graphical strategic planning assumption. While that is an impressive sounding statement it really does not provide any insight to what the Magic Quadrant is all about and how it helps in software selection.

The purpose or value of the Magic Quadrant is to assess or rate a vendor along two major dimensions. The first dimension is referred to as completeness of vision and forms the vertical axis of a quadrant or graph. The second dimension is referred to as the vendor's ability to execute and forms the horizontal axis of the same quadrant or graph. Based upon Gartner's assessment process, a vendor can fall into any one of the four quadrants. These quadrants are more precisely market position categories and represent niche player, challenger, visionary, or market leader positions. A vendor positioned in the market leader quadrant has obtained the highest possible stature or position within its given market.

Gartner's assessment includes four assessment categories along each dimension. With regard to completeness of vision, vendors are evaluated by how well they rate based upon the following criteria:

- Does the vendor have a vision or statement of direction?
- Is this vision or statement of direction consistent with market trends?
- Is the vendor's vision consistent with Gartner Group's assessment of what vendors in this market segment should be doing?
- Can the vendor gain critical mass in the form of a sufficiently sized installed base software given its software vision?

With regard to the ability to execute, vendors are evaluated by how well they rate based upon the following criteria:

- The vendor's financial health
- The vendor's success at managing its research and development process
- The vendor's success in developing new business through multiple distribution channels
- The vendor's success in forming alliances that aligns its software to industry trends

Based upon these two criteria, the values or scores awarded in the assessment process are then plotted along the Magic Quadrant™ graph

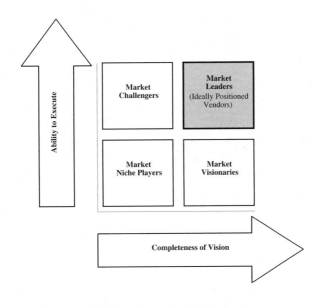

The Gartner Group's Magic Quadrant

Figure 11.3 The Gartner Group Magic Quadrant: A Conceptual Overview

axes. Figure 11.3 provides a generic illustration of the Gartner Group Magic Quadrant.

I have chosen to profile only three of the many industry analysts that I know exist. To find the right industry research provider or report is not always easy. Here is a technique that may help: Request sample reports or outdated copies of reports to ensure the reports are what you expect in terms of depth and general applicability. Oftentimes an organization will spend several hundred, if not thousand, dollars for a report that provides very little value. For the right report that confirms the informed software package decision your organization has or will make, the price will seem rather trivial given the overall size of the investment being made.

Disposable Solutions

Given where the future is headed, as a consultant I am inclined to only recommend software acquisitions from vendors who have adopted or are embracing the concept of plug-and-play software. Practically speaking, that may not be desirable, especially for the smallest of firms. In such cases, the concept of a disposable solution may make some sense.

How does this work? Buy a package that satisfies today's business requirements and expected business growth. For the moment, ignore the trends in industry, with the understanding that today's solution may in effect be obsolete and will need to be replaced in a relatively short period of time. How real is this approach? Not very real unless the implementation time is short (less than three months) and the payback or return on investment is quick (ideally, less than one year). The disposable solution strategy does not work well given the high acquisition and implementation costs and the lengthy install period associated with most software packages.

Gaps and Concerns about Functionality

On several occasions now I have mentioned that few, if any, software packages will satisfy 100% of your business requirements. Some requirements have less weight, or more precisely, less value than others have. Gaps that are deemed critical or essential to the organization represent gaps in functionality. In addition to gaps, there will be other causes of concern that arise during the vendor and product evaluation process. All such gaps and concerns should be documented by package (or vendor) as they arise.

In addition, each software package will likely have gaps that are specific or unique to that package alone. It is important to understand the importance of any gaps or unresolved issues and not hastily proceed with a selection until they can all be resolved. Understand that any gaps left on the table will affect the overall implementation plan, your organization's prospects for success with the software, and the unknown budget required to close any such gaps.

Once the gap list has been developed for a given package, sit down with the vendor and discuss how to address each gap or concern on the list. In many cases, the vendor has previously dealt with the same concerns and may be able to offer acceptable solutions. The next step is to negotiate the cost dimensions of closing gaps. Sometimes vendors will concede on these issues and provide consulting or technical services at no or very little cost.

This is a win-win situation for both the vendor and the prospective software buyer in many cases. It is a new piece of functionality to address a specific business practice or industry concern that can be remarketed. It also sets the stage for obtaining a new client now. Vendors who are new to the market, such as a vendor that is entering North America or adding a new feature to its package (e.g., an ERP vendor introducing a CRM module for its ERP system) are frequently the most willing to pony up the resources on their tab.

CONTRACT NEGOTIATIONS

The last thing anyone wants to do is pay list price. One of the negotiating objectives is to arrive at is the lowest cost possible. If two semifinalists are very close (if not identical) in meeting functionality, technical, and vendor relationship requirements, then cost is truly the final frontier in making the business decision.

Negotiate to win as many cost and add-on or throw-in concessions for as long as possible. It is also wise to fix or lock-in as many costs as possible. For long-term costs, such as maintenance, include an annual cost escalator cap (for instance the consumer price index or the GDP price deflator) that covers a 3-, 5- or 7-year period from the date of the original agreement.

I believe that a software package acquisition is the formation of a long-term strategic partnership with the vendor. I prefer to select a finalist and enter into negotiations with that vendor. At this point, I have not disqualified the runner-up completely; I have just chosen to use my time and the runner-up's time more effectively. Neither party will benefit from ruthless negotiation that sets the stage for an adversarial future relationship. If the finalist vendor is unyielding, consider working with the runner-up instead, especially when there is near parity on other requirement dimensions. The vendor should make it easier, not more difficult, for the buyer.

As for the nonprice negotiations, these are the details of hammering out the final contractual agreement between two consenting parties. Every vendor will offer up a standard contractual agreement that will favor the vendor, not the buyer. Legal counsel can be used to review the finalist vendor's contract documents and assist an organization in adding, modifying, or striking unfavorable contract conditions and language. This is not a step to be taken lightly. There are many issues to be considered, including:

- Does the contract require that any future disputes must be submitted to binding arbitration?
- Does the contract allow for the transferability of the software (and license) to a new owner given only written notice to the vendor?
- Does the contract prohibit the lockout of functionality or the restricting of access to business data should the buyer forgo future payments during a dispute, or should the buyer discontinue maintenance services on the software at any future date after implementation?

There are many other aspects of software licensing and implementation and support service contracting that must be considered. Your legal counsel should be able to assist your organization in restructuring the vendor's contractual documents to provide for or to protect your organization's rights as a buyer or licensee of the software.

Some consultants can or will offer to provide vendor negotiation assistance. Consultants are not attorneys, so counsel should still review their recommendations. You are relying on the consultant for the technical expertise and the attorney for the legal expertise in crafting the final contract negotiations. Some midsize and larger law firms have technology practices that deal with computer-related technology law. In addition, there are a number of helpful books and guides available from legal publishers on the ins-and-outs of technology-related contracts. These resources are particularly helpful if your organization will rely on in-house counsel to draft the final vendor contract.

MAKING THE SOFTWARE DECISION

The concluding and most important decision in the overall software selection and evaluation process is obvious — the choice of the actual software package to be acquired and implemented. This is not an easy decision. This chapter provided a series of evaluation methods and tools to make this process as objective as possible. In the final analysis, selection of the software package remains a calculated business risk. The evaluation methods and tools recommended are all intended to reduce or mitigate such risks. However, they will not and can never completely reduce the business risks involved in the decision-making process.

The selection team must evaluate the entire array of information — factual and opinion — along with each member's informed opinions. The selection team must then combine all fact and opinion in a consensus-reaching manner, in order to arrive at a knowledgeable, informed, and objective decision.

SOFTWARE SELECTION: AN EPILOGUE

Much of this chapter discussed both tools and techniques that make the process of deciding which software package is a good choice for your organization more objective, less stressful, and less risky. It is also about your organization's confidence level in the vendor on its ability to achieve its promises and remain in business for the foreseeable future. The holistic software selection must consider a multitude of factors.

12

SOFTWARE PACKAGE IMPLEMENTATION: PLANNING YIELDS SUCCESS

This chapter is about the end stages of the software package life cycle (SPLC) concept that was introduced earlier in this book. If you thought making the software decision was tough, buckle up, as implementation is really the more difficult task. This chapter is also about the reason why you have come this far — implementing the software package and achieving the envisioned business value from the software package itself.

Almost three decades ago, I found inspiration in a book titled *Successfully Managing by Objectives* by Karl Albrecht. In his book Albrecht proposed a simple, three-stage management model. I have used this model throughout the course of my professional career. These three stages are:

- Look ahead
- Plan ahead
- Move ahead

Although I have seen a variation of this model with the stage labels of seeing, aiming, and doing, I like the former model for one powerful reason: it explicitly emphasizes planning. In complex business projects, such as developing and launching a new product, building a new plant facility, and more germane to this book, implementing a new software package, planning is essential to the success of the project.

One of the most important practices that you must adopt to ensure success when implementing any software package is to adopt, organize, preach, and live by a workflow process, or more simply put, a plan. Consultants and software vendors will often refer to their workflow process as an implementation approach or methodology. No matter what you decide to call it, in the end it is about planning the work and working the plan.

This chapter represents an experiential-based approach or model — in short, a plan — for software package implementation. This model is a culmination of my experience and the insights of my most trusted and experienced colleagues with implementing different software packages in different industries. Although this model was first introduced several years ago as a presentation topic at ERP World, it remains a work in process. This model incorporates many best practice based concepts that are considered *critical* to a successful software package implementation. More important, this chapter is based upon my experience and first-hand knowledge of what works — and what does not.

THE SOFTWARE PACKAGE IMPLEMENTATION: A BEST PRACTICE BASED MODEL FOR SUCCESS

First, let me begin by saying that both software package vendors and the consultants who implement software packages will, in all likelihood, have their own proprietary implementation models or approaches. In general, those models will likely have a similar overall work or process flow. In some cases, that flow may be identical, saving for the naming conventions of the underlying stages or phases. While there may subtle differences between this model and other models, there should not be substantial differences. For best results, the implementation model that your organization ultimately adopts should include the planning components that approximate or parallel the stages of the software package implementation approach presented here.

The Evolution of this Model

Since this model was first developed and presented several years ago as a paper at ERP World, there have been several important changes to the model. First and most notably, a parallel technology infrastructure track has been added. The purpose is to elevate the importance of these tasks. The software package acquisition will often infer the introduction of one or more other new technologies into an organization to support that package. Therefore, it stands to reason that although they are separate events, they should not be managed separately.

Second, I have elevated the stature of the production readiness stage to represent the point of convergence. This is the point where the technical or infrastructure components of the implementation workflow intersect with the business process or functional components of the implementation workflow. This is an important point in the implementation project where everything must come together in order for the software package rollout to happen.

Third, the implementation model now presupposes that it is a part of a larger, overall software package process management model. I have previously referred to this as the SPLC model in earlier chapters of this book. This is important in two regards. First, the model is now more adaptable to any business application software package implementation rather than being narrowly focused toward just enterprise resource planning (ERP) software packages. Second, some steps have been moved out of the implementation stream and into the overall life cycle model for a software package.

Applying the Model to Your Implementation Project

I have previously stated that no two given business organizations are identical. It also stands to reason that no two software package implementations will ever likely be identical for that reason alone. So at best, this or any other implementation model or approach represents merely the starting point that should serve to jump-start the overall project planning effort. It is important to understand that the major work process components defined by this model represent areas where the nature or volume of the work is greatest, or where potential project risks are greatest. It is best not to overlook or disregard any of the steps presented here until the implications for doing so are fully understood.

The model implementation approach presented here serves only as a framework for the design and development of a detailed project plan. Such a plan is specifically tailored to achieve the successful implementation of a specific software package for a specific organization under a specific set of assumptions, circumstances, and requirements.

Some of the steps may not be necessary, for instance, in some cases some of the steps suggested by this model may be organized differently into overall, larger steps. The model presented herein can be used as a guide in helping your organization to assess and fine tune another implementation model to one that better suits the needs of your organization.

Before illustrating the implementation model, some general discussion of important project management practices and techniques related to software package implementation will be reviewed.

Focus on Plannable Units of Work

The project should be divided into plannable units of work — a series of project stages and ultimately into specific, granular activities that logically relate to the challenges and complexities of software package implementation. The importance of any workflow process is to provide a framework for organizing what is, in the case of the typical software package implementation, an enormous amount of work. This includes developing project timelines, building teams, assigning resources to tasks, defining milestones, resolving issues, meeting deadlines, and controlling project scope.

The project workflow process should include steps to ensure deliverables are created as needed and reviewed by the appropriate process owners and managers to expedite the work. This will help you to ensure all bases are covered as you walk process owners through each step. For instance, when evaluating the vendor or consultant's workflow process for a software package implementation, it should minimally include a standard set of procedures for completing each task in a model project plan. When appropriate, it should also include templates for deliverables for any such task.

Use a Project Planning Tool

For a complex project like a software package implementation, it is best to use a robust, computer-based project-planning tool, such as Microsoft Project, Primavera Systems Primavera Project Planner, or Primavera Suretrak. Another alternative is a product called TurboProject from IMSI.

Although TurboProject is not as powerful as the Microsoft or Primavera options, it does offer one specific feature I like. That feature is the ability to organize a project visually, from the perspective of a work breakdown structure. In addition, it is able to print a work breakdown structure that TurboProject refers to as a project tree; this is something that Microsoft or Primavera cannot do easily, or at all. Several project plan templates built around the model approach illustrated in this chapter are a part of the author's template collection. The templates may prove to be a good starting point for your project planning efforts. Consult Appendix A for more information.

The Project Plan: What to Include

As I previously alluded to, there are two approaches to building work plans. First, work plans can be built that are function-oriented. The functional work plan would start with a list of the software package modules to be implemented (e.g., accounts payable, accounts receivable, general ledger accounting, inventory control, and procurement).

Second, work plans can be built that are process-oriented. A process or workflow-oriented work plan would build out the task list based on all of the software package business functions that your organization would use. For instance, all of the steps related to purchase order processing would be included on the procure to pay script. This may include:

- Item and vendor setup
- Request quote
- Compare quotes
- Select vendor
- Approve order
- Convert quote to order
- Print order
- Receive order
- Voucher order
- Write payment to vendor

Function-oriented task plans are great for controlling the tasks at a microlevel. These module-specific plans can ensure a specific module is being configured and unit tested. They are not too good for planning the overall or integrated configuration planning and testing. Enter the process-oriented task plan. This process-oriented task plan is typically used to facilitate process or macrolevel validation.

Once the task plan orientation is decided, the next step is identifying the configuration and testing tasks associated with each functional module or business process step. The identification can generally be divided into these areas of activity:

- Identify any system level setup steps that apply.
- Complete any system level setup steps that apply.
- Identify any functional or process level setup steps that apply.
- Complete any functional or process level setup steps that apply.
- Identify any master data level setup steps that apply.
- Complete any master data level setup steps that apply.
- Identify any transaction-specific setup steps that apply.
- Complete any transaction-specific setup steps that apply.
- Setup sample master data for testing purposes.
- Enter test transaction scenarios to exercise the configured function or process.
- Review the testing results.
- Identify any role-based setup steps that apply.
- Complete any role level setup steps that apply.
- Enter test transaction scenarios by role to exercise the configured function or process.
- Review the testing results.

This is a relatively generic or conceptual guide to configuring and testing software package functionality. It may vary by software package, but not dramatically. Notice that I recommend configuring and testing general functionality first — where any given user has complete authorization to software features and functions. Once the general functionality is working as desired, the next step would be to conduct role-based configuration and testing. This is where a given user has only authorization to perform or use specific software features and functions based upon the user's usual or proposed job role. Again, I make use of a document template to develop such user roles. This user role template is a part of the author's template collection. Consult Appendix A for more information.

Using the above guide as a framework, the software vendor's system documentation will be the likely starting point in identifying the specific tasks to be conducted. For example, the table of contents in each user reference guide will detail the setup activities to be completed, but be assured there can be some gotchas in the form of unidentified steps. Some vendors and consultants have ready-made templates or scripts related to the configuration of their specific software functionality that preidentify these steps. Some vendors even have online configuration step browsers or explorers that equate to such a list or template.

By building your task plan using a reference guide's table of contents, you may find yourself unsure if a report or processing step applies to your project. Using this approach, you can quickly reference that section of the user guide and research its applicability to your project. This will not resolve all of your questions, but it should resolve many of them. Understand that virtually every program or screen form, report, or process workflow step likely has some form of required setup.

Many software packages are delivered with one or more preconfigured versions for each configurable component of the system. Sometimes the vendor or implementation consultant will be able to utilize such a template for your implementation. Even when adopting these preconfigured components, a minimal review of their applicability to your organization must be performed.

Rollout Strategies and Project Planning

As I mentioned in a previous chapter, there are a number of different options available regarding how the software package is rolled out to your organization at large. These rollout options include:

The big bang — In this case, the decision is made to go live with the complete software package system all at once for your entire organization.

The staged approach — In this case, your organization decides to go live with only portions of the software package. For instance, your organization could decide on financial modules initially, then start up other modules at a later date.

The location-by-location approach — In this the case, your organization decides on a geographic-based rollout, going live with the complete software package system all at once for a given geographically isolated business unit within the organization. In this case, the experience and lessons learned in this implementation are used to refine the project plan into a template for use in implementing the remaining business units.

Regardless of the rollout strategy your organization decides on, it is imperative to the success of your software package to thoroughly plan those efforts. This is accomplished by using a robust computer-based project planning and management tool.

Iterative Project Plan Refinement

Time and time again I see project plans that are established initially and often in intricate detail. However, I then find the schedule is not subsequently updated over the course of a project to reflect schedule progress or variations. Unfortunately, this is an inappropriate and ineffective way to use a computer-based project planning and management tool. My recommendation is to ensure these schedules are kept up to date. This can be helpful in managing the project and in guiding project status discussions. The latest versions of Microsoft and Primavera software support team-level collaboration for project scheduling and for schedule updating.

Schedule updates alone are only a part of the story. I recommend regular, periodic project meetings to review the progress on each of the tasks that is scheduled for work within a given time period. Task status is then updated in the schedule to reflect progress, including task completions and estimates of any delays or possible project bottlenecks. This information can then be used to determine corrective actions needed, including changing priorities, adding resources or adjusting deadlines and targets.

In addition, I highly recommend the use of a baseline plan. This helps to illustrate plan variances. Such variances may be small at the task level, but may have dramatic project impact. Progress tracking of activities can be considered as a form of continuous improvement for your baseline project plan. Actual results versus baseline plans can form the basis for the calculation of an estimating margin of error for each task in your time line and for the project on an overall or cumulative basis. This information can subsequently be used to refine the details of the ongoing project plan.

Schedule refinements are particularly beneficial when your organization has multiple rollouts of a software package to perform (e.g., multiple geographic locations within the organization). Although there will typically be variations in each of the subsequent rollouts, the knowledge gain made possible by progress tracking can be instrumental in helping you to provide project budgets and time lines of increasing accuracy as your organization initiates each subsequent rollout or implementation.

A Well-Managed Project Minimizes Business Risk

A planned, deliberate approach to executing the selection and implementation of software packages minimizes business risk. A good project manager will tell you that some of the most serious risks associated with any project include:

- A failure to plan the project
- A failure to follow a project plan once it has been outlined
- A failure to monitor and revise the project plan as project circumstances change

Active risk management is considered a project management best practice — a prerequisite that is considered critical to the project's chance of success.

There are two dimensions to risk management. The first dimension is to anticipate problems before they happen. Few experienced project managers will argue otherwise. The time to begin identifying possible risks is in the earliest stages of any project. When risks are identified early, appropriate contingencies can be developed. As more information becomes available, appropriate aversive measures that are outlined in the form of a contingency plan can be taken as needed.

The second dimension of risk management is swift and continuous action. This means that a continuous assessment of the project schedule, any gaps and issues of resource usage is needed. Quick identification and resolution of issues that may impact the project budget, schedule, or scope is essential. Such issues can arise at any time during the life of a project. Left unchecked, even small problems or issues have a nasty habit of growing in magnitude, especially when they are not identified and assessed at the earliest point in time. Frequently such issues can be resolved quickly and the end result will be little, if any, impact on the overall project.

Mitigating Project Risk

Managing project risk is largely about anticipating problems, assessing the impact these potential problems may have on the project and developing appropriate contingencies for dealing with these problems. A three-stage model for actively managing project risks is suggested. The three-stage model is as follows:

- Anticipate a problem.
- Assess its impact.
- Develop an appropriate contingency plan.

A discussion of these three stages follows.

Anticipate Problems

Active risk management requires a top-to-bottom review of the entire project plan. It is important to assess and categorize the different types of risks associated with the project plan. For instance, a review of the resource plan would yield information about which outside or external suppliers, such as hardware and software vendors, consultants, and common carriers, will be relied upon. Potential failure points must be identified, especially those that may occur during the critical go-live chain of events. Once a project has started, project managers must periodically review the state of the project to identify any possible issues that might pose a risk or threat to the project in some way.

Assess Their Impact

Once a problem or issue is identified, it is necessary to make an assessment about what impact, if any, the issue or problem would likely have on the project. Quantitatively speaking, risk can be assessed along two dimensions. First, consider the likelihood of occurrence. Often a likelihood of occurrence is assigned by the project manager, usually on a scale of 1 to 10, with 1 representing the lowest likelihood of occurrence and 10 representing the highest. Second, the project manager considers what the potential business impact of a given risk or threat is, again usually on a scale of 1 to 10 as well. A score of 1 would represent low impact, while of score of 10 would represent high impact. By multiplying the likelihood of occurrence by the level of perceived business risk, a severity level is then attached to a given problem or issue. The following formula summarizes the impact assessment process:

Likelihood of Occurrence × Business Risk = Severity Level

It can be said that any issue or problem that has a high severity level will likely have a very real risk to the project as a whole.

Develop Appropriate Contingency Plans

Guidelines should be developed that suggest within what time frame an issue remains unresolved before a contingency plan is developed to address the problem or issue. Generally speaking, the higher the severity level, the shorter an organization's time frame should be. Note that in some cases the impact may be considered so severe as to require immediate action. Major project dependencies must be reviewed. Some issues may be mundane, but can have a decided impact on the project. Sometimes even for the most mundane of issues, appropriate contingency measures must be in place.

The Gaps and Issues List

All problems or issues, no matter how minor they may appear to be, should be logged to a list as they arise throughout the course of the implementation project. The project manager is generally responsible for tracking issues and for facilitating their resolution by team members. This person is also responsible for developing an acceptable contingency plan if resolution is not made within an acceptable period of time. Issues and gaps can be managed in an overall list or as two separate lists. Such lists are considered the centerpiece of an active risk management effort. Figure 12.1 depicts a gaps and issues list document. This list template is part of the author's template collection. Consult Appendix A for more information.

A significant amount of time is typically devoted to reviewing, understanding, and resolving both real and perceived issues in software package implementation. When the project team cannot resolve issues, the steering committee is called upon to provide guidance as to the criticality of issue.

A STEP-BY-STEP REVIEW OF THE IMPLEMENTATION MODEL

The successful software package implementation approach will include stages that approximate or parallel these stages. The functional stages of the overall model approach are as follows:

- Project kickoff
- Educate team
- Model processes
- Align processes

Rolling Gaps and Issues List
Client: ABC Manufacturing

TradewindsGroup
Tradewinds Group, Incorporated
Consultants to Management
Box 3601
Oak Brook, Illinois 60522

Problem	Problem Description	Expectation of Occurrence	Business Impact	Severity Level	Resolution Status	Type of Resolution Action Proposed or Taken	Proposed or Actual Resolution Action	Contingency Plan
Negative Inventory	Software package does not allow inventory transactions to occur if the inventory balance is negative or would be brought to negative. As a result shipment paper work can not be prepared in advance of receipt on dock to dock transfer.	10	7	70	Unresolved	Customization	Pre-Receive the "In Transit" Stock. Requires supplier pre-notification.	None
Statements and Envelopes	The new mailing address on the customer statement in the Accounts Receivable module does not align into current window envelope.	10	2	20	Unresolved	Customization	Change Accounts Receivable customer statement document layout to fit current enveloped.	Order new envelopes.
Training Schedule Conflict	The Materials Manager is unavailable the second week of July for Procure to Pay training at the vendor's local training center.	10	1	10	Resolved	Workaround	Scheduled training for a later week in the month at a training facility in another city. This will prevent any delays in the work efforts of the overall project team.	None
				0				
				0				
				0				
				0				
				0				
				0				
				0				
				0				
				0				
Summary Status		10	3	33				

Explanations:
Score Likelihood of Occurrence on a 0-10 scale, with 10 being highest (10 = Event has occured, 1 = Event unlikely to or won't occur)
Score on a 1 - 10 scale, with 10 being highest value (10 = Possible Business Disruption, 0 = No or Minimal Business Disruption)
Severity Level = Business Impact x Likelihood of Occurrence

Figure 12.1 The Gaps and Issues List

- Configure software
- Prototype configuration
- Identify gaps
- Document the as-built configuration
- Establish production readiness
- Training end users
- Go live
- Establish steady state

In addition to these functional stages there is a parallel, technical track or path within the model. The technical stages of the overall model approach are as follows:

- Install technical infrastructure
- Install software package
- Create test environment
- System integration planning
- Design/build integration components
- Complementary products deployment
- Data migration planning
- Design/build migration components
- Migrate production data

Figure 12.2 illustrates this model as a largely sequential, or waterfall, style of structure. It roughly corresponds to the critical path that a software package implementation will have.

These stages represent the highest level of the project plan. It is a high-level master project plan for all of the stages of your project and any subprojects. For instance, you may want to consider as subprojects the implementation of each major functional area (e.g., accounting, procurement) or business process (e.g., order to cash or procure to pay). You may also use subprojects to distinguish each location being implemented. Figure 12.3 illustrates a page from a typical project plan. This illustration is from a template included in the author's template collection. Consult Appendix A for more information.

Lower-level or detailed work breakdown structures and work packages must be developed for each stage of the software package implementation project. The details must identify specific activities or tasks. Associated with each activity or task will be resources (largely people) and deliverables or outcomes, such as a completed configuration step, creation of a training manual or a custom program to fulfill a functionality gap. Figure 12.4 illustrates a typical work breakdown structure. Note also that this work breakdown structure illustration or project tree was produced using

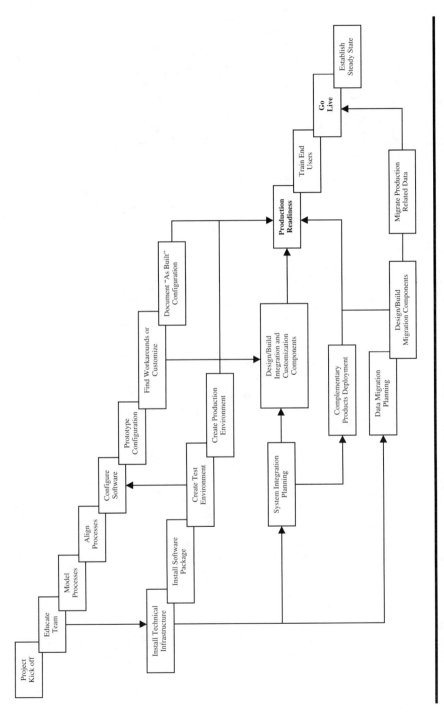

Figure 12.2 The Software Package Implementation Model

336 ■ Maximizing Business Performance through Software Packages

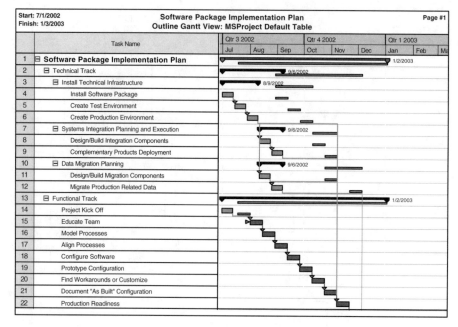

Figure 12.3 The Typical Project Plan: A High-Level Example

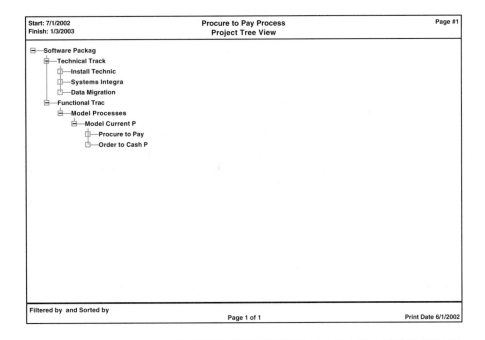

| Start: 7/1/2002 | Procure to Pay Process | Page #1 |
| Finish: 1/3/2003 | Project Tree View | |

Filtered by and Sorted by
Page 1 of 1
Print Date 6/1/2002

Figure 12.4 A Typical Work Breakdown Structure

the TurboProject project management software tool that was discussed earlier in this chapter. This illustration is based on a project plan template that is part of the author's template collection. Consult Appendix A for more information.

Project Kickoff

During this project stage, a clear understanding of your software package system implementation strategy should be developed. The project scope and objectives should be defined. The approach should be affirmed or finalized. During this stage, the project working and executive teams should be defined and staffed. Once these teams are in place, a kickoff meeting is held to review the project charter and to begin planning the project.

The Project Charter

Before embarking on the software package implementation, it is necessary to establish both the scope and objectives of the project and the approach to be taken to complete the implementation. The result of this work is the completion of a project charter document. Several important tasks occur when formalizing or defining the project charter.

First, the project scope must be defined. The project must be defined in terms of the business processes, organizational functions, business units, and perhaps even products or product lines to be affected. Here are some examples of questions that help to define project scope:

- Will the implementation impact the entire organization or just the domestic portion of a multinational organization?
- Will the implementation impact all business units or just the manufacturing business units handling specific product lines?
- Are all processes affected or does the implementation affect only financial-related processes and business units?

The actual questions that will apply to your implementation project should be framed in terms of the overall makeup of the organization. This includes business processes, organizational functions, business units, products and services, and the organization's overall business model. These questions and their answers will become an integral part of the formal project charter.

Depending upon the degree of work done during the earliest stages of the SPLC, it is possible that only a reaffirmation of a project's scope will be necessary during this prerequisite step. One of the problems I see clients frequently encounter is scope creep.

If significant changes to the project scope are determined to exist from what had originally been envisioned, then the business case will in all likelihood need to be reviewed as well. Generally speaking, when the project scope changes, the economics of the project will change as well. In many cases this can be dramatic. Project benefits can disappear quickly due to the high burn rates associated with a software package implementation project.

In addition, the project approach must be defined. The project approach must take into consideration how the software package will be introduced into, or rolled out to, the organization. There are a number of approaches or combinations that are possible. Depending upon the degree of work completed during earlier stages in the SPLC or the structure defined within a winning vendor proposal, only a reaffirmation of project approach is necessary during this prerequisite step.

Combining the project scope and approach will yield the project plan and ultimately the project time line. If the project time line has a mandated deadline, then its existence will largely define the duration of each project stage and ultimately each task.

The Steering Committee

Formal project executive sponsorship is established. This is usually done through commissioning a formal project executive team or project steering committee. The team or committee will meet to review progress; assess project risks; and decide on project scope, budget, or schedule changes. The basic agenda for these meetings will be to review the overall project status using the project plan, the project budget, and the project issues list as guiding documents. For the steering committee, the project plan can be summarized into major functional and technical tasks and reported on a scorecard basis. The mechanism I use for this purpose is called a stoplight report. The stoplight color indicates severity or risk to the project schedule or budget. This report is constructed using a Microsoft Word document template or Microsoft PowerPoint slideshow. Templates for these reports are a part of the author's template collection. Consult Appendix A for more information.

The Working Team

A working team is formed. The team should include both internal personnel and implementation consultants. Internal personnel should be selected from among the best and brightest the organization can offer. It should be assembled from a cross section of the representative business areas that will be impacted. This working team is usually known simply as the project team. A leader is appointed for this project working team. Consulting participants are interviewed and added to the team. After the team is established, the next task is to develop a detailed implementation plan and project time table. This plan should include the identification of what needs to be accomplished and who is going to accomplish it. This is considered a draft or baseline plan. It may be reviewed and revised after the team education process has been completed.

The project working team will meet on a regular basis, perhaps weekly or biweekly, to review progress, determine project status, identify issues and tasks, and identify project risks and project scope changes. The basic agenda for these meetings will be to review the project plan, individual action plans, task status, and project issues. Also, resolutions to issues will be proposed. The working team will produce periodic updates for the steering committee and the organization on the state of the project.

For larger implementations, such as a multiple site ERP rollout, the project working team may be broken into functional or process-related subteams or purposed subteams, such as a master data definition subteam or a site rollout training team. In such cases, a working team member will often be a member of multiple subteams. Figure 12.5 illustrates the recommended project organizational structure that was described in this section.

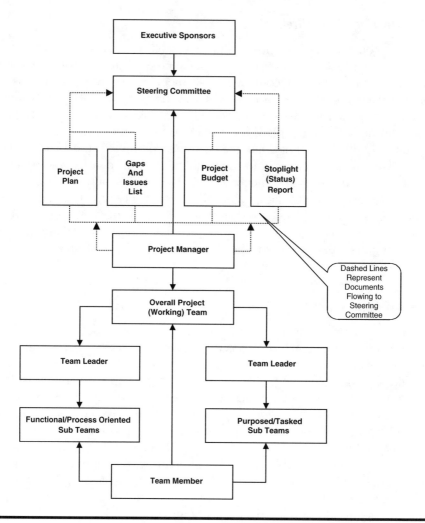

Figure 12.5 A Typical Project Organizational Structure

Educate Project Team

The project team receives overview training in project and change management, business process analysis and modeling techniques, and specialized education related to the software package. It is not unusual for the cumulative required classroom education to extend anywhere from 4 to 6 weeks for each member of the team. Once education is complete, the project team can reconvene and reconsider the initial project plan and make adjustments to its plan and estimates of work effort based upon its newfound knowledge.

Typically, the project team training has multiple purposes. First, the goal is to plant the seeds for these individuals to become the internal subject matter experts for the software package. Of course their training is put to the test and their expertise is developed while going through the process of configuring and testing the software package functionality. In many cases, training alone will be insufficient and implementation consultants will still be needed. This should be expected. Be sure that knowledge transfer occurs from the consultants to your own subject matter experts in every step of the process.

A second purpose of project team training on the software package is to develop an army of internal trainers. Generally speaking, most software vendors expect that your organization will do its own end user training. Their training classes are typically geared toward building subject matter experts and trainers, not building specific end user skills. In addition, vendor training is usually too generic to be of much value as end user training. The trained project team members would provide either one-on-one or classroom style training to the end users of the system prior to the go-live date.

The third purpose of training is that it provides the background necessary to construct or assist other individuals with the construction of training materials and other courseware. Fourth, training and all of the experience learned to the point of go live builds the support team your organization will need for those first few hectic weeks or months after go live.

The project team likely needs additional training. For instance, process modeling, interviewing, project scheduling, word processing, spreadsheet usage, technical writing and classroom audience presentation, and training skills are notable areas where those selected for the project team may be lacking. Outside training resources and the implementation consultants can often provide such training. For both project team and end user training, I make use of the training planner template. The training planner template is a part of the author's template collection. Consult Appendix A for more information.

Install Technical Infrastructure

During this stage of the implementation project, central site preparations are completed. The central site hardware is delivered, installed, and made ready for software loading. The operating system is licensed and installed. The database and middleware software components are licensed and installed. The software package itself is licensed and installed. Also, the software package baseline environments are established. Usually this will consist of both a testing and a production environment, at a minimum.

Other environments may be needed or desired (i.e., a separate development or training environment). Any necessary project team hardware, such as client workstations, are delivered and installed and the appropriate client software environments are deployed.

It is quite important during this stage that the integrity of your environments be confirmed. Unfortunately many organizations that implement a new software package simply do not realize the technical complexities of the client server and the software package environments. Until you get the base configuration right, your organization should not proceed with the software package implementation. An improperly configured environment will result in a continuous series of problems during your software package implementation. These problems can cause project delays and substantial rework. In addition, if left unresolved, these problems can result in production environment inconsistencies and may present difficulties when attempting to make any software upgrades. Most important, your organization should thoroughly understand and validate what environments are created and used and what interrelationships exist between them in its software package implementation.

Model Processes

Ideally, much of the process modeling activities will have occurred at a much earlier stage in the overall SPLC as described by this book. Usually process modeling, or at least the as-is or current state modeling, occurs as a part of any business process improvement or reengineering activities. If that has not been done, then current state process modeling should be completed at this time.

During this stage of the project, a full understanding of your current business environment, including business practices and processes and an understanding of the roles and responsibilities of each member of your user community, should be developed. Best practices that are contained in the software package are also identified and considered as to their applicability to your processes. What is necessary is a complete picture of the business processes affected by the software package in the context of an as-is or current state process model.

Figure 12.6 illustrates the early stage process flow of deliverables associated with the implementation model. The process modeling deliverables include business process maps and SIPOC process models. It is also possible that a to-be or future state process model was developed or derived through process visioning in an earlier stage. If available, that model would be the starting point instead of an as-is or current state model. If future state process modeling was not done, then as-is models and process vision statements will have to suffice for guidance on the

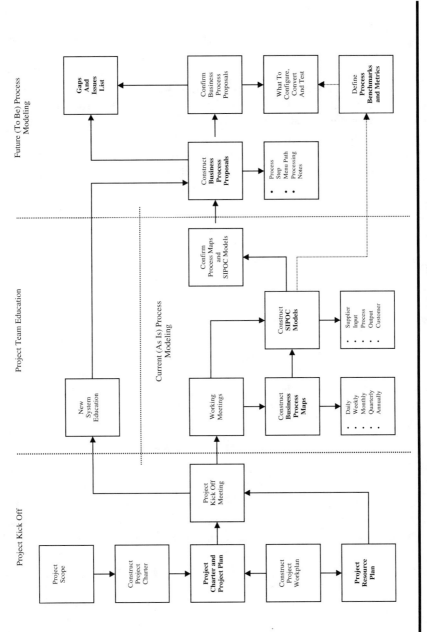

Figure 12.6 Implementation Model Process Flow and Deliverables: The Early Stages

future state in the next stage. Refer to Chapter 5 for a complete discussion and illustrations of process modeling deliverables.

When building business process models, it is also important to gather current written procedures and samples of transactions. This includes examples of any manually created documents and input forms used in the current process. Examples of entry screens, inquiry screens, and reports or forms created in the current process should also be gathered. These documents will be instrumental in mapping data and in replicating current process steps using available functions within the software package. Organize, index, and store all documents along with the appropriate process model documentation for continuing reference.

In addition, pay attention to the business rules used and routing workflow steps that are involved in a process. If there are standard rules or regulations that must be considered in future procedures, gather these as well. The process models should be confirmed with the current process enablers.

Align Processes

In this stage, business process models and software functionality must meet. The intersection of process models and software package functionality is accomplished through a scripting document that is referred to as a business process proposal. A business process proposal is developed by first extracting processes from the business process model and then linking these to the appropriate processing steps within the software package. Minimally, the menu path in the software package is noted on the business process proposal, but the content can be extended to include processing steps and any related processing notes. Figure 12.7 illustrates the business process proposal document. The process proposals should be confirmed with the current process enablers.

As I mentioned earlier, my general preference is to limit the amount of business modeling to a minimum, especially the as is or current process flow portion. Your efforts should focus on modeling current processes only for understanding. The greater emphasis should be placed on modeling future business processes in terms of the software package functionality to be implemented. This is ideally done with current state process models in hand and after receiving formal software package education. This way one is able to leverage both dimensions of knowledge into a future process model. One last note: This build out of new business models is an area where software package implementation consultants can provide valuable overall direction and guidance.

Business Process Proposal

TradewindsGroup

Client	ABC Manufacturing
Document Number	BPP-PUR-DSHIP-D
Overall Business Process	Purchasing
Process Description	Direct (Drop) Ship Purchasing
Process Frequency	Daily

Proposed Step(s)	Menu Path	Notes
Enter Purchase Order for a drop stock item; Optionally, use an order template order to retrieve Items and prices for placing drop ship order with specific vendors	Foundation (G) > Distribution/Logistics (G4) > Procurement (G43) > Daily Processing (G4310) > Stock Based (G43A) > Purchase Order Processing (G43A11) > Enter Purchase Orders > Work With Purchase Orders > Add	Enter Supplier Number, Enter Ship To Number for Direct Ship Enter Customer Name and Address for Direct Ship Order Enter Requested Delivery Date Enter Item Number and Quantity Requested
Print Purchase Order	Foundation (G) > Distribution/Logistics (G4) > Procurement (G43) > Daily Processing (G4310) > Stock Based (G43A) > Purchase Order Processing (G43A11) > Enter Purchase Orders > Work With Purchase Orders	Enter PO Number, then select Row > Print Order Print order printing is an optional, on demand step for a drop ship order
When acknowledgement is received, use speed status update to enter the scheduled ship date into the requested date	Foundation (G) > Distribution/Logistics (G4) > Procurement (G43) > Daily Processing (G4310) > Stock Based (G43A) > Purchase Order Processing (G43A11) > Order Gen/Approve/Release (G43A14) > Purchasing Date Revisions	Enter new requested delivery date or promised delivery date (from vendor acknowledgement)
When vendor invoice is received: Enter invoice date as receipt date, receive PO	Procurement (G43) > Daily Processing (G4310) > Stock Based (G43A) > Purchase Order Processing (G43A11) > Enter Receipts by PO	Enter PO Number then click on "Find" Highlight First Row, Click on "Select" Enter Vendor's Invoice date as the "Receipt" Date Enter Vendor's Invoice Number as the Receipt Document (Number) Enter quantity invoiced on a line for line basis

Figure 12.7a The Business Process Proposal Document: An Example

Business Process Proposal **TradewindsGroup**

Client	ABC Manufacturing
Document Number	BPP-PUR-DSHIP-D
Overall Business Process	Purchasing
Process Description	Direct (Drop) Ship Purchasing
Process Frequency	Daily

Proposed Step(s)	Menu Path	Notes
Enter freight charge on Purchase Order as an additional line	Foundation (G) > Distribution/Logistics (G4) > Procurement (G43) > Daily Processing (G4310) > Stock Based (G43A) > Purchase Order Processing (**G43A11**) > Enter Purchase Orders > Work With Purchase Orders	Enter PO Number then click on "Find" Highlight First Row, Click on "Select" Add line item referred to as "Freight In" to the order Enter Dollar amount of freight in charge
Forward invoice to Accounting for Accounts Receivable Billing and Accounts Payable Invoice Vouchering		

Process Related Decisions Necessary

1. Create Address Book record for Ship To on Direct Ship orders.
2. Create freight in item with G/L category to freight in account.

Printed on 08/01/02 – Confidential and Proprietary – Page 2 of 2

Figure 12.7b The Business Process Proposal Document: An Example

Configure Software

In this stage, the software package is configured. It is configured using the document produced or gathered in the two previous stages. Generally speaking, software package configuration requires:

- Setting software switches to control certain system, process, and even data type or transaction specific functionality in the software
- Establishing common values in shared tables
- Establishing variants for certain system components (e.g., reports)
- Setting up user roles or authorizations to specific system functions

Additional guidance about configuration activities appeared earlier in this chapter in the section labeled, "The Project Plan: What to Include," and in Chapter 8. Figure 12.8 continues the process flow of deliverables associated with the implementation model.

It is important to note that configuration does not include the modification or customization of any part of the software package as delivered. Recall that a key tenet of any successful software package implementation is to avoid customization of the core product where and when possible. This recommendation does not preclude work on known gaps that emanated from the software selection process and that require customization.

This is also the stage where test scenarios are created. A testing scenario consists of two elements: a test scenario and test data. The test scenario is based upon conducting a specific type of business activity or process. For example, procuring an inventory good versus procuring a service are two distinct types of business activities and each should be tested. However, at times portions of any given test scenario may be reusable. A test scenario should exercise the transaction or process from inception to completion or from cradle to grave. Let us take a look at an ERP example. This means every step in a process (i.e., the procure to pay thread) would be exercised and tested under each of the two scenarios given here as examples (i.e., procuring an inventory good versus procuring a service). Checkpoints should be established in the test plan to verify all steps are working correctly in a process against known results. For example, after placing a purchase order for an inventory item, inventory should be inquired upon to see if the on order quantity has been updated for the item on the order.

As for known results, the test data are usually the detail of a previously executed business transaction. The transaction may have been manually produced, systemically produced, or a combination of the two. In the case of an inventory purchase, it might be the original requisition, a purchase order, a delivery ticket or packing list, a putaway ticket, a bill of lading, an invoice, and a check payment (or voucher). The key to a

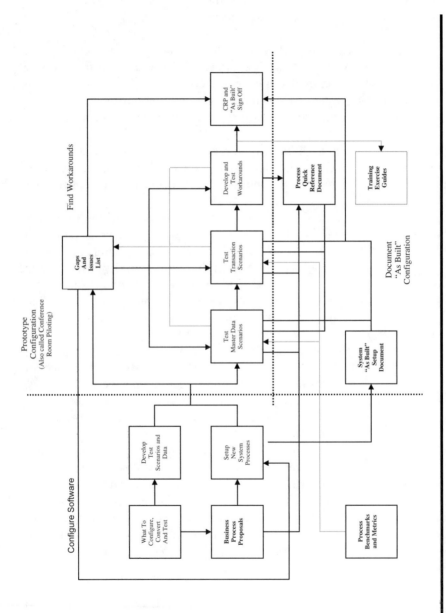

Figure 12.8 Implementation Model Process Flow and Deliverables: The Middle Stages

test scenario and test data development is to understand that you will test everything about the system relevant to a given transaction, including a review of all data entered, calculations performed or produced, and any audit trails that exist in the system. This is what is frequently called an integrated test scenario.

Besides transaction details, that previously executed business transaction also relied on master data — data that does not change from transaction to transaction. In the case of an inventory procurement, master data would consist of a supplier or vendor and an inventory item, such as a raw material or manufacturing component item. In addition to the transaction processing steps, master data entry steps should be verified typically through a separate associated business data test scenario. In this given scenario, the presumption is that both the vendor and the end product or item must be set in this system.

The test scripts and the associated test data (or source documents) should be organized, indexed, and stored along with a copy of the appropriate business process proposals used to execute the test scripts in a binder that is available for continuing reference. The next step is exercising or prototyping system functionality by executing the test scripts developed in the previous stage.

Prototyping Your Business Processes

Proof of concept occurs in this stage. Both business data and transaction scenarios are exercised. A complete understanding of how the software package works is sought and these processes are documented. Any software gaps are identified for further action. This is a time-consuming and iterative task. All features and functions that will be used in a given software package should be thoroughly tested. Generally speaking, new gaps will likely emerge during testing. Until a feature can be proven to work as intended or desired in support of a given business process or function, it is a candidate for the gaps and issues list.

When tests fail, the reasons why must be understood. Most errors in processing occur because of missing, incomplete, or incorrect configuration details, master data, or transaction data. The missing elements must be identified and corrected and retesting must occur. As prototyping or proof of concept occurs for a given process, the as-built documentation is completed or updated. If proof of concept does not occur, the newly identified software gap, issue, or error must be added to the gaps and issues list.

Testing can also fail due to software package defects. It is not unusual for any given software package to have dozens or even hundreds of known defects. Examples of software package defects that can impede implementation include program bugs, missing or corrupted software components, documentation errors, and omissions. Defect detection is one of the reasons why your testing must be deliberate and exhaustive. The cause of the error must be isolated. Possibilities must be eliminated.

At this point, the vendor should be contacted regarding the perceived defect, but the vendor may not resolve the problem. The vendor may deem the problem to be a customer specific problem related to your data or configuration. The problem may be deemed an infrastructure or an environment specific problem, meaning it relates to your specific installation. The vendor may be unable to duplicate the problem and does not do anything to solve it. If the software vendor is unable to provide a satisfactory solution, the newly identified software defect must be added to the gaps and issues list.

Usually the initial or base version of the software along with all known fixes to a given point in time will be contained in the installation kit you receive from the vendor. The vendor will likely, over time, find or be notified of additional defects in the software. The vendor will correct and catalogue all defects through additional fixes, patches, code changes, PTFs, service packs, or alerts. These items are then made available on request to the customer (at least those under warranty or who pay for software maintenance). Often these code changes can be downloaded from a software vendor's Web site.

As more software vendors move toward electronic distribution of software, the latency between defect detection and correction and inclusion into the software product should diminish. This will be a blessing to anyone involved in software package implementation, installation, or maintenance work.

Find Workarounds or Customize

In this stage, any previously identified software gaps will be reviewed and attempts to develop workaround solutions can be made and subsequently tested in the system. If the workarounds are successful, the as built documentation is completed or updated and the gap is marked as closed on the gaps and issues list. If the workaround is unsuccessful or unworkable, then custom transactions are designed to replace or extend the functionality of the delivered software package.

I have worked on many system implementations involving software packages. With few exceptions, these systems have gone live with known show-stopper problems or defects (a handful at the most). The most common way outside of customizing or making changes to the software to accommodate exceptions is through what are called workarounds. Some workarounds are quire simple while others can be complex and laborious.

In these cases the workaround is often a complex machination requiring a number of steps, usually both systemic and manual.

Sometimes a workaround is necessary because of a specific problem or issue (i.e., a known but uncorrected defect) in the current version of the software that will be remedied in the future, usually through some form of patch or update from the vendor. Sometimes the issues are not really defects; they are merely idiosyncrasies attributed to a given software product, usually the result of a poor or ill-conceived vendor design. Clearly, the software buyer wants to avoid the use of workarounds whenever possible.

Workarounds are always a potential failure point in any new system implementation. When system features are not intuitive, they also represent potential failure points. In both cases, training end users how to use a workaround or the clumsy system feature can make a big difference in how quickly steady state is reached in a new system implementation. It also helps to eliminate the system as the source of an organization's business problems.

System Integration Planning and Execution

This stage is a part of the parallel technical track that I previously identified as an integral part of the overall software package implementation project. During this stage, technical plans and solutions are developed to fulfill software gaps.

In addition, if complementary products or software will be deployed as part of the software package implementation, those technologies must be installed and unit tested. They must then be integrated and tested in conjunction with the software package functionality that they complement. Examples of such complementary technologies include bar code scanners and printers, handheld data collection devices, and report writing software. This work must be completed and tested prior to the production readiness checkpoint review meeting.

The third set of activities is the planning for and the design and build of any required integration or interoperability components that may be needed to execute the software package implementation.

Data Migration Planning and Execution

This stage is part of the parallel technical track that I previously identified within the overall software package implementation project. A data migration or conversion plan is devised and executed. Master data and transaction-related data from existing legacy systems are identified and analyzed. Tools or programs are used to extract, scrub, edit, and load such data into the appropriate software package system data files or data tables. In some cases, data may be so incompatible that offline reentry is necessary. In other cases, data volume may not warrant automated conversion. Do not take lightly the significance of this work. This work must be completed and tested prior to the production readiness checkpoint review meeting.

Oftentimes the implementation of a new software package can either mandate or give rise to the elective wholesale conversion of data. There are two reasons that I encounter why this need arises. The first problem is data quality. Call it bad data, dirty data, incomplete or inconsistent data, or simply no data. While the data migration planning can automate most, if not all, of your data cleanup, once done it will be necessary to keep up with this task on an ongoing basis. Simply put, bad data will cause problems — some minor and others severe. Transaction failures and errors lead to lost or wrong customer orders, lost customers, and ultimately to lost revenues. The choice on data quality is yours to make and so too are the costs of avoiding it.

The second problem is data format. A new software package will often have a different way of formatting or handling data than your organization's current method or procedure. Developing mappings of old business data using guidelines and standards for business data in the new system can be a significant task. This understanding between new and old and how to transform old to new is one of the primary tasks in data migration planning. It is the prerequisite to any design/build activities that would establish automated processes that will transform and migrate data to the new software package's database.

Suppose your organization has not previously maintained formal data administration policies governing changes, additions, and deletions to your business data files or a centralized data administrator or administration function. This may be the time to reconsider the need for formalized data administration within your organization. A formal change management request process and system security that restricts business data changes to trained database administrators is ideal. A good data administration policy will also include standards.

Data administration standards should be written. They codify the rules of business data relevant to the software package. These standards should cover the details for the creation of new business data records. Once proof of concept of the configuration of your system is achieved and how and what data fields will be used, it is a good practice to immediately codify this knowledge for future reference and training purposes. This is particularly true with regard to all master business data tables for the software package. For example, in an ERP system this will minimally include customers, suppliers, items, and bills of materials.

Document As-Built Configuration

During this stage, all prior deliverables are quality assured for consistency to the As-Built configuration of the system. Your organization should develop any specific end user and technical documentation during this time. In addition, develop any specific training materials such as reference guides, exercise guides, quick-reference cards, overviews, data sheets, or training exercise-related data.

I find in many cases that the previously developed business process proposals and test scenarios can serve a dual role; they can be used during both testing and end user training. This can take some clean-up effort, but the time saved over crafting new materials from scratch can be significant. This stage will commence as workflow and functionality issues are finalized. Business policies and procedures are revised and rewritten as needed to support the new software package system. A training plan must be devised. The design and construction of training classes and classroom collateral materials must be undertaken.

Next, a training schedule is devised and participants are identified and scheduled. A training environment is defined and training data for hands-on exercises is constructed and created in this environment. Any necessary training facilities and hardware is obtained and made operational. You will want to provide the trainer education. Trainers will practice their timing and presentation skills. Trainers must ensure they have complete competency in the software functions and business processes they will be expected to train. I have devised and use several templates to produce training materials. These training document templates are part of the author's template collection. Consult Appendix A for more information.

Establish Production Readiness

This stage represents a final verification that all prerequisite tasks are completed and all processes or components — functional and technical — are deemed operationally ready. This stage also represents that the software package, as a whole, is deemed operationally ready. Assuming that all functional testing of the base or core software occurred during configuration prototyping and was accepted as built, then this stage is more so a quality assurance stage. This stage assures that technical track activities sync up with the functional readiness of the software package.

Among the activities that must occur includes a verification of the actual stored data and the validation of all business process audit trails contained in the business data. This includes testing of all converted business data that go-forward processes will rely on. This is an especially important step to assure the accuracy, consistency, and usability of the converted data.

All customizations must be tested and verified for completeness, accuracy, and error-free operation, if not previously done. Integration and interoperability must be tested and verified for completeness, accuracy and error-free operation, if not previously done. Testing plans should allow for individual component, module, interface testing, and end-to-end testing of the entire software package and any external systems. All of the detailed work during prototyping and production readiness makes "going live" a decision point rather than an additional task to fulfill at the end of a project.

Third-party software and any other complementary products must be tested and verified for accuracy and error-free operation, as well as for correct and consistent integration to the software package. Stress testing of the software package and any complementary products or customization components should be performed. This is especially true of interfaces, data migrations, and interoperability transactions where throughput can be of major concern.

An important deliverable is also produced in this stage. It is the go-live checklist. The go-live checklist is the equivalent of the preflight checklist that a pilot might run through before a takeoff. Every possible prerequisite in the chain of events leading up to the start-up date or time — the point in time when day-to-day business transaction processing can commence in the software package — must be identified and associated with where in the chain it must occur leading up to the start-up date or time. The go-live checklist will become the document to live by during the go-live chain of events. Once again, I use a ready-made template for such a go-live checklist. This go-live checklist template is a part of the author's template collection. Consult Appendix A for more.

The conclusion of this stage is a production readiness checkpoint review meeting. If all project tasks are considered complete, then production readiness has been achieved. This completeness means that all processes or components are deemed operationally ready and all gaps and issues raised to this point are deemed noncritical.

Train End Users

In this stage of the model, the primary attention is given to the delivery of end user training. Training should be conducted as near as possible to the go-live date. Hands-on training should be provided. Some suggestions for conducting an effective software package training program are as follows:

■ Walk participants through an overview of the business process as a part of the training.

- Provide participants with exercises built on sample or demonstration data drawn from data that they are accustomed to.
- Demonstrate first, then ask participants to perform the same transaction.
- Provide ample time to practice during formal training classes.
- Provide a sandbox environment where participants can continue to practice and improve their competency with the new software package until and after the go-live date.
- Use a classroom whiteboard as a parking lot for unresolved questions, problems, or issues that arise.
- Use breaks between classes to address and resolve these issues.
- Review the previous day's topics and parking lot issues before moving on.
- If needed, provide written follow-up of all parking lot issues resolved after training ends.
- Train 10 to 12 users at a time.
- Each user should have a private, rather than a shared workstation to use in the training class.
- Ideally, training will be team taught, allowing one member to float and assist and the other to lecture or demonstrate.

Obviously the above rules apply to formal classroom training. For one-on-one instruction, not all of these best practices apply. Implementation consultants can be used to produce the courseware and conduct the end user training if more desirable.

Go Live

At this stage, the all-important go-live chain of events has been reached. Before this actually happens, a final checkpoint review meeting is held. The management and working teams assess the overall readiness to go live with the software. A readiness assessment is completed and the go-live checklist and gaps and issues list are reviewed. Assuming all go-live prerequisite steps are complete, the decision is to proceed with the software package start-up and the launch countdown begins.

Certainly, most of the prerequisites involve the loading of all configuration, master, historical, opening balance, and past transactional data into the production environment. Also included is loading any pending or unfulfilled transactions into the production environment, such as unshipped sales orders, in progress production runs, undelivered purchase orders, and unpaid invoices.

It is important to understand that Go Live is usually not simply a set or fixed date or event. It has been my experience that a software package go live is a chain or series of events. It consists of multiple prerequisites that must be satisfied before any day-to-day business transaction processing can commence within the software package. During the countdown to when such processing can occur, all of the prerequisites must be fulfilled. Each is usually given a target milestone along the go-live countdown clock.

During this time the project team will meet frequently to assess and reassess the countdown and whether to stop the clock based upon the significance of failure for a prerequisite step. Usually this means postponing the point in time when day-to-day business transaction processing can commence. This delay could be for an hour, a day, or more. Contingency plans are activated. While the countdown is delayed, most physical business processes, such as the movement of goods or the taking of orders, will usually continue. Transactions might be held back or processed manually until the software package is made available. In some cases even physical activities may be suspended. Once a prerequisite failure is brought under control, the clock can be restarted. When all the prerequisites are fulfilled, the organization has reached the first stop on its software package destination and may begin conducting business using the new software package.

Go live may or may not be done in a parallel mode with the dual entry of business transactions into the new software package and any legacy systems. It is my experience that most attempts at parallels — whether they are tests or the real thing, using all business transactions or merely a subset of the business transactions — will typically fail. The best way to negate the need for parallels is testing, retesting, and more testing. This is especially true for any complementary products, configuration, customization, data migration, integration, or interoperability components related to the software package.

Establish Steady State

The final implementation stage revolves around achieving steady state. This stage begins coincidentally with live production. During this stage problem resolution and change management procedures are critical.

System performance monitoring should be conducted to ensure that both online and batch processing standards are met. The amount of tuning required of the technical infrastructure will depend on the initial results in production. There may also be performance issues encountered that require changing processes, software configurations, or the technical architecture supporting the software package. During this stage a smooth and orderly transfer of knowledge to your personnel should occur and the implementation consultants should begin rolling out.

POSTIMPLEMENTATION STAGES IN THE SOFTWARE PACKAGE LIFE CYCLE

Is a software package implementation ever really complete? The astute reader already knows the answer to this question. No, the successful software package implementation is never really complete. The SPLC does not conclude when go live occurs or steady state is reached. While the implementation may be considered as complete at this time, the software package endures until the software package becomes the next legacy system to be shut down. This may occur in 5, 10, or 15 years. During such time, change is very much the rule. The end stages of the SPLC represent a fitting end to this chapter and to this book.

Your organization will periodically, if not constantly, assess whether or not the software package is achieving its original objectives, promises, and desired benefits. There are several reasons why this is so. First, there are performance issues related primarily to growth and throughput. Second, there are business change issues. These issues were discussed in Chapter 8. Third, there are upgrades to the software package from the vendor for any number of reasons. In short, keeping the software package healthy and in tune with the business is an ongoing process.

It can be said that the successful software package implementation is best represented by a continuous, closed loop system — known as the software package lifecycle (SPLC) — with the software package health check providing the impetus for continuous improvement and tuning. Achieving greater business value from a software package is a journey, not a destination.

Periodic health checks should assess both the functional and technical results of the software package over time. Tuning and upgrading of the software package to achieve higher performance and throughput levels must also be considered as the business grows.

There is another way to answer this question: Your business organization is not static; it is dynamic. By definition your business processes and infrastructure, which includes your software package, must constantly change to reflect the dynamics of your business. Again, Chapter 8 discussed many change management issues that are quite relevant in the postimplementation setting.

Periodic Health Checks

Keeping your software package system healthy is an ongoing process. It begins once the software package enters production and extends throughout the lifetime that the software package remains in active use by your organization. Periodic health checks should assess both the functional and technical results of the system. You will constantly want to address whether the software package is achieving its original objectives and whether its full benefits are being realized. For these purposes, I previously recommended the use of the management audit as a postimplementation assessment tool (see Chapter 4).

Perform Software Updates

A periodic health check assesses both the functional and technical performance of the software package. But that alone is not enough. Active involvement in user groups, vendor notification programs, or an upgrade subscription service will allow the organization to continuously monitor that state of the software package and to assess. The organization will also be able to assess whether an upgrade is necessary or desirable.

Upgrades generally provide cumulative fixes to known software bugs and often provide performance enhancements through design changes that leverage system performance through other middleware, operating system, and database infrastructure upgrades. The software vendor should also be making functionality enhancements that may further extend the value of your software package or possibly eliminate the need for a remaining legacy system.

Upgrades can pose a significant challenge on an ongoing basis if your organization has made extensive customizations or has significant integration points with other legacy systems. Several other considerations about upgrades include:

- Do not upgrade immediately when a new release is available. Wait about 6 months, while you let others shake out any problems.
- Try to stay no more than one release level behind the current version of the software.

There are several reasons for following this last recommendation:

- Straying too far from the pack lessens the quality of vendor support your organization will likely receive.
- Most upgrades must be sequentially applied. This may require that if you fall behind several release levels, it will need to catch up before applying the latest release.

Software package users can be bombarded with lesser releases that need to be applied against the base software. These are known as interim releases, bridge releases, quick fixes, patches, service packs, or temporary fixes. These releases are used to resolve specific problems. The problems they address will span from the mundane to the severe. Carefully weigh the merits of each patch to your system and what ramifications it may have. This is especially important if your organization has invested in substantial customization or has significant integration or interoperability components involved or related to the software package.

Another release category may be the year-end release. In the case of financial and ERP software packages, these are generally available for specific regulatory changes (i.e., new 1099 or W2 information reporting formats). Most vendors will provide these updates for all supported versions of their software.

Tuning and upgrading of other aspects of the infrastructure that support the software package may be needed as well. Software package databases seem to grow exponentially. Software package performance slows over time. Certainly database size is one issue here. A data retention and archiving policy must be instituted. Transaction volumes also increase over time. This may give rise to network bandwidth or processor performance enhancements. In short, consistent performance and throughput levels must be maintained as the business grows.

SOFTWARE IMPLEMENTATION: AN EPILOGUE

This chapter reviewed the end stage of the SPLC. The end stage includes both implementation and postimplementation stages in the life cycle. The implementation of a software package requires careful planning, attention to detail, and risk management. Much of this chapter focused on planning the software package implementation through a model approach to software package implementation. Once an implementation plan is formulated, the real work begins. There are no substitutes available for the enormous amount of work needed to complete the implementation of the typical software package.

Appendix A:

OBTAINING REFERENCED TEMPLATES

At various times throughout this book the author has made reference to or has illustrated a number of ready-made Microsoft Office templates. This collection of templates may be of value to your organization in "jump-starting" its own business improvement, software package selection, business case development, or software implementation initiative. The template collection, along with an associated implementation guide, which is published in portable document format (PDF) format, is available for purchase directly from the author.

There is nominal charge of $95 for the template collection. The charge includes surface delivery. Payment should be in the form of a check or money order, payable in U.S. funds, made to the order of *Tradewinds Group, Incorporated*. To obtain the Microsoft Office-based document template collection from the author, please forward your payment and shipping information to the author's mailing address provided in Appendix B.

Thank you for your interest in the template collection.

Appendix B:

HOW TO CONTACT THE AUTHOR

The author enjoys comments and questions and will make every attempt to provide brief, timely replies to them. Questions or inquiries should be sent via e-mail or surface mail to the address below. In addition, template orders should be sent to this mailing address.

The author is also available to serve in a consulting or educational capacity to organizations within the continental United States. The author also welcomes invitations from business organizations and industry and trade associations to speak before their assembled groups at business meetings and other events.

Robert W. Starinsky
Tradewinds Group, Incorporated
Box 3601
Oak Brook, Illinois 60522
rwstarinsky@tradewindsgroupinc.com

INDEX

M

Macintosh computer, 171
Magic Quadrant, 312, 314, 318–319
Maintenance, *see* Service operations management (SOM) systems
Maintenance agreement from vendor, 167
Management audits
    assessment, 72–75
    basics, 68–69
    business cases, 70–71
    concept to deliverable, 71–75
    conducting, 71
    discovery instrument, 70
    level of detail, 88
    manufacturing environment, 71–72
    necessity, 70
    nonmanufacturing environment, 72
    postimplementation, 86–88
    purpose, 88
    SWOT analysis deliverable, 75
Management organizational needs, 46–47
Manufacturing environment, 71–72
Manufacturing execution systems (MES), 20
Manufacturing planning and control, 20–21
Manugistics, 14
MAPICS, 169
Maps, processes, 102, 342
Market timeliness, 5
Maslow, Abraham, 43
Mass customization, 13
Materials billing, 281–283
Materials requirements planning (MRP) software
    APS, 27, 28
    basics, 16
    process improvements, 92
Meal expenses, 282
Media protocols, 188
MES, *see* Manufacturing execution systems (MES)
Messaging, client server computing, 180–181
Micrographix, 107
Microsoft company, 311–312
Microsoft Project software, 326
Middle businesses and markets
    process reengineering, 95
    scorecard systems, 53
    software packages, 13

technical and infrastructure objectives, 277
Middleware, 188–190
Mindset, supply chain management, 23–25
Modularity, 180
Monetary metrics, 148
Money, time value, 132
MQ Series (IBM), 40
MRP software, *see* Materials requirements planning (MRP) software

N

National Aeronautics and Space Administration (NASA), 17
Navison, 14, 311
Navy, *see* U.S. Navy
NCR, 166
Needs of organizations, 43–47
Negotiations, *see* Contract negotiations
Netscape Navigator, 187
Networks of computers, 181
Nike, 10
Nonfeatures requirements, 254–256
Norton, David, 47–49, 53
N-tier architecture, 184
Numetrix (J.D. Edwards), 26

O

Object Management Group, 40
Objects
    basics, 172–174
    building blocks, 176–178
    classes and inheritance, 177
    features of software, 242
    impact, 178
    importance, 174–175
    methods, 176
    reusability and composition, 177–178
    screen scraping, 176
    software by assembly, 174
    traditional software comparison, 175
ODBC compliant database system, 189–190, 196
Office Suite software, 222, 264, 312
One-time charges, 284–285
One-to-one marketing, 36

W

Walker, William, 97
Wang Laboratories, 166
Warehouse management system (WMS), 29-32
Warranty from vendor, 167
WebMethods software, 40
Weighted average cost of capital (WACC), 134
Weights, developing, 298-299
White papers, *see* Best practices
WholeView research strategy, 316
Windows NT
    client server communications support, 188
    infrastructure, 170
    midrange market, 166
    open systems, 165, 167
Wintel platform

Word software, 107, 264, 296, 339
Workarounds, 214-215, 350-351
Workbooks *vs.* worksheets, 296-297

Work breakdown structures, 334
Working team, implementation, 339-340
Work order role, 34-35

X

Xerox, 171
XML, *see* Extensible markup language (XML)
XSL, *see* Extensible stylesheet language (XLS)

Y

Y2K (Year 2000)
    compliance, 8, 120, 125
    ERP, 13, 18
    Internet-based technologies updating, 187
    management audit, 70-71
    software purchased before, 203
    technology-enabled change, 97
    XML compliance, 203